BRIGHT START MUSIC:

A DEVELOPMENTAL PROGRAM FOR MUSIC THERAPISTS, PARENTS, AND TEACHERS OF YOUNG CHILDREN

Darcy Walworth, PhD, MT-BC
University of Louisville

AMERICAN
MUSIC
THERAPY
ASSOCIATION

American Music Therapy Association
www.musictherapy.org

Neither the American Music Therapy Association nor its Board of Directors is responsible for the conclusions reached or the opinions expressed by the authors of this book.

The American Music Therapy Association is a non-profit association dedicated to increasing access to quality music therapy services for individuals with disabilities or illnesses or for those who are interested in personal growth and wellness. AMTA provides extensive educational and research information about the music therapy profession. Referrals for qualified music therapists are also provided to consumers and parents. AMTA holds an annual conference every autumn and its seven regions hold conferences every spring.

For up-to-date information, please access the AMTA website at *www.musictherapy.org*

ISBN: 978-1-884914-30-0

Copyright Information: ©American Music Therapy Association, Inc., 2013
                                      8455 Colesville Road, Suite 1000
                                      Silver Spring, MD 20910 USA
                                      www.musictherapy.org
                                      info@musictherapy.org

Technical Assistance: Wordsetters
                                      Kalamazoo, Michigan

                                      Marcia Humpal, MEd, MT-BC

Cover Design and Layout: Tawna Grasty, Grass T Design

Printed in the United States of America

ACKNOWLEDGMENTS

The author would like to thank Judy Engel for her unending support and for modifying this developmental program to use in a hospital setting for children at risk of developmental delays, the music therapy staff at Tallahassee Memorial Healthcare for their tireless support and feedback while field testing this program, and Jocelyn Fish for researching and field testing this program in an early intervention setting. Many thanks are given to Julie Alley and the music therapists, song writers, and music therapy students who contributed their creativity to this work. This book would not have been possible without the guidance of Marcia Humpal, whose expertise in early childhood education and music therapy proved invaluable. Additional thanks is given to Dr. Jayne Standley, who continually provides countless hours of feedback, resources, and motivation to promote and expand music therapy interventions to underserved populations.

CONTENTS

INTRODUCTION AND SUPPORTING
BACKGROUND INFORMATION

The Bright Start program evolved from research, experiential music therapy clinical work with infants and toddlers, and a general belief that very young children can benefit from structured group music involvement prior to 2 years of age. This book provides a protocol for a developmental music program for very young children that is delivered in a group setting. Background information, session plans across various types of group settings that target developmental skills, plus skill charts, and lyric and chord sheets are included.

STRUCTURED MUSIC ACTIVITIES

Providing infants and toddlers with opportunities to explore and immerse themselves in a variety of environments and experiences is an ever-increasing aim for those concerned with child development. Children learn through the social and communicative exchanges with their peers and caregivers throughout each day. Simultaneous cross-domain learning occurs when children interact in various activities.

Structured music activities help a child process multiple sensory inputs. For example, a song traditionally seen as a movement activity actually requires a child to process visual input from a peer or adult model, auditory input from the music source, receptive language to decode directions in the song, cognitive functioning to enable decision making, expressive language to communicate within the activity, emotional regulation to remain engaged, and kinesthetic inputs to implement the motor skills demonstrated in the activity. Much research supports the multisensory learning paradigm that learning-rich environments provide to children. Illuminating the multiple learning areas extended to infants during music activities strengthens the developmental impact of music intervention. Music therapists, early childhood music educators, and childcare providers can all provide developmentally appropriate music interactions for infants and children and also can share these experiences with the families of the children.

MUSIC THERAPY

Many people ask what separates music therapists from musicians leading songs and groups. As a profession, music therapy is defined as "the clinical and evidence-based use of music interventions to accomplish individualized goals within a therapeutic relationship by a credentialed professional who has completed an approved music therapy program. Music Therapy is an established health profession in which music is used within a therapeutic relationship to address physical, emotional, cognitive, and social needs of individuals" (American Music Therapy Association, 2012). Within the early childhood setting, music therapists draw on their training to identify and address needs of children of all ability levels and their family systems to increase their developmental progress over time (Knight, 2010). Knight explains that overlapping can occur among music therapists, music educators, and community music professionals pertaining to children served, music curricula used, and musical backgrounds. This overlapping enables music therapists and related professionals to work alongside each other in exposing young children to the many benefits of music listening, interactions, and interventions.

Within early intervention settings, music therapy is a related service that targets need areas for children including cognitive development, hearing ability, motor skills, receptive and expressive language, self-regulation skills, social-emotional skills, and visual skills (Humpal & Colwell, 2006). Pederson and Reuer (2010) found that functional skills in motor, language, and social areas increased for at-risk children ages 0–3 who attended the "Sound Minds" music therapy groups with their caregivers. For kindergarteners, phonological memory and metacognitive abilities were increased for students participating in a music therapy program led by a music educator versus students participating in the standard music education program (Bolduc, 2009). Hanson-Abromeit (2011) identified seven therapeutic functions that music serves for infant language development:

1. melodic contour to regulate attention;

2. rhythm as a sensory organizer;

3. style and tonality to support cultural familiarity and context;

4. form and tempo to regulate emotion;

5. pitch to encourage vocalizations, reciprocal and therapist initiated;

6. dynamics to organize sensory integration; and

7. lyrics to facilitate language (gestures, intentional babbling, and words).

One explanation for why music interactions enhance developmental skills for young children is that the mirror neuron system is activated during shared musical experiences (Overy & Molnar-Szakacs, 2009). The Shared Affective Motion Experience model posits that expressive motor acts are heightened through the imitation, synchronization, and shared experiences that naturally occur through music interactions. After reviewing the recent early childhood literature, LaGasse (2011) postulates that music interactions have the ability to alter the young child's developing brain to allow acquisitions of new skills, due in part to the brain's plasticity at the infant stage.

DEVELOPMENTAL SKILLS AND DOMAINS

Children are commonly drawn to music activities and willingly engage in musical play. Just as adults commonly listen to music while exercising or working to increase their enjoyment while completing tasks, children who are having fun at music time are learning and practicing important skill development without realizing they are "working." With the knowledge that music does positively impact developmental learning areas such as reading and literacy skills for pre-K and school-aged children (Standley, 2008), it stands to reason that early music can have an impact on developmental learning for infant and toddlers in the following areas.

Social Skills

When exploring the evolution of music, researchers have focused on music's ability to reinforce social bonds (Balter, 2004). Music can teach social skills by encouraging interaction through directions in the lyrics, by taking turns playing instruments, and by telling stories in the music (Gourgey, 1998). To investigate the ecological impact on music play behaviors, Littleton (1991) observed preschool children in a music-specific play area and non-music house play setting. When the children played in the music setting, more functional and constructive play was observed, whereas children who played in the house setting engaged in more dramatic play. Music therapy groups targeting social skill acquisition for infants 0–3 with their caregivers were successful in increasing skill levels for the infants (Nicholson, Berthelsen, Abad, Williams, & Bradley, 2008; Pederson & Reuer, 2010; Walworth, 2009).

Cognitive Skills

Cognition is addressed in all music therapy interventions for young children when a child is integrating the words in the songs, movements, playing instruments, and observing their surroundings. Very young children demonstrated improvement after engaging in the current program (Standley, Walworth, Nguyen, & Hillmer, 2011). Targeting gains for clients in cognitive goal areas is recommended for all early childhood music therapists (Wellman, 2011).

Language and Communication Skills

Language and communication permeate all goal areas. Communication and language skills have improved for various age groups participating in music interactions (Nicholson et al., 2008; Register, 2001; Schwartz, 2008; Standley, Walworth, & Nguyen, 2009).

Motor Skills

Motor skills are addressed within music therapy sessions when children dance, play instruments, and move around the environment. Children have shown improvement in their motor skills after exposure to music therapy groups (Pederson & Reuer, 2010; Standley et al., 2009).

FACTORS THAT IMPACT CAREGIVER AND INFANT INTERACTIONS

A large body of research has focused on the impact of maternal interaction on infants' development. Maternal responsiveness, play behaviors, affect, depression, joint attention, and synchrony with their infants have all been investigated. Research continues to show that mothers and other caregivers have a very large impact on the developmental outcome of a child.

For example, variations in the onset of language for infants are linked to variations in the amount of symbol-infused joint engagement seen between mothers and infants (Adamson & Bakeman, 2004). When parents placed a target item within their 6-month-old infant's visual field, a significant number of infants were able to match the parent's direction of gaze toward the object, but were not able to do so when the target object was placed out of the infant's visual field (Morales, Mundy, & Rojas, 1998). These findings indicate that some infants develop important socialization joint attention skills as early as 6 months old when interacting with a parent.

A large sample of 111 mother–infant pairs was investigated by Laakso, Poikkeus, Eklund, and Lyytinen (1999) to assess 14-month-old children's symbolic play competence and early social interactional behaviors. Results indicated that an infant's social attention coordination serves as a prerequisite for expressive language, and maternal interactional strategies have a positive influence on symbolic play behaviors. Both aid in later language development for the infant.

CAREGIVER MOOD STATE

Mothers suffering from a depressed mood state may not only impact interaction with their infants, but may also influence how their infants interact with other individuals in their environment. When 112 infants were assessed at 15 months, infants with chronically depressed mothers performed significantly lower on motor and cognitive tests compared to infants whose mothers were not depressed (Cornish et al., 2005). However, early language scores were not affected by maternal depression.

In a sample of 260 infants, differences in infant development between infants whose mothers showed depressive symptoms versus infants born to mothers without depressive symptoms were measured with mental and motor scores at a 12-month follow-up after mothers were randomly assigned to the control or intervention group (Field et al., 2000). Intervention groups consisted of maternal relaxation therapy, music mood induction, massage therapy, and mother–infant coaching. Mothers in the intervention group showed significantly improved interactions, biochemical values, and normalized vagal tone. Infants whose mothers were in the intervention group also demonstrated more positive maternal interaction, better growth, and normalized biochemical values. At the 12-month follow-up, they had higher mental and motor scores than infants in the control group.

The importance of maternal–infant bonding has been established and such bonding can be facilitated by music therapy interventions (Edwards, 2011). Music therapy interventions can address what Register (2011) identifies as three fundamental goals for caregiver–infant interactions:

1. providing children and their families with support for safe, secure, and appropriate attachment to one another;

2. modeling situations for children to self-regulate and cope with change; and

3. offering play-based opportunities for families, particularly young children, to communicate in meaningful, positive ways.

Parents who have difficulty forming healthy attachments with their children are able to learn observation skills to increase their ability to read and respond to their child's emotional cues (Betz, 2011). Music provides a safe and nurturing environment for parents who are practicing new interaction styles with their infants and young children.

PREMATURITY/LOW BIRTH WEIGHT

The preterm birth rate has risen by roughly 30% since the late 1980s and currently no evidence indicates that the premature birth rate will decline in the future (Eunice Kennedy Shriver National Institute of Child Health and Human Development, 2008). Therefore, for children born prematurely who are at risk of developmental delays, identifying effective interventions targeted at increasing developmental skill achievement is critical. Children born with extremely low birth weight are at risk of developing poorer social skills and adaptive behaviors and having more attention and behavior problems when they are school aged (Msall & Tremont, 2002). Many parents are faced with increased levels of care when their preterm infants come home from the hospital. Donohue (2002) found that most parents of preterm infants adjust well to their change in lifestyle, but some did report having psychological distress for years after their preterm child's birth due to their child's health problems.

Health-related quality of life (HRQL) was measured at preschool age for infants admitted to the Newborn Intensive Care Unit (NICU) and also for their parents (Klassen et al., 2004). Parents reported more worry and stress as well as less time to meet their own needs. Parents of infants admitted to a NICU reported more maladaptation from fathers and need for support during the first year after delivery, as well as more child behavior problems at 3 years of age and less time for themselves due to the intensity of child care than did parents of low-risk and no hospitalization control infants (Rautava, Lehtonen, Helenius, & Sillanpää, 2003).

CAREGIVER TRAINING AND SUPPORT

Parent training programs have had positive effects on premature infant development over time. A Mother-Infant Transaction Program targeting responsiveness of parents to their premature infants has shown favorable results and is low in cost to hospital systems (Nordhov et al., 2010). While their premature infants were still hospitalized, parents were counseled through the emotions of having a preterm infant and were taught specific interaction techniques, the signs of infant distress, and the various behavioral states their infants would cycle through. Infants whose parents completed the in-hospital training and received follow-up visits for the first 3 months following discharge had increased cognitive intelligence scores at 5 years of age.

Because the stresses and challenges faced by children born prematurely and their caregivers, as well as by infants of depressed mothers, are substantial, a community group setting may offer many benefits to them. Attending a developmental music group can provide a supportive network of other parents who are caring for young children. Additionally, the other children attending the group provide peer models of various developmental skills for children at risk for delays.

MUSIC AND EARLY INTERVENTION/ EARLY CHILDHOOD SPECIAL EDUCATION

UNIFIED THEORY OF PRACTICE

Early intervention/early childhood special education (EI/ECSE) programs in every state primarily provide services for infants and preschool children with disabilities and their families. A unified theory of practice is currently supported by the EI/ECSE fields. This theory consists of the following tenets:

1. Families and homes are primary nurturing contexts; strengthening relationships is an essential feature of EI/ECSE.

2. Children learn through acting on and observing their environment.

3. Adults mediate children's experiences to promote learning.

4. Participation in more developmentally advanced settings is essential.

5. Program transitions are enhanced by adults or experiences.

6. Broader ecological contexts influence families and EI/ECSE programs.
   (Odom & Wolery, 2003)

Group music activities can promote each of the tenets of the unified theory through facilitating interaction between caregiver–infant dyads. A group music setting may provide a rich environment for children to act on and explore to promote learning across a variety of developmental domains.

LEARNING THROUGH MUSIC

While there is much literature that discusses the importance of early childhood learning through music for pre-K and elementary-aged children, the literature addressing developmental learning through music for children under the age of 2 is just beginning to emerge. How infants respond to music stimuli is well documented. Simultaneous cross-domain learning for infants among music and language, music and social awareness, or music and motor development is an area needing further investigation. Many music therapists can attest to the fact that infants and toddlers with developmental delays make gains as a result of music therapy intervention in multiple developmental areas such as language, cognition, motor, and social-emotional skills (Abad & Williams, 2007; Nicholson et al., 2008; Pederson & Reuer, 2010; Schwartz, 2008). The development and implementation of Bright Start Music substantiate this premise.

BRIGHT START PILOT PROJECT

The current program was implemented and investigated to determine the impact of music on developmental learning for infants and toddlers. Infants who regularly attended the groups using the current program were compared with infants of the same ages who attended only one time (Standley et al., 2009). Regularly attending infants demonstrated significantly advanced music, cognitive, and social skills. The infants who participated in the targeted program groups clapped in time, moved in time, and played instruments independently. They also followed directions to retrieve and return objects, pointed to their own body parts when named, and performed sign language and other gestures at a significantly higher rate than infants who came to the group only once. Additionally, infants regularly attending the groups shared with others more often, socialized with peers in the group, and responded to other people's names with higher frequency.

A follow-up study with group participants investigated the impact of group involvement on the caregiver–infant interaction (Walworth, 2009). All subjects were matched according to developmental age and were also matched by group for socioeconomic status and for maternal depression. Types of infant play and parent responsiveness were measured using observation of a standardized toy play for parent–infant dyads, a demonstrated measurement tool used in similar mother–infant dyad research. The toy play time that was observed occurred at a time other than during the music group. The amount of time caregivers and infants spent in social play versus non-social play was recorded.

The infants attending the music groups using the targeted program's curriculum with their parents demonstrated significantly more social toy play during the standardized parent–infant toy play than infants who did not attend the music groups. While not significant, graphic analysis of parent responsiveness showed parents who attended the developmental music groups engaged in more positive and less negative play behaviors with their infants than parents who did not attend the music groups. Another interesting finding involved the premature infants who attended the music groups. While the amount of their social toy play time was not as great as the full-term infants attending the groups, the premature infants did spend more time in social play than full-term babies who did not come to the music groups. This investigation supported the positive effects a developmental music group can have on social behaviors for both premature and full-term infants under 2 years old. In addition to the studies discussed above, this program was pilot tested in hospital settings for children at risk of developmental delay due to their hospitalization and with children receiving early intervention services in a community setting.

BRIGHT START MUSIC

CURRICULUM

DESIGN

The Bright Start curriculum described in this book is designed to support a caregiver–infant program, based on findings that mother–infant coaching can positively impact infant development. Specific instructions are given to caregivers throughout each session to train mothers and caregivers in ways to provide developmentally appropriate interactions in their home and community environments, helping the adult caregiver mediate the child's experience to increase learning. Developmental checklists are provided to enable the music therapist or educator to identify the developmental level of each child and the specific skills he or she is accomplishing. Modifications of the curriculum are also presented for settings where mothers and caregivers are not able to be present.

Interventions were designed for parent–child groups and for school settings such as early intervention and child care centers. The session plans are divided into three groups by developmental age. All curricular content was chosen based on the literature findings that music is effective for addressing developmental skill achievement in cognitive, language (encompasses all forms of communication, receptive, as well as expressive), motor, and social-emotional domain areas.

CONTENT

Designed as an infant developmental learning curriculum, Bright Start's content and specific interventions offer systematic developmental scaffolding for cognitive, language, motor, and social-emotional domains. The group session format also provides behaviors, skills, and interactions for infants and caregivers to observe and integrate into their repertoire. The experiences and input of other caregivers within sessions give an ever-changing and expanding experiential learning opportunity for caregivers and infants. The sequence of intervention sessions follows the development of skills acquisition in each domain for each of the three age groups. As groups advance through the curriculum, the developmental skills addressed in each session increase in complexity. Because the groups are divided by developmental age, the curricular content is appropriate for typically developing children as well as children at risk for developmental delays. For example, a child who is functioning at the 10-month developmental level and is 14 months old chronologically would attend the 6–12 month age group session. When a child is in the appropriate group for his or her developmental age, developmentally appropriate activities are provided across domains, which decreases the child's frustration and increases his or her success in acquiring new skills.

This developmental music curriculum is designed for caregiver and infants to attend groups together, with the groups separated by developmental age. Additionally, sections of this curriculum are devoted to implementing developmental music interventions in settings where parents and caregivers are not present. In either format, the youngest age group is 6 months to 12 months, the second group is 12 months to 18 months, and the oldest group is 18 months to 24 months. Each session is designed to last approximately 30 minutes, which provides many cross-domain learning opportunities for infants and toddlers.

There are 12 sessions per age group. If a group meets weekly, the 12 sessions for each age group will be repeated once during a 6-month time span. If a group meets twice a month, the sessions will each occur only once during the 6-month time span for each age group.

The songs used throughout the curriculum are designed to repeat with enough frequency for caregivers to learn the songs in order to encourage implementation of songs in the home environment. However, new songs are introduced at a frequency intended to keep caregivers and children interested in the activity and to prevent boredom from repetition of songs.

FORMAT

The session format is similar across age groups, but does vary based on the increased mobility of infants as they approach 24 months. All sessions address all the developmental domain areas in which infants are progressively developing. Because infants who attend the groups represent a variety of ages within each 6-month age range, the developmental skills are presented as a continuum determined by ability level, not static within one stage. For example, in the 6- to 12-month age group, some infants will not be crawling, some will be crawling, and some may be already walking. All movement activities within the sessions are presented to facilitate motor learning regardless of the exact stage of the infant. Caregivers should provide supportive assistance as infants advance their current skills through practice.

While an onlooker might perceive music play to be the only task the infants are engaged in, the parent instructions in each session highlight the simultaneous cross-domain learning that is actually occurring within each activity.

Music therapists and early childhood educators using this curriculum are encouraged to discuss with caregivers what is being learned by the infant at the beginning or end of each activity. Infant and toddler attention spans do not allow a long discourse on the learning taking place, so a quick reminder and application for that skill at home is suggested next to each activity within the session plans. The following is an excerpt of a parent instruction from a movement song for the 18–24-month age group:

Encourage your child to follow the movement directions in the song. Coordinating complex movements through space develops many skill areas at the same time. Cognitive processing and visual input are at work to analyze what motion your child is observing and how to imitate it; kinesthetic skills are being developed as your child tries the new motion without falling over; social skills and emotional awareness are being developed as your child watches other people's reactions to performing the movements; interpersonal awareness is developing as your child forms his or her own reaction to the activity! That's a lot going on!!

HOW TO INCLUDE CHILDREN WITH SENSORY ISSUES

For children with sensory input challenges, attending group music sessions can be overwhelming. Slowly acclimating to complete inclusion in the full group circle takes time and patience for the parent, but it can result in a child successfully attending and participating in full sessions. Some children may need to listen outside the door where the music group is meeting for an entire session before being ready to step inside the room. Forcing a child to participate in an activity that is overstimulating can result in a negative association with music for that child. It can also cause a child to become dysregulated, upsetting not only the parent but other children participating in the music group. If a child with sensory processing difficulties needs to observe a session several times from a peripheral location before sitting with the group circle, communication with the parent may be necessary. The best approach is to assure the parent that the child is welcome to join the group when he or she is able to process what is going on within the group activities and stay regulated.

ASSESSMENT AND DOCUMENTATION

For music therapists and early childhood educators who are interested in providing documentation of the cross-domain learning that is occurring within each session, a tool is made available within the current curriculum. The developmental skill charts provide numbers for each developmental skill a child demonstrates with each age group. The charts are coded by domain area as follows: C = cognitive, L = language (both expressive and receptive), M = motor, and SE = social-emotional. While these charts are not designed to be used as assessment tools, they do offer a way for music therapists and early childhood educators to document learning that is occurring within and across sessions.

The developmental skills charts were compiled from traditional developmental milestone achievements demonstrated during each 6-month age group targeted in the music sessions (The Centers for Disease Control and Prevention [CDC], 2012). The charts are not designed to be exhaustive of all developmental milestones reached during each age group. They are a list of targeted milestones addressed within the music group sessions for infants at each age grouping. The specificity of skills identified within each domain provides concrete actions adults can address during infant and toddler interactions. Because infant learning occurs across domains simultaneously, some of the skills are directly related to a skill in a different domain. For those skills, a ▶ symbol is included, pointing to the developmental skill that is directly related to the skill being described. The following excerpt shows some of the cognitive developmental skills for infants attending the 6–12-month age group:

6–12 Months Cognitive Developmental Skills

Skill Number	Skill Description
C1	Looks for dropped object by turning his/her head (e.g., spoon dropped from high chair, toy dropped when lying on back)
C2	Grasps toy with both hands voluntarily to obtain a desired toy (▶M18)
C3	Attempts to retrieve a toy that has been dropped (e.g., toy dropped when lying on back) (▶SE7)
C4	Explores objects by picking up toys and putting in mouth

Therefore, music therapists and educators can identify broad goal areas within music activities such as improving cognitive or gross motor skills, or focus on a slightly more specific objective such as increasing use of both hands during toy play.

The section titled "Developmental Skills Addressed in Each Session" provides the skill chart numbers for every activity addressed within each session. At the beginning of each age group within that section, there is a list of developmental skills that are addressed or can be seen in all songs and all sessions. This represents a group of skills or developmentally appropriate behaviors for each age group that an infant can demonstrate at any point during any song. Examples include:

C13	Watches and observes action in environment (attends to activity)
L10	Gets and keeps attention using non-crying sounds
L11	Imitates by repeating back to you different speech sounds
L12	Uses Dada/Mama appropriately
M27	Runs independently
M28	Walks quickly without falling
SE32	Enjoys "performing" for an audience (likes applause) and adult attention
SE33	Explores environment and objects freely (▶C19)
SE37	Gets upset if things do not happen NOW (has difficulty waiting)
SE38	Will have a temper tantrum or get angry when upset

When documenting learning that occurs in each session, it is important that the music therapist or early childhood educator include the list of skills that are covered in every session at the beginning of the "Skills Addressed" section for each age group. The skills listed next to each activity are skills addressed specifically within that activity and not generally across all songs and all sessions. The excerpt below is from the 12–18-month group:

Bright Start Music   12–18 Month Group Session Plan #12

SKILL AREA & SONGS	DEVELOPMENTAL SKILLS ADDRESSED
Hello Song **When I Meet a New Friend**	L17, L18, L19
Sign Language Song **Birdie Beat**	L17, L18, L19, L27, SE31
Instruments – Rhythm Instruments **Click! Click! Click! Go the Castanets**	C16, C17, C18, L29, L30, M23, M24, M25, M29, M32, M36, M41, SE18, SE26, SE29, SE30
Movement **Flower Power**	L17, L18, L25, L27, M30, M31, M39, SE31

ADVANCING THROUGH LEVELS

As children progress through the curriculum and become more independent, instructions are given for each activity to increase the child's independence while engaged in each song. For example, once children are able to pick up an instrument off the floor themselves, instruments are no longer handed to them by the group leader or caregiver. Similarly, once a child is able to put a puppet away in the bag or storage container where it belongs, the group leader does not walk around the group collecting the puppets. Instead, the child is encouraged to take the puppet to the bag and put it inside. While this takes longer than having an adult collect the manipulatives, it is an important part of developing an awareness of where items belong, as well as fostering awareness of social rules.

There are not as many songs in the 18–24-month age group as there are in the 6–12-month age group. The engagement of retrieving and putting away manipulatives takes time. Furthermore, because of the cognitive advancement that occurs between 6 and 24 months, older children are able to stay actively engaged in songs that last longer, have more verses, and take longer to complete.

AIDS TO CROSS-DOMAIN LEARNING

Visual aids, labeled for the songs they are designed to accompany, are provided in the curricular content to help facilitate the simultaneous cross-domain learning occurring within each music activity. These may be reproduced for use only by the purchaser of this program. For the visual aids designed for songbooks, bind the pictures together in whatever format you think best. Binding can be as simple as hole punches and string, or as complex as professional binding. It is recommended that an image be printed in black and white and colored in manually. Colored images printed in black and white lose the visual contrast needed for an image to be visually appealing.

For those who play guitar or piano, lyric and chord sheets are provided. All the songs used in this curriculum either are public domain songs or were written specifically for this curriculum. Multicultural songs are included to incorporate traditional songs from Australian, Israeli, Mexican, Native American, Spanish, South African, and West African cultures. While the original music is copyrighted by the songwriter, each songwriter has granted permission for the lyric and chord sheets to appear in the curriculum content.

Recordings of all songs used within the curriculum are included within the program as well, to facilitate learning the melodies and tempos of the songs. It is highly recommended that live music be used when implementing the curriculum as it allows the group leader to modify each song as it is progressing, based on input from the children attending the group. For those who do not play guitar, feel free to use the recordings within the classroom. However, plan ahead if implementing an entire session, as songs are arranged alphabetically and not by session format.

GETTING STARTED

INSTRUMENTS AND MATERIALS

A list of instruments and materials needed to implement the program as designed is included in this book. While it is costly to acquire this extensive list, note that children and parents benefit from a rich learning environment. Recommendations for brands of instruments and materials are made based on the author's experience with products that survive the wear and tear of use by young children over time.

LOCATION

When choosing a location for a music group, consider the ease of access to the location. If the target audience is clustered around a certain location, finding a place near that area will improve attendance. Similarly, if your target audience uses public transportation, finding a location on the public transit route is important. For the actual room, it is imperative to find a space large enough to allow a great deal of movement. Once children become mobile, they like to move! Movement activities are interspersed throughout each session to allow for just that.

STORAGE

Another consideration is storage of materials and manipulatives during the session. To keep each child's attention piqued, manipulatives are handed out and put away multiple times throughout each session. Visually block the manipulatives from the children's view during non-manipulative songs. For example, during a movement song, puppets are not used. However, if children are moving around the room (which they should be if following the directions in the song), they could become easily distracted by the sight of a bag or clear plastic container of puppets. At that point, children will most likely forget about the movement activity they were so actively engaged in and go investigate the various animal puppets that have been discovered. The same can be said for all the very colorful instruments and scarves used during the session. A visual block such as a long folding table turned on its side works well for storing bags of manipulatives away from the children's view, while still providing easy access for the music therapist or educator leading the session.

FORMAT MODIFICATIONS

While this program is designed in the format of a 30-minute parent–child group, modifications can be made for the music therapist or early childhood educator in a different situation. Within a classroom, it might not be feasible to set aside 30 minutes for a music group, even as beneficial as that is! If there are specific domain areas that can be addressed in a 5- or 10-minute slot each day, the session can be broken into several small sections to be implemented each day instead of grouped together in the 30-minute format. For a music therapist or educator providing individual intervention services targeted at specific developmental skill areas, session content can be chosen that addresses each child's specific need area. For example, for a child with a motor and language delay who is not delayed in his or her social-emotional skills, the motor skill and language skill specific songs can be pooled together to form appropriate session content for individual intervention.

START SINGING!

For the non-singers out there who are using this program, remember that children love to engage in singing and are also learning from adult and peer models! If you are using the recordings of these songs and not singing along, start singing! Children who are watching the group leader for behavioral cues can be confused when they are told to sing along, but then do not see the group leader singing. Even if you think you cannot "carry a tune in a bucket," you will increase the children's participation level if you sing along. And who knows? You might actually find yourself enjoying the activities more!

REFERENCES

Abad, Vicky, & Williams, K. E. (2007). Early intervention music therapy: Reporting on a 3-year project to address needs with at-risk families. *Music Therapy Perspectives, 25*(1), 52–58.

Adamson, L. B., & Bakeman, R. (2004). The development of symbol-infused joint engagement. *Child Development, 75*, 1171–1187.

American Music Therapy Association. (2012, June 5). Retrieved from http://www. musictherapy.org/about/quotes/

Balter, M. (2004). Seeking keys to music. *Science, 306*, 1120–1122.

Betz, S. (2011). Attachment-based music therapy: New opportunities and requirements for music therapists working with young children. *imagine, 2*, 50–52.

Bolduc, J. (2009). Effects of a music programme on kindergarteners' phonological awareness skills 1. *International Journal of Music Education, 27*, 37–47.

Centers for Disease Control and Prevention. (2012). Developmental milestones. Retrieved July 5, 2012 from http://www.cdc.gov/ncbddd/actearly/milestones/index.html

Cornish, A. M., McMahon, C. A., Ungerer, J. A., Barnett, B., Kowalenko, N., & Tennant, C. (2005). Postnatal depression and infant cognitive and motor development in the second postnatal year: The impact of depression chronicity and infant gender. *Infant Behavior and Development, 28*, 407–417.

Donohue, P. K. (2002). Health related quality of life of preterm children and their caregivers. *Mental Retardation and Developmental Disabilities Research Reviews, 8*, 293–297.

Edwards, J. (2011). *Music therapy and parent-infant bonding*. Oxford, UK: Oxford University Press.

Eunice Kennedy Shriver, National Institute of Child Health and Human Development, NIH, DHHS. (2008). *Prematurity research at the NIH (NA)*. Washington, DC: U.S. Government Printing Office.

Field, T., Pickens, J., Prodromidis, M., Malphurs, J., Fox, N., Bendell, et al. (2000). Targeting adolescent mothers with depressive symptoms for early intervention. *Adolescence, 35*, 381–414.

Gourgey, C. (1998). Music therapy in the treatment of social isolation in visually impaired children. *RE:view, 29*, 157–162.

Hanson-Abromeit, D. (2011). Early music therapy intervention for language development with at-risk infants. *imagine, 2*, 34–35.

Humpal, M., & Colwell, C. (2006). *Early childhood and school age educational settings: Using music to maximize learning.* Silver Spring, MD: American Music Therapy Association.

Klassen, A. F., Lee, S. K., Raina, P., Chan, H. W. P., Matthew, D., & Brabyn, D. (2004). Health status and health related quality of life in a population-based sample of neonatal intensive care unit graduates. *Pediatrics, 113,* 594–600.

Knight, A. (2010). Collaboration in music: Therapy and early childhood music educators. *imagine, 1,* 21.

Laakso, M. L., Poikkeus, A. M., Eklund, K., & Lyytinen, P. (1999). Social interactional behaviors and symbolic play competence as predictors of language development and their associations with maternal attention-directing strategies. *Infant Behavior and Development, 22,* 541–556.

LaGasse, B. (2011). Research snapshots 2011: Music and early childhood development. *imagine, 2,* 28–30.

Littleton, D. (1991). Influence of play settings on preschool children's music and play behaviors. *Dissertation Abstracts International, 52*(04), 1198A. (UMI No. 9128294)

Morales, M., Mundy, P., & Rojas, J. (1998). Following the direction of gaze and language development in 6-month-olds. *Infant Behavior and Development, 21,* 373–377.

Msall, M. E., & Tremont, M. R. (2002). Measuring functional outcomes after prematurity: Developmental impact of very low birth weight and extremely low birth weight status on childhood disability. *Mental Retardation and Developmental Disabilities Research Reviews, 8,* 258–272.

Nicholson, J. M., Berthelsen, D., Abad, V., Williams, K., & Bradley, J. (2008). Impact of music therapy to promote positive parenting and child development. *Journal of Health Psychology, 13,* 226–238.

Nordhov, S. M., Rønning, J. A., Dahl, L. B., Ulvund, S. V., Tunby, J., & Kaaresen, P. I. (2010). Early intervention improves cognitive outcomes for premature infants: Randomized controlled trial. *Pediatrics, 126,* e1088–e1094.

Odom, S. L., & Wolery, M. (2003). A unified theory of practice in early intervention/ early childhood special education: Evidence-based practices. *Journal of Special Education, 37,* 164–173.

Overy, K., & Molnar-Szakacs, I. (2009). Being together in time: Musical experience and the mirror neuron system. *Music Perception: An Interdisciplinary Journal, 26,* 489–504.

Pederson, N., & Reuer, B. (2010). Sound minds: Musical bonding for teens and their babies. *imagine, 1,* 44–47.

Rautava, P., Lehtonen, L., Helenius, H., & Sillanpää, M. (2003). Effect of newborn hospitalization on family and child behavior: A 12-year follow-up study. *Pediatrics, 111*, 277–283.

Register, D. (2001). The effects of an early intervention music curriculum on prereading/ writing. *Journal of Music Therapy, 13*, 154–162.

Register, D. (2011). Imagine why music matters: Advocating for music as an essential early childhood experience. *imagine, 2*, 20–23.

Schwartz, E. (2008). *Music therapy and early childhood: A developmental approach.* Gilsum, NH: Barcelona.

Standley, J., Walworth, D., Nguyen, J., & Hillmer, M. (2011). A descriptive analysis of infant attentiveness in structured group music classes. *Music Therapy Perspectives, 29*(2), 112–116.

Standley, J., Walworth, D., & Nguyen, J. (2009). Effect of parent/child group music activities on toddler development: A pilot study. *Music Therapy Perspectives, 27*(1), 11–15.

Standley, J. M. (2008). Does music instruction help children learn to read? Evidence of a meta analysis. *Update: Applications of Research in Music Education, 27*, 17–32.

Walworth, D. (2009). Effects of developmental music groups for parents and premature or typical infants under two years on parental responsiveness and infant social development. *Journal of Music Therapy, 46*(1), 32–52.

Wellman, B. (2011). Understanding development in early childhood music therapy. *imagine, 2*, 61–63.

SETTINGS AND SESSION PLANS

SESSION PLANS FOR CAREGIVERS PRESENT
(Parent Instructions or Comments Included)
Darcy Walworth, PhD, MT-BC, and Judy Nguyen, MM, MT-BC

This grouping of session plans is designed to address the full range of developmental skill areas in a 30–45-minute session time for infants with caregivers present. The session plans are provided with parent instructions to highlight various reasons developmental skills are being targeted in each song. The parent instructions are not exhaustive and can be easily modified based on the individual needs of each group. Therefore, session plans without parent instructions also will be provided in a subsequent section. For a seasoned music therapist or developmental specialist, the session plans without parent instructions may be preferable.

Bright Start Music   6–12 Month Group   Session Plan #1

SKILL AREAS & SONGS	PARENT INSTRUCTION
Hello Song **My Right Hand Says Hello**	Help your baby greet other babies in the group by orienting their body to other babies. Direct his/her attention by pointing to the baby you are waving hello to!
Sing and Sign Song **Clap Your Hands** (signs: more, music)	Take your child's hands and form the signs for your child. Sign with your child routinely so you don't forget to do it at home such as at meal times, bath time, play time, and bedtime. At her next bath you could model and encourage her to ask for "more" bubbles. Babies do not sign back to you for the first time until they are 10-14 months old, but they are learning every time you show them signs!
Instruments- Shakers **Shake, Shake, Shake!**	Encourage your child to reach by placing the shaker in front of your child on the carpet to see if she will reach for it…or hold the shaker slightly out of his reach in front of him to encourage reaching. Make sure he is not getting frustrated! Everyday objects he/she can reach for include toys, spoons, sippie cups, and bath toys.
Movement **Pat a Cake** **Itsy Bitsy Spider** **Ten in the Bed**	Depending on your child's movement ability encourage him by: A) Back time- bringing feet to mouth B) Lifting head with chin tucked toward chest C) Holding head in line with trunk when pulled from lying to sitting D) Rolling back to tummy E) If already crawling or about to crawl, encouraging crawling by laying infant on tummy and putting your hands flat against your infant's feet and slightly pushing F) If already standing or about to stand, encouraging supported or unsupported standing G) If your child is about to walk, then helping them walk by holding both of their hands

Visual- Scarves **Blow Me Some Bubbles** **I Can Name the Colors**	Point to the bubbles to encourage visual tracking and play Peek-a-boo with scarves with your child. Everyday you can encourage this type of visual tracking, by drawing your child's attention to birds flying by, planes flying in the sky, or when driving in your car pointing out things you see like school buses and garbage trucks.
Animals/Puppets **Old MacDonald** **Brown Bear, Brown Bear*** (with book) *Sung to tune of Twinkle, Twinkle, Little Star	Let your child feel and explore puppet's features, encourage interaction with the puppet by puppet pretending to kiss, nudge, and play with child.
Body Parts **Head, Shoulders, Knees, and Toes**	Take your child's hands and touch each body feature in song.
Mirror Time **If You're Happy and You Know It** (with different expressions)	Hold the mirror in front of your child so you can see your child's face and make different faces for the different emotions in song. You can have fun with mirror time at home by facing your baby towards a large mirror and telling him/her a story while using animated facial expressions, or singing songs while facing the mirror.
Affection/Bonding **Never Let Me Go**	Show your child affection during this song by hugging, kissing, and rocking with your child. It is always good for your child to hear "I Love You."
Instruments- Ocean Drums/Rain Sticks **Hush Little Baby**	Massaging your baby before bedtime can help your baby fall asleep more quickly and sleep more soundly!
Goodbye Song **It's Time to Go** (using sign language)	Take your child's hands and form the signs for your child. Using this song is perfect for transitions (for instance, when it is time to get in the car when you are leaving home, the grocery store, or the mall).

Bright Start Music   6–12 Month Group   Session Plan #2

SKILL AREAS & SONGS	PARENT INSTRUCTION
Hello Song **My Right Hand Says Hello**	Help your baby greet other babies in the group by orienting their body to other babies. Direct his/her attention by pointing to the baby you are waving hello to!
Sing and Sign Songs **This is the Mommy Wiggle** (signs: mommy, daddy) Review: **Clap your Hands** (signs: more, music)	Take your child's hands and form the signs for your child. Find a routine time to sign with your child so you don't forget to do it at home. At her next meal you could model and encourage for her to ask "mommy" for "more" to eat. Babies do not sign back to you for the first time until they are 10–14 months old, but they are learning every time you show them signs!
Instruments- Shakers **Shake, Shake, Shake!**	Encourage reaching for your child by placing the shaker in front of your child on the carpet to see if she will reach for it…or hold the shaker slightly out of his reach in front of him to encourage reaching. Make sure he is not getting frustrated! Everyday objects he/she can reach for include toys, spoons, sippie cups, and bath toys.
Movement **Going Over the Sea** (MT use **ocean drum**)	Depending on your child's movement ability encourage him by: A) Back time- bringing feet to mouth B) Lifting head with chin tucked toward chest C) Holding head in line with trunk when pulled from lying to sitting D) Rolling back to tummy E) If already crawling or about to crawl, encouraging crawling by laying infant on tummy and putting your hands flat against your infant's feet and slightly pushing F) If already standing or about to stand, encouraging supported or unsupported standing G) If your child is about to walk, then helping them walk by holding both of their hands

Visual- Scarves **Twinkle Twinkle**- with **bubbles** **Little Red Caboose**- with **train** moving	Point to the bubbles and the train moving to encourage your child's visual tracking. Everyday you can encourage this type of visual tracking, by drawing your child's attention to birds flying by, planes flying in the sky, or when driving in your car pointing out things you see like school buses and garbage trucks.
Animals/Puppets **Old MacDonald** **Brown Bear, Brown Bear*** (with book) *Sung to tune of Twinkle, Twinkle, Little Star	Let your child feel and explore puppet's features; encourage interaction with the puppet by puppet pretending to kiss, nudge, and play with child.
Body Parts **If I Arr a Pirate**	Take your child's hands and touch each body feature in the song.
Mirror Time **If You're Happy and You Know It** (with different expressions)	Hold the mirror in front of your child so you can see your child's face and make different faces for the different emotions in song. You can have fun with mirror time at home by facing your baby towards a large mirror and telling him/her a story while using animated facial expressions, or singing songs while facing the mirror.
Affection/Bonding **Never Let Me Go**	Show your child affection during this song by hugging, kissing, and rocking with your child. It is always good for your child to hear "I Love You."
Instruments - Ocean Drums/Rain Sticks **Hush Little Baby**	Massaging your baby before bedtime can help your baby fall asleep more quickly and sleep more soundly!
Goodbye Song **It's Time to Go** (using sign language)	Take your child's hands and form the signs for your child. Using this song is perfect for transitions (for instance, when it is time to get in the car when you are leaving home, the grocery store, or the mall).

Bright Start Music   6–12 Month Group   Session Plan #3

SKILL AREAS & SONGS	PARENT INSTRUCTION
Hello Song **My Right Hand Says Hello**	Help your baby greet other babies in the group by orienting their body to other babies while you help your baby wave.
Sing and Sign Songs Song: **Mommy Go' Round the Sun** (signs: chair/sit, play/toy) Review: **This Is the Mommy Wiggle** (signs: mommy, daddy) Review: **Clap Your Hands** (signs: more, music)	Take your child's hands and form the signs for your child. Find a routine time to sign with your child so you don't forget to do it at home. Examples of routine times include: meal times, bath time, play time, and bedtime. While playing with your baby you can model the signs and encourage for him/her to ask "mommy" for "more" "toy." Babies do not sign to you for the first time until they are 10–14 months old. They are learning every time you show them signs!
Instruments- Drums **Humpty Dumpty** **One, Two, Buckle My Shoe** **Two Little Blackbirds**	Try to hide the drum for your child to find under your legs or behind your back. Also, encourage your child to move the mallet from one hand to the other while they are playing the drum. If your child needs help playing the drum, place the mallet in his hand and help him hit the drum by moving his hand. During play time encourage your baby to find "hidden" toys that they see you hide.
Movement **Ten in the Bed**	Depending on your child's movement ability encourage him by: A) Back time- bringing feet to mouth B) Lifting head with chin tucked to chest C) Holding head in line with trunk when pulled from lying to sitting D) Rolling back to tummy E) If already crawling or about to crawl, encouraging by laying infant on tummy and putting your hands flat against your infant's feet and slightly pushing F) If already standing or about to stand, encouraging supported or unsupported standing G) If your child is about to walk, then helping them walk by holding both of their hands

Visual- Scarves **I Can Name the Colors** with **scarves** **Little Red Caboose**- with **train** moving	Play Peek-a-boo with scarves with your child and point to the train moving to encourage your child's visual tracking. Playing games like peek-a-boo helps develop your child's social skills by giving him/her a "reward" for making eye contact and connecting with another person (you!).
Animals/Puppets **Had a Little Rooster**	Let your child feel and explore puppet's features; encourage interaction with the puppet by puppet pretending to kiss, nudge, and play with child.
Body Parts **Head, Shoulders, Knees, and Toes**	Take your child's hands and touch each body feature in song.
Mirror Time **You Are My Sunshine** (with different expressions)	Hold the mirror in front of your child so you can see your child's face and make different faces for the different emotions in song. Labeling facial expressions for different emotions teaches your child what to expect during different emotional situations.
Affection/Bonding **Never Let Me Go**	Show your child affection during this song by hugging, kissing, and rocking with your child. It is always good for your child to hear "I Love You."
Instruments - Ocean Drums/Rain Sticks **Soon the Moon Will Rise**	Massage before bedtime has been linked with better quality sleep for babies!
Goodbye Song **It's Time to Go** (using sign language)	Take your child's hands and form the signs for your child. Using this song is perfect for transition times such as when it is time to go eat when play time is done, or when it is time to get in the car when playground time is done.

Bright Start Music   6–12 Month Group   Session Plan #4

SKILL AREAS & SONGS	PARENT INSTRUCTION
Hello Song **My Right Hand Says Hello**	Help your baby greet other babies in the group by orienting their body to other babies. Direct his/her attention by pointing to the baby you are waving hello to!
Sing and Sign Songs **Doggie Doggie** (signs: dog, cat, ball) Review: **Mommy Go 'Round the Sun** (signs: chair/sit, play/toy) Review: **This Is the Mommy Wiggle** (signs: mommy, daddy)	Take your child's hands and form the signs for your child. Find a routine time to sign with your child so you don't forget to do it at home. Examples of routine times include: meal times, bath time, play time, and bedtime. While playing with your baby, encourage signing by modeling "play" "ball" with "mommy." Babies do not sign back to you for the first time until they are 10–14 months old, but they are learning every time you show them signs!
Instruments - Drums **This Old Man** **One, Two, Buckle My Shoe**	Try to hide the drum for your child to find under your legs or behind your back. Also, encourage your child to move the mallet from one hand to the other while they are playing the drum. If your child needs help playing the drum, place the mallet in his hand and help him hit the drum by moving his hand. Help your baby transfer toys from one hand to the other at home.
Movement **London Bridge** **Row, Row, Row Your Boat**	Depending on your child's movement ability encourage him by: A) Back time- bringing feet to mouth B) Lifting head with chin tucked to chest C) Holding head in line with trunk when pulled from lying to sitting D) Rolling back to tummy E) If already crawling or about to crawl, encouraging crawling by laying infant on tummy and putting your hands flat against your infant's feet and slightly pushing F) If already standing or about to stand, encouraging supported or unsupported standing G) If your child is about to walk, then helping them walk by holding both of their hands

Visual- Scarves **Twinkle Twinkle**- with **bubbles** **Little Red Caboose**- with **train** moving	Point to the bubbles and the train moving to encourage your child's visual tracking. Everyday you can encourage this type of visual tracking by pointing out when a dog is running by you at the park, or when a train is going by if you are stopped at the train tracks.
Animals/Puppets **Had a Little Rooster**	Let your child feel and explore puppet's features; encourage interaction with the puppet by puppet pretending to kiss, nudge, and play with child.
Body Parts **If I Arr a Pirate**	Take your child's hands and touch each body feature in song.
Mirror Time **You Are My Sunshine** (with different expressions)	Hold the mirror in front of your child so you can see your child's face and make different faces for the different emotions in song. Make a game out of making faces in the mirror at home!
Affection/Bonding **Never Let Me Go**	Show your child affection during this song by hugging, kissing, and rocking with your child. It is always good for your child to hear "I Love You."
Instruments - Ocean Drums/Rain Sticks **Soon the Moon Will Rise**	Massage encourages good circulation and promotes relaxation!
Goodbye Song **It's Time to Go** (using sign language)	Take your child's hands and form the signs for your child. Using this song is perfect for transition times such as when it is time to go after a play date or when leaving grandpa's or grandma's house.

Bright Start Music   6–12 Month Group   Session Plan #5

SKILL AREAS & SONGS	PARENT INSTRUCTION
Hello Song **My Right Hand Says Hello**	Help your baby greet other babies in the group by orienting their body to other babies. Direct his/her attention by pointing to the baby you are waving hello to!
Sing and Sign Songs **Roll the Ball** (signs: want, please, help, sorry) Review: **Doggie Doggie** (signs: dog, cat, ball) Review: **Mommy Go 'Round the Sun** (signs: chair/sit, play/toy)	Take your child's hands and form the signs for your child. Find a routine time to sign with your child so you don't forget to do it at home. Examples of routine times include: meal times, bath time, play time, and bedtime.
Instruments - Shakers **Mister Golden Sun** **Oh Where Has My Little Dog Gone?**	Try to hide the drum for your child to find under your legs or behind your back. Also, encourage your child to move the mallet from one hand to the other while they are playing the drum. If your child needs help playing the drum, place the mallet in his hand and help him hit the drum by moving his hand.
Movement **London Bridge** **Row, Row, Row Your Boat**	Depending on your child's movement ability encourage him by: A) Back time- bringing feet to mouth B) Lifting head with chin tucked toward chest C) Holding head in line with trunk when pulled from lying to sitting D) Rolling back to tummy E) If about to crawl, encouraging crawling by laying infant on tummy and putting your hands flat against your infant's feet and slightly pushing F) If already standing or about to stand, encouraging supported or unsupported standing G) If needed, helping your child walk by holding both of their hands

Visual - Scarves **Blow Me Some Bubbles**- with **bubbles** **Little Red Caboose**- with **train** moving	Point to the bubbles and the train moving to encourage your child's visual tracking.
Animals/Puppets **Polar Bear, Polar Bear*** (with book) *Sung to tune of Twinkle, Twinkle, Little Star **Old MacDonald**- with **puppets**	Let your child feel and explore puppet's features; encourage interaction with the puppet by puppet pretending to kiss, nudge, and play with child.
Body Parts **Head, Shoulders, Knees, and Toes**	Take your child's hands and touch each body feature in song.
Mirror Time **If You're Happy and You Know It** (with different expressions)	Hold the mirror in front of your child so you can see your child's face and make different faces for the different emotions in song.
Affection/Bonding **Always in My Heart**	Show your child affection during this song by hugging, kissing, and rocking with your child. It is always good for your child to hear "I Love You."
Instruments- Ocean Drums/Rain Sticks **Big Bright Moon**	Massage encourages good circulation and promotes relaxation!
Goodbye Song **It's Time to Go** (using sign language)	Take your child's hands and form the signs for your child. Find a routine time to sign with your child so you don't forget to do it at home. Examples of routine times include: meal times, bath time, play time, and bedtime.

Bright Start Music   6–12 Month Group   Session Plan #6

SKILL AREAS & SONGS	PARENT INSTRUCTION
Hello Song **My Right Hand Says Hello**	Help your baby greet other babies in the group by orienting their body to other babies. Direct his/her attention by pointing to the baby you are waving hello to!
Sing and Sign Songs **The Walking Song** (signs: all-done, stop, ouch/hurt, hot) Review: **Roll the Ball** (signs: want, please, help, sorry) **Doggie Doggie** (signs: dog, cat, ball)	Take your child's hands and form the signs for your child. Find a routine time to sign with your child so you don't forget to do it at home. Examples of routine times include: meal times, bath time, play time, and bedtime.
Instruments- Drums **Click, Click, Click, Go the Castanets** **This Old Man**	Try to hide the drum for your child to find under your legs or behind your back. Also, encourage your child to move the mallet from one hand to the other while they are playing the drum. If your child needs help playing the drum, place the mallet in his hand and help him hit the drum by moving his hand.
Movement **The Ants Go Marching**	Depending on your child's movement ability encourage him by: A) Back time- bringing feet to mouth B) Lifting head with chin tucked toward chest C) Holding head in line with trunk when pulled from lying to sitting D) Rolling back to tummy E) If already crawling or about to crawl, encouraging crawling by laying infant on tummy and putting your hands flat against your infant's feet and slightly pushing F) If already standing or about to stand, encouraging supported or unsupported standing G) If needed, helping your child walk by holding both of their hands

Visual- Scarves **Blow Me Some Bubbles**- with **bubbles** **Little Red Caboose**- with **train** moving **I Can Name the Colors**- with color circles	Point to the bubbles and the train moving to encourage your child's visual tracking, point to the color circles that are being held up to identify color name.
Animals/Puppets **Polar Bear, Polar Bear*** (with book) *Sung to tune of Twinkle, Twinkle Little Star **Old MacDonald**- with puppets	Let your child feel and explore puppet's features; encourage interaction with the puppet by puppet pretending to kiss, nudge, and play with child.
Body Parts **If I Arr a Pirate**	Take your child's hands and touch each body feature in song.
Mirror Time **You Are My Sunshine** (with different expressions)	Hold the mirror in front of your child so you can see your child's face and make different faces for the different emotions in song.
Affection/Bonding **How Will You Grow?**	Show your child affection during this song by hugging, kissing, and rocking with your child. It is always good for your child to hear "I Love You."
Instruments- Ocean Drums/Rain Sticks **Big Bright Moon**	Massage encourages good circulation and promotes relaxation!
Goodbye Song **It's Time to Go** (using sign language)	Take your child's hands and form the signs for your child.

Bright Start Music   6–12 Month Group   Session Plan #7

SKILL AREAS & SONGS	PARENT INSTRUCTION
Hello Song **My Right Hand Says Hello**	Help your baby greet other babies in the group by orienting their body to other babies. Direct his/her attention by pointing to the baby you are waving hello to!
Sing and Sign Songs **Where's Baby** (signs: eat/food/spoon, boy, girl) **The Walking Song** (signs: all-done, stop, ouch/hurt, hot) **Roll the Ball** (signs: want, please, help, sorry)	Take your child's hands and form the signs for your child. Find a routine time to sign with your child so you don't forget to do it at home. Examples of routine times include: meal times, bath time, play time, and bedtime.
Instruments- Triangles/Wood Blocks **The Alphabet Song** **My Favorite Spot**	Tell your child that the stick hits the triangle and the wood blocks hit each other to make a sound; we are focusing on making a paired connection between two things.
Movement **The Ants Go Marching** **I've Been Working on the Railroad** (for children who can walk, you can walk in a circle like a train)	Depending on your child's movement ability encourage him by: A) Back time- bringing feet to mouth B) Lifting head with chin tucked toward chest C) Holding head in line with trunk when pulled from lying to sitting D) Rolling back to tummy E) If already crawling or about to crawl, encouraging crawling by laying infant on tummy and putting your hands flat against your infant's feet and slightly pushing F) If already standing or about to stand, encouraging supported or unsupported standing G) If your child is about to walk, then helping them walk by holding both of their hands

Visual - Tracking Let child choose from instrument choices **Skip to My Lou** **Mister Golden Sun** **Tingalayo**	Parent plays instruments while moving them around your child to encourage tracking.
Animals/Puppets Put puppets out in middle of circle out of reach for child to crawl/scoot/reach to get **Had a Little Rooster**	Let your child feel and explore puppet's features; encourage interaction with the puppet by puppet pretending to kiss, nudge, and play with child.
Body Parts **Hokey Pokey**	Take your child's hands and touch each body feature in song.
Mirror Time **The More We Get Together** (with different emotions written in song)	Hold the mirror in front of your child so you can see your child's face and make different faces for the different emotions in song.
Affection/Bonding **How Will You Grow?**	Show your child affection during this song by hugging, kissing, and rocking with your child. It is always good for your child to hear "I Love You."
Instruments - Ocean Drums/Rain Sticks **Big Bright Moon**	Massage before sleep has been linked with better quality and longer sleep!
Goodbye Song **It's Time to Go** (using sign language)	Take your child's hands and form the signs for your child.

Bright Start Music   6–12 Month Group   Session Plan #8

SKILL AREAS & SONGS	PARENT INSTRUCTION
Hello Song **My Right Hand Says Hello**	Help your baby greet other babies in the group by orienting their body to other babies. Direct his/her attention by pointing to the baby you are waving hello to!
Sing and Sign Songs **Miss Mary Jane** (signs: car, airplane) Review: **Where's Baby** (signs: eat/food/spoon, boy, girl) Review: **The Walking Song** (signs: all-done, stop, ouch/hurt, hot)	Take your child's hands and form the signs for your child. Find a routine time to sign with your child so you don't forget to do it at home. Examples of routine times include: meal times, bath time, play time, and bedtime.
Instruments- Triangles/Wood Blocks **The Alphabet Song** **My Favorite Spot**	Tell your child that the stick hits the triangle and the wood blocks hit each other to make a sound; we are focusing on making a paired connection between two things.
Movement **The Ants Go Marching** **I've Been Working on the Railroad** (for children who can walk, you can walk in a circle like a train)	Depending on your child's movement ability encourage him by: A) Back time- bringing feet to mouth B) Lifting head with chin tucked toward chest C) Holding head in line with trunk when pulled from lying to sitting D) Rolling back to tummy E) If already crawling or about to crawl, encouraging crawling by laying infant on tummy and putting your hands flat against your infant's feet and slightly pushing F) If already standing or about to stand, encouraging supported or unsupported standing G) If your child is about to walk, then helping them walk by holding both of their hands

__Visual- Tracking__ Let child choose from instrument choices. **Blow Me Some Bubbles** **Kookabura**	Parent plays instruments while moving them around your child to encourage tracking.
__Animals/Puppets__ Put puppets out in middle of circle out of reach for child to crawl/scoot/reach to get **Animal Song**	Let your child feel and explore puppet's features; encourage interaction with the puppet by puppet pretending to kiss, nudge, and play with child.
__Body Parts__ **My Hand on My Head** Ask: Where is your <u>hand</u>? (fill in blank with other body parts)	Take your child's hands and touch each body feature in song.
__Mirror Time__ **Peek-A-Boo** (with different emotions written in song)	Hold the mirror in front of your child so you can see your child's face and make different faces for the different emotions in song.
__Affection/Bonding__ **How Will You Grow?**	Show your child affection during this song by hugging, kissing, and rocking with your child. It is always good for your child to hear "I Love You."
__Instruments- Ocean Drums/Rain Sticks__ **Big Bright Moon**	Massaging your infant routinely before bed can cue your child this it is time for bed!
__Goodbye Song__ **It's Time to Go** (using sign language)	Take your child's hands and form the signs for your child.

Bright Start Music   6–12 Month Group   Session Plan #9

SKILL AREAS & SONGS	PARENT INSTRUCTION
Hello Song **My Right Hand Says Hello**	Help your baby greet other babies in the group by orienting their body to other babies. Direct his/her attention by pointing to the baby you are waving hello to!
Sing and Sign Songs **The Little Cat Goes Creeping** (signs: sleep/bed, fish, thank you) Review: **Miss Mary Jane** (signs: car, airplane) Review: **Where's Baby** (signs: eat/food/spoon, boy, girl)	Take your child's hands and form the signs for your child. Find a routine time to sign with your child so you don't forget to do it at home. Examples of routine times include: meal times, bath time, play time, and bedtime.
Instruments - Claves/Wood Blocks/Drums **The Alphabet Song** **My Favorite Spot**	Tell your child that the mallet hits the drum and the claves/wood blocks hit each other to make a sound; we are focusing on making a paired connection between two things.
Movement **Five Little Ducks**	Depending on your child's movement ability encourage him by: A) Back time- bringing feet to mouth B) Lifting head with chin tucked toward chest C) Holding head in line with trunk when pulled from lying to sitting D) Rolling back to tummy E) If already crawling or about to crawl, encouraging crawling by laying infant on tummy and putting your hands flat against your infant's feet and slightly pushing F) If already standing or about to stand, encouraging supported or unsupported standing G) If your child is about to walk, then helping them walk by holding both of their hands

**Visual- Tracking** Let child choose from instrument choices **Kookabura** **Whack the Drum**	Parent plays instruments while moving then around your child to encourage tracking.
**Animals/Puppets** Put puppets out in middle of circle out of reach for child to crawl/scoot/reach to get **Had a Little Rooster**	Let your child feel and explore puppets features; encourage interaction with the puppet by puppet pretending to kiss, nudge, and play with child.
**Body Parts** **If I Arr a Pirate** Ask: Where is your <u>hand</u>? (fill in blank with other body parts)	Take your child's hands and touch each body feature in song.
**Mirror Time** **Peek-A-Boo** (with different emotions written in song)	Hold the mirror in front of your child so you can see your child's face and make different faces for the different emotions in song.
**Affection/Bonding** **Always in My Heart**	Show your child affection during this song by hugging, kissing, and rocking with your child. It is always good for your child to hear "I Love You."
**Instruments- Ocean Drums/Rain Sticks** **Soon the Moon Will Rise**	Massaging your infant routinely before bed can cue your child this it is time for bed!
**Goodbye Song** **It's Time to Go** (using sign language)	Take your child's hands and form the signs for your child.

Bright Start Music   6–12 Month Group   Session Plan #10

SKILL AREAS & SONGS	PARENT INSTRUCTION
Hello Song **My Right Hand Says Hello**	Help your baby greet other babies in the group by orienting their body to other babies. Direct his/her attention by pointing to the baby you are waving hello to!
Sing and Sign Songs **Bunny Boogie** (signs: bunny) Review: **The Little Cat Goes Creeping** (signs: sleep/bed, fish, thank you) Review: **Miss Mary Jane** (signs: car, airplane)	Take your child's hands and form the signs for your child. Find a routine time to sign with your child so you don't forget to do it at home. Examples of routine times include: meal times, bath time, play time, and bedtime.
Instruments - Claves/Wood Blocks/Drums **My Favorite Spot** **BINGO**	Tell your child that the mallet hits the drum and the claves/wood blocks hit each other to make a sound; we are focusing on making a paired connection between two things.
Movement **London Bridge** **Row, Row, Row Your Boat** **I Roll the Ball to You*** *Roll balls from MT to each child/parent	Depending on your child's movement ability encourage him by: A) Back time- bringing feet to mouth B) Lifting head with chin tucked toward chest C) Holding head in line with trunk when pulled from lying to sitting D) Rolling back to tummy E) If already crawling or about to crawl; encouraging crawling by laying infant on tummy and putting your hands flat against your infant's feet and slightly pushing F) If already standing or about to stand, encouraging supported or unsupported standing G) If your child is about to walk, then helping them walk by holding both of their hands

Visual- Tracking Create shaker instrument from beans in a can (let child put beans in can and take out when songs are done) **Blow Me Some Bubbles** **Five Green and Speckled Frogs**	Point to the bubbles and play the shaker can while moving it around child to encourage your child's visual tracking.
Animals/Puppets Put puppets out in middle of circle out of reach for child to crawl/scoot/reach to get **Animal Song**	Let your child feel and explore puppet's features; encourage interaction with the puppet by puppet pretending to kiss, nudge, and play with child
Body Parts **My Hand on My Head** Ask: Where is your <u>hand</u>? (fill in blank with other body parts)	Take your child's hands and touch each body feature in song.
Mirror Time **Where is Thumbkin?** (with different emotions written in song)	Hold the mirror in front of your child so you can see your child's face and make different faces for the different emotions in song.
Affection/Bonding **Always in My Heart**	Show your child affection during this song by hugging, kissing, and rocking with your child. It is always good for your child to hear "I Love You."
Instruments- Ocean Drums/Rain Sticks **Soon the Moon Will Rise**	Massaging your infant routinely before bed can cue your child this it is time for bed!
Goodbye Song **It's Time to Go** (using sign language)	Take your child's hands and form the signs for your child.

Bright Start Music   6–12 Month Group   Session Plan #11

SKILL AREAS & SONGS	PARENT INSTRUCTION
Hello Song **My Right Hand Says Hello**	Help your baby greet other babies in the group by orienting their body to other babies. Direct his/her attention by pointing to the baby you are waving hello to!
Sing and Sign Songs **Charlie Over the Water** (signs: water) Review: **Bunny Boogie** (signs: bunny) Review: **The Little Cat Goes Creeping** (signs: sleep/bed, fish, thank you)	Take your child's hands and form the signs for your child. Find a routine time to sign with your child so you don't forget to do it at home. Examples of routine times include: meal times, bath time, play time, and bedtime.
Instruments- Triangles/Wood Blocks **Twinkle Twinkle** **Itsy Bitsy Spider**	Tell your child that the mallet hits the drum and the claves/wood blocks hit each other to make a sound; we are focusing on making a paired connection between two things.
Movement **London Bridge** **Row, Row, Row Your Boat** **I Roll the Ball to You*** *Roll balls from MT to each child/parent	Depending on your child's movement ability encourage him by: A) Back time- bringing feet to mouth B) Lifting head with chin tucked toward chest C) Holding head in line with trunk when pulled from lying to sitting D) Rolling back to tummy E) If already crawling or about to crawl, encouraging crawling by laying infant on tummy and putting your hands flat against your infant's feet and slightly pushing F) If already standing or about to stand, encouraging supported or unsupported standing G) If your child is about to walk, then helping them walk by holding both of their hands

Visual- Tracking Create shaker instrument from beans in a can (let child put beans in can & take out when songs are done) **Blow Me Some Bubbles** **Five Green and Speckled Frogs**	Point to the bubbles and play the shaker can while moving it around child to encourage your child's visual tracking.
Animals/Puppets Use **Picture Cards** of birds or **Scarves** to mimic bird movement **Birdie Beat**- Allow children to explore activity circle freely during this activity	Let your child feel and explore puppet's features; encourage interaction with the puppet by puppet pretending to kiss, nudge, and play with child.
Body Parts **Loop De Loop** Ask: Where is your <u>hand</u>? (fill in blank with other body parts)	Take your child's hands and touch each body feature in song.
Mirror Time Put mirror wrong side up to let child find functional side **Where is Thumbkin?** (with different emotions written in song)	Hold the mirror in front of your child so you can see your child's face and make different faces for the different emotions in song.
Affection/Bonding **How You Will Grow?**	Show your child affection during this song by hugging, kissing, and rocking with your child. It is always good for your child to hear "I Love You."
Instruments- Ocean Drums/Rain Sticks **Goodnight, My Sweet One**	Massaging your infant routinely before bed can cue your child this it is time for bed!
Goodbye Song **It's Time to Go** (using sign language)	Take your child's hands and form the signs for your child.

Bright Start Music   6–12 Month Group   Session Plan #12

SKILL AREAS & SONGS	PARENT INSTRUCTION
Hello Song **My Right Hand Says Hello**	Help your baby greet other babies in the group by orienting their body to other babies. Direct his/her attention by pointing to the baby you are waving hello to!
Sing and Sign Songs **My World** (signs: book) Review: **Charlie Over the Water** (signs: water) Review: **Bunny Boogie** (signs: bunny)	Take your child's hands and form the signs for your child. Find a routine time to sign with your child so you don't forget to do it at home. Examples of routine times include: meal times, bath time, play time, and bedtime.
Instruments- Claves/Wood Blocks/Drums **Skip to My Lou** **Humpty Dumpty**	Tell your child that the mallet hits the drum and the claves/wood blocks hit each other to make a sound; we are focusing on making a paired connection between two things.
Movement **Five Little Monkeys Jumping on the Bed** **I Roll the Ball to You*** *Roll balls from MT to each child/parent	Depending on your child's movement ability encourage him by: A) Back time- bringing feet to mouth B) Lifting head with chin tucked toward chest C) Holding head in line with trunk when pulled from lying to sitting D) Rolling back to tummy E) If already crawling or about to crawl, encouraging crawling by laying infant on tummy and putting your hands flat against your infant's feet and slightly pushing F) If already standing or about to stand, encouraging supported or unsupported standing G) If your child is about to walk, then helping them walk by holding both of their hands

Visual- Tracking Create shaker instrument from beans in a can (let child put beans in can and take out when songs are done) **I'm a Little Teapot** **If All the Raindrops**	Play the shaker can while moving it around child to encourage your child's visual tracking.
Animals/Puppets Use **Picture Cards** of birds or **Scarves** to mimic bird movement. **Birdie Beat** Allow children to explore activity circle freely during this activity.	Let your child feel and explore puppet's features; encourage interaction with the puppet by puppet pretending to kiss, nudge, and play with child.
Body Parts **Loop De Loop** Ask: Where is your <u>hand</u>? (fill in blank with other body parts)	Take your child's hands and touch each body feature in song.
Mirror Time Put mirror wrong side up to let child find functional side. **Where is Thumbkin?** (with different emotions written in song)	Hold the mirror in front of your child so you can see your child's face and make different faces for the different emotions in song.
Affection/Bonding **Always in My Heart**	Show your child affection during this song by hugging, kissing, and rocking with your child. It is always good for your child to hear "I Love You."
Instruments- Ocean Drums/Rain Sticks **Goodnight, My Sweet One**	Massaging your infant routinely before bed can cue your child this it is time for bed!
Goodbye Song **It's Time to Go** (using sign language)	Take your child's hands and form the signs for your child.

Bright Start Music   12–18 Month Group Session Plan #1

*Throughout Session - Use verbal directions for activities for child to follow. Avoid giving gestural cues; give directions while pointing to objects.

SKILL AREAS & SONGS	PARENT INSTRUCTION
Hello Song **When I Meet a New Friend**	Encourage your child to greet their friends at music by going up to them to say hello, shake hands, or give a hug.
Sing and Sign Songs **La La La Lullaby** Signs: Sleep/bed, I love you **Review: Skye Boat Song** Signs: stars, blanket, moon, I love you **Review: My World** Signs: book	Take your child's hands and form the signs for your child. Find a routine time to sign with your child so you don't forget to do it at home. Reading bedtime books and signing bedtime songs provides a great opportunity to practice signs such as "moon" and "stars" and "book." During the transition time to bed you can encourage your child to sign "sleep/bed." When your baby starts signing back to you, he/she may tell you when they are tired and want to go to "sleep/bed"!
Instruments- Rhythm Instruments **Playing Along** Create shaker instrument from beans in a can (let child put beans in can and take out when songs are done).	Have your child stand up and pick up an instrument off the floor from standing. Ask your child to hand you an instrument to play together. Ask your child, "What's this?" Play an instrument while moving around your child, helping him/her to follow and localize sound. Encourage children's independence by letting them pick up items they want instead of doing it for them.
Movement **The Owl**	Pretend to fly like an owl as you walk with your child (holding hands if needed) to the front, to the side, and backwards. Pretend play helps your child organize and understand how things work in the world!
Visual- Scarves **I Can Name the Color**	Encourage your child to imitate/copy your movements with the scarf. Children learn many skills by imitating adult and speech.
Animals/Puppets **Hello Mr. Animal**	Let your child feel and explore puppet's features; encourage interaction with the puppet by puppet pretending to kiss, nudge, and play with child.
Books **Ten Little Monkeys** (Big Book)	Pat the beat on your child's knees or bounce your child to the beat in your lap. We have rhythm in our speech and our steps. Internalizing a rhythmic beat can help your child in more ways than singing!

Body Parts **If I Arr a Pirate**	Take your child's hands and touch each body part mentioned in the song, or have your child hold the mirror while you point to each body part.
Mirror Time **Look in the Mirror**	Have your child hold the mirror so you can see your face in the mirror, too. Make the different emotional faces in the mirror for your child to see. Reading nonverbal cues from other people is an important social and communication skill your child is developing!
Movement **Hot Air Balloon**	Face each other in a circle with children facing center of circle. Pick children up and fly them through the air to the center of the circle and back out. Your child will be processing lots of visual and sensory input during this activity! Coordinating input from multiple senses is complicated...even for adults!
Affection/Bonding **In My Own Little Way**	Show your child affection during this song by hugging, kissing, and rocking with your child. It is always good for your child to hear "I Love You." Emotional attachment is an important indicator of a child being secure in new or novel situations later in life.
Goodbye Song **It's Time to Go** (using sign language)	Take your child's hands and form the signs for your child if they are not signing on their own yet. Establishing routines with your child will help them predict what is happening next in their world, which can decrease temper tantrums!

Bright Start Music   12–18 Month Group   Session Plan #2

*Throughout Session - Use verbal directions for activities for child to follow. Avoid giving gestural cues; give directions while pointing to objects.

SKILL AREAS & SONGS	PARENT INSTRUCTION
Hello Song **When I Meet a New Friend**	Encourage your child to greet their friends at music by going up to them to say hello, shake hands, or give a hug.
Sing and Sign Songs **La La La Lullaby** Signs: Sleep/bed, I love you Review: **Skye Boat Song** Signs: stars, blanket, moon, I love you Review: **My World** Sign: book	Take your child's hands and form the signs for your child. Find a routine time to sign with your child so you don't forget to do it at home. Reading bedtime books and signing bedtime songs provides a great opportunity to practice signs such as "moon" and "stars" and "book." During the transition time to bed you can encourage your child to sign "sleep/bed." When your baby starts signing back to you, he/she may tell you when they are tired and want to go to "sleep/bed"!
Instruments- Rhythm Instruments **Playing Along**	Have your child stand up and pick up an instrument off the floor from standing. Ask your child to hand you an instrument to play together. Ask your child, "What's this?" Play an instrument while moving around your child, helping him/her to follow and localize sound. Encourage children's independence by letting them pick up items they want instead of doing it for them.
Movement **The Owl**	Pretend to fly like an owl as you walk with your child (holding hands if needed) to the front, to the side, and backwards. Pretend play helps your child organize and understand how things work in the world!
Visual- Scarves **I Can Name the Color**	Encourage your child to imitate/copy your movements with the scarf. Children learn many skills by imitating adult and speech.
Animals/Puppets **Hello Mr. Animal**	Let your child feel and explore puppet's features; encourage interaction with the puppet by puppet pretending to kiss, nudge, and play with child.
Books **Ten Little Monkeys** (Big Book)	Pat the beat on your child's knees or bounce your child to the beat in your lap. We have rhythm in our speech and our steps. Internalizing a rhythmic beat can help your child in more ways than singing!

Body Parts **You Do the Same** Incorporate rolling and throwing small balls.	Take your child's hands and touch each body part mentioned in the song, or have your child hold the mirror while you point to each body part.
Mirror Time **Look in the Mirror**	Have your child hold the mirror so you can see your face in the mirror, too. Make the different emotional faces in the mirror for your child to see. Reading nonverbal cues from other people is an important social and communication skill your child is developing!
Movement **Hot Air Balloon**	Face each other in a circle with children facing center of circle. Pick children up and fly them through the air to the center of the circle and back out. Your child will be processing lots of visual and sensory input during this activity! Coordinating input from multiple senses is complicated...even for adults!
Affection/Bonding **In My Own Little Way**	Show your child affection during this song by hugging, kissing, and rocking with your child. It is always good for your child to hear "I Love You." Emotional attachment is an important indicator of a child being secure in new or novel situations later in life.
Goodbye Song **It's Time to Go** (using sign language)	Take your child's hands and form the signs for your child if they are not signing on their own yet. Establishing routines with your child will help them predict what is happening next in their world, which can decrease temper tantrums!

Bright Start Music   12–18 Month Group   Session Plan #3

*Throughout Session - Use verbal directions for activities for child to follow. Avoid giving gestural cues; give directions while pointing to objects.

SKILL AREAS & SONGS	PARENT INSTRUCTION
Hello Song **When I Meet a New Friend**	Encourage your child to greet their friends at music by going up to them to say hello, shake hands, or give a hug.
Sing and Sign Songs **La La La Lullaby** Signs: Sleep/bed, I love you Review: **Skye Boat Song** Signs: stars, blanket, moon, I love you	Take your child's hands and form the signs for your child. Reading bedtime books and signing bedtime songs provides a great opportunity to practice signs such as "moon" and "stars" and "book." During the transition time to bed you can encourage your child to sign "sleep/bed." When your baby starts signing back to you, he/she may tell you when they are tired and want to go to "sleep/bed"!
Instruments- Rhythm Instruments **Razzle Dazzle 'Em** Create shaker instrument from beans in a can (let child put beans in can and take out when songs are done)	Have your child stand up and pick up an instrument off the floor from standing. Ask your child to hand you an instrument to play together. Ask your child, "What's this?" Play an instrument while moving around your child to follow and localize sound. When you are outside of your house notice the sounds around you. Describe what you are hearing to your child while trying to locate the source of the sound.
Movement **The Owl**	Pretend to fly like an owl as you walk with your child (holding hands if needed) to the front, to the side, and backwards. Pretend play helps your child organize and understand how things work in the world!
Visual- Scarves **I Can Name the Color**	Encourage your child to imitate/copy your movements with the scarf. Children learn through imitation! Remember, they are watching what you do!
Animals/Puppets **Animal Song**	Let your child feel and explore puppet's features; encourage interaction with the puppet by puppet pretending to kiss, nudge, and play with child.
Books **Mulberry Bush** (Big Book)	Pat the beat on your child's knees or bounce your child to the beat in your lap. We have rhythm in our speech and our steps. Internalizing a rhythmic beat can help your child in more ways than singing!

Body Parts **Look in the Mirror**	Take your child's hands and touch each body part mentioned in the song, or have your child hold the mirror while you point to each body part.
Mirror Time **This is How I Look**	Have your child hold the mirror so you can see your face in the mirror, too. Make the different emotional faces in the mirror for your child to see. Have fun with mirror time at home...play games and act silly in front of the mirror with your child.
Movement **Pitter Patter** Can incorporate rain sticks or ocean drums	Children stand for this song. Model to children rain falling down with your fingers. Splash hands from side to side and stomp with your children. Using gestures with words will help increase your child's communication ability!
Affection/Bonding **In My Own Little Way**	Show your child affection during this song by hugging, kissing, and rocking with your child. It is always good for your child to hear "I Love You." Emotional attachment is an important indicator of a child being secure in new or novel situations later in life.
Goodbye Song **It's Time to Go** (using sign language)	Take your child's hands and form the signs for your child if they are not signing on their own yet. Establishing routines with your child will help them predict what is happening next in their world, which can decrease temper tantrums!

Bright Start Music   12–18 Month Group   Session Plan #4

*Throughout Session - Use verbal directions for activities for child to follow. Avoid giving gestural cues; give directions while pointing to objects.

SKILL AREAS & SONGS	PARENT INSTRUCTION
Hello Song **When I Meet a New Friend**	Encourage your child to greet their friends at music by going up to them to say hello, shake hands, or give a hug.
Sign Language Song **Brown Bear, Brown Bear*** *Sung to the tune of Twinkle, Twinkle, Little Star	Take your child's hands and form the signs for your child. If your child is now signing know that as they begin to say a word they used to sign, they may stop doing using that sign and instead will replace it with a new sign they are learning!
Instruments- Rhythm Instruments **Playing Along**	Have your child stand up and pick up an instrument off the floor from standing. Ask your child to hand you an instrument to play together. Ask your child "what's this?" Play an instrument while moving around your child to follow and localize sound. Discovering sources of sounds in your environment will open up new conversation topics. Describe everything you hear to your child to provide a language rich environment!
Movement **Let's Go for a Ride**	Pretend to drive a car or ride on a motorcycle while walking with your child (holding hands if needed) - to the front, to the side, and backwards. Pretend play is important for development of inter- and intra-personal skills.
Visual- Scarves **I Can Name the Color**	Encourage your child to imitate/copy your movements with the scarf. Your child will get practice with hand/eye coordination as well as imitation skill improvement!
Animals/Puppets **Monkey Hug**	Let your child feel and explore puppet's features; encourage interaction with the puppet by puppet pretending to kiss, nudge, and play with child.
Books **Farmer in the Dell** (Big Book)	Pat the beat on your child's knees or bounce your child to the beat in your lap. Rhythmic activities help foster language development.
Body Parts **You Do the Same** Incorporate rolling and throwing small balls.	Take your child's hands and touch each body part mentioned in the song, or have your child hold the mirror while you point to each body part.

Mirror Time **This is How I Look**	Have your child hold the mirror so you can see your face in the mirror, too. Make the different emotional faces in the mirror for your child to see. When your baby sees a mirror at home watch to see if he/she initiates a bid for interaction by "asking" you to play with him/her in front of the mirror.
Movement **There's a Tickle Under My Skin**	Children stand for this song. Play drums while dancing to the beat. Pairing the drum with a mallet helps solidify the idea that some items come in pairs.
Affection/Bonding **Doo Wop Love**	Show your child affection during this song by hugging, kissing, and rocking with your child. It is always good for your child to hear "I Love You."
Goodbye Song **It's Time to Go** (using sign language)	Take your child's hands and form the signs for your child. When your child starts signing, he/she may tell you when he/she is all done with an activity and is ready to go!

Bright Start Music   12–18 Month Group Session Plan #5

*Throughout Session - Use verbal directions for activities for child to follow. Avoid giving gestural cues; give directions while pointing to objects.

SKILL AREAS & SONGS	PARENT INSTRUCTION
Hello Song **When I Meet a New Friend**	Encourage your child to greet their friends at music by going up to them to say hello, shake hands, or give a hug.
Sign Language Song **Brown Bear, Brown Bear*** *Sung to the tune of Twinkle, Twinkle, Little Star	Take your child's hands and form the signs for your child. Find a routine time to sign with your child so you don't forget to do it at home. Examples of routine times include: meal times, bath time, play time, and bedtime.
Instruments- Rhythm Instruments **Razzle Dazzle 'Em** Create shaker instrument from beans in a can (let child put beans in can and take out when songs are done.)	Have your child stand up and pick up an instrument off the floor from standing. Ask your child to hand you an instrument to play together. Ask your child, "What's this?" Play an instrument while moving around your child to follow and localize sound.
Movement **Let's Go for a Ride**	Pretend to drive a car or ride on a motorcycle while walking with your child (holding hands if needed)- to the front, to the side, and backwards.
Visual- Scarves **I Can Name the Color**	Encourage your child to imitate/copy your movements with the scarf.
Animals/Puppets **Animal Song** with **Picture Cards**	Hold up the correct animal picture card as the song progresses in front of your child or place the correct picture card in their hand each time the animal changes in the song.
Books **This Old Man** (Big Book)	Pat the beat on your child's knees or bounce your child to the beat in your lap.
Body Parts **Look in the Mirror**	Take your child's hands and touch each body part mentioned in the song, or have your child hold the mirror while you point to each body part.
Mirror Time **I Feel Silly**	Have your child hold the mirror so you can see your face in the mirror, too. Make the different emotional faces in the mirror for your child to see.

Movement **Pitter Patter** Can incorporate rain sticks or ocean drums.	Children stand for this song. Model to children rain falling down with your fingers. Splash hands from side to side and stomp with your children.
Affection/Bonding **Baby Baby**	Show your child affection during this song by hugging, kissing, and rocking with your child. It is always good for your child to hear "I Love You."
Goodbye Song **It's Time to Go** (using sign language)	Take your child's hands and form the signs for your child.

Bright Start Music   12–18 Month Group   Session Plan #6

*Throughout Session - Use verbal directions for activities for child to follow. Avoid giving gestural cues; give directions while pointing to objects.

SKILL AREAS & SONGS	PARENT INSTRUCTION
Hello Song **When I Meet a New Friend**	Encourage your child to greet their friends at music by going up to them to say hello, shake hands, or give a hug.
Sign Language Song **Brown Bear, Brown Bear*** *Sung to the tune of Twinkle, Twinkle, Little Star	Take your child's hands and form the signs for your child. Find a routine time to sign with your child so you don't forget to do it at home. Examples of routine times include: meal times, bath time, play time, and bedtime.
Instruments- Rhythm Instruments **Playing Along**	Have your child stand up and pick up an instrument off the floor from standing. Ask your child to hand you an instrument to play together. Ask your child, "What's this?" Play an instrument while moving around your child to follow and localize sound.
Movement **Let's Go for a Ride**	Pretend to drive a car or ride on a motorcycle while walking with your child (holding hands if needed) - to the front, to the side, and backwards.
Visual- Scarves **I Can Name the Color**	Encourage your child to imitate/copy your movements with the scarf.
Animals/Puppets **Mr. Animal** with **Picture Cards**	Hold up the correct animal picture card as the song progresses in front of your child or place the correct picture card in their hand each time the animal changes in the song.
Books **Nine Ducks Nine** (Big Book)	Pat the beat on your child's knees or bounce your child to the beat in your lap.
Body Parts **You Do the Same** Incorporate rolling and throwing small balls.	Take your child's hands and touch each body part mentioned in the song, or have your child hold the mirror while you point to each body part.
Mirror Time **I Feel Silly**	Have your child hold the mirror so you can see your face in the mirror, too. Make the different emotional faces in the mirror for your child to see.

Movement **There's a Tickle Under My Skin**	Children stand for this song. Play drums while dancing to the beat.
Affection/Bonding **Baby Baby**	Show your child affection during this song by hugging, kissing, and rocking with your child. It is always good for your child to hear "I Love You."
Goodbye Song **It's Time to Go** (using sign language)	Take your child's hands and form the signs for your child.

Bright Start Music   12–18 Month Group   Session Plan #7

*Throughout Session - Use verbal directions for activities for child to follow. Avoid giving gestural cues; give directions while pointing to objects.

SKILL AREAS & SONGS	PARENT INSTRUCTION
Hello Song **When I Meet a New Friend**	Encourage your child to greet their friends at music by going up to them to say hello, shake hands, or give a hug.
Sign Language Song **Polar Bear, Polar Bear** (with Big Book)	Take your child's hands and form the signs for your child. Find a routine time to sign with your child so you don't forget to do it at home. Examples of routine times include: meal times, bath time, play time, and bed-time.
Instruments - Rhythm Instruments **Whack That Drum**	Have your child stand up and pick up an instrument off the floor from standing. Ask your child to hand you an instrument to play together. Ask your child, "What's this?" Play an instrument while moving around your child to follow and localize sound.
Movement **Tree Hugs**	Encourage your child to do the movements in the song. Model the movements for your child!
Visual- Picture Cards **My Favorite Spot**	Encourage your child to pick up the picture card when they hear it in the song and move it through the air.
Animals/Puppets **Animal Song**	Let your child feel and explore puppet's features; encourage interaction with the puppet by pretending to kiss, nudge, and play with your child.
Books **Walking Through the Jungle** (Big Book)	Pat the beat on your child's knees or bounce your child to the beat in your lap.
Body Parts **You Do the Same** Incorporate rolling and throwing small balls	Take your child's hands and touch each body part mentioned in the song, or have your child hold the mirror while you point to each body part.
Mirror Time **I Feel Silly**	Have your child hold the mirror so you can see your face in the mirror, too. Make the different emotional faces in the mirror for your child to see.

Movement **Pitter Patter** Can incorporate rain sticks or ocean drums.	Children stand for this song. Model to children rain falling down with your fingers. Splash hands from side to side and stomp with your children.
Affection/Bonding **Baby Baby**	Show your child affection during this song by hugging, kissing, and rocking with your child. It is always good for your child to hear "I Love You."
Goodbye Song **It's Time to Go** (using sign language)	Take your child's hands and form the signs for your child.

Bright Start Music   12–18 Month Group Session Plan #8

*Throughout Session - Use verbal directions for activities for child to follow. Avoid giving gestural cues; give directions while pointing to objects.

SKILL AREAS & SONGS	PARENT INSTRUCTION
Hello Song **When I Meet a New Friend**	Encourage your child to greet their friends at music by going up to them to say hello, shake hands, or give a hug.
Sign Language Song **Polar Bear, Polar Bear** (with Big Book)	Take your child's hands and form the signs for your child. Find a routine time to sign with your child so you don't forget to do it at home. Examples of routine times include: meal times, bath time, play time, and bedtime.
Instruments- Rhythm Instruments **Whack That Drum**	Have your child stand up and pick up an instrument off the floor from standing. Ask your child to hand you an instrument to play together. Ask your child, "What's this?" Play an instrument while moving around your child to follow and localize sound.
Movement **Flower Power**	Encourage your child to do the movements in the song. Model the movements for your child!
Visual- Picture Cards **My Favorite Spot**	Encourage your child to pick up the picture card when they hear it in the song and move it through the air.
Animals/Puppets **Monkey Hug**	Let your child feel and explore puppet's features; encourage interaction with the puppet by pretending to kiss, nudge, and play with your child.

Books **Panda Bear, Panda Bear, What Do You See?** (Big Book)	Pat the beat on your child's knees or bounce your child to the beat in your lap.
Body Parts **My Hand on My Head**	Take your child's hands and touch each body part mentioned in the song, or have your child hold the mirror while you point to each body part.
Mirror Time **Look in the Mirror**	Have your child hold the mirror so you can see your face in the mirror, too. Make the different emotional faces in the mirror for your child to see.
Movement **There's a Tickle Under My Skin**	Pretend to fly like an owl as you walk with your child (holding hands if needed) - to the front, to the side, and backwards.
Affection/Bonding **Doo Wop Love**	Show your child affection during this song by hugging, kissing, and rocking with your child. It is always good for your child to hear "I Love You."
Goodbye Song **It's Time to Go** (using sign language)	Take your child's hands and form the signs for your child.

Bright Start Music   12–18 Month Group Session Plan #9

*Throughout Session - Use verbal directions for activities for child to follow. Avoid giving gestural cues; give directions while pointing to objects.

SKILL AREAS & SONGS	PARENT INSTRUCTION
Hello Song **When I Meet a New Friend**	Encourage your child to greet their friends at music by going up to them to say hello, shake hands, or give a hug.
Sign Language Song **Polar Bear, Polar Bear** (with Big Book)	Take your child's hands and form the signs for your child. Find a routine time to sign with your child so you don't forget to do it at home. Examples of routine times include: meal times, bath time, play time, and bedtime.
Instruments- Rhythm Instruments **I'm the Sun**	Have your child stand up and pick up an instrument off the floor from standing. Ask your child to hand you an instrument to play together. Ask your child, "What's this?" Play an instrument while moving around your child to follow and localize sound.
Movement **Flower Power**	Encourage your child to do the movements in the song. Model the movements for your child!
Visual- Picture Cards **My Favorite Spot**	Encourage your child to pick up the picture card when they hear it in the song and move it through the air.
Animals/Puppets **Animal Song**	Let your child feel and explore puppet's features; encourage interaction with the puppet by pretending to kiss, nudge, and play with your child.
Book **Wheels on the Bus** (Big Book)	Pat the beat on your child's knees or bounce your child to the beat in your lap.
Body Parts **You Do the Same** Incorporate rolling and throwing small balls	Take your child's hands and touch each body part mentioned in the song, or have your child hold the mirror while you point to each body part.
Mirror Time **This is How I Look**	Have your child hold the mirror so you can see your face in the mirror, too. Make the different emotional faces in the mirror for your child to see.

Movement **Hot Air Balloon**	Face each other in a circle with children facing center of circle. Pick children up and fly them through the air to the center of the circle and back out.
Affection/Bonding **Doo Wop Love**	Show your child affection during this song by hugging, kissing, and rocking with your child. It is always good for your child to hear "I Love You."
Goodbye Song **It's Time to Go** (using sign language)	Take your child's hands and form the signs for your child.

Bright Start Music   12–18 Month Group Session Plan #10

*Throughout Session - Use verbal directions for activities for child to follow. Avoid giving gestural cues; give directions while pointing to objects.

SKILL AREAS & SONGS	PARENT INSTRUCTION
Hello Song **When I Meet a New Friend**	Encourage your child to greet their friends at music by going up to them to say hello, shake hands, or give a hug.
Sign Language Song **Birdie Beat** Signs: **Bird, Tree, Fly, Wind**	Take your child's hands and form the signs for your child. Find a routine time to sign with your child so you don't forget to do it at home. Examples of routine times include: meal times, bath time, play time, and bedtime.
Instruments- Rhythm Instruments **I'm the Sun**	Have your child stand up and pick up an instrument off the floor from standing. Ask your child to hand you an instrument to play together. Ask your child, "What's this?" Play an instrument while moving around your child to follow and localize sound.
Movement **Tree Hugs**	Encourage your child to do the movements in the song. Model the movements for your child!
Visual- Picture Cards **My Favorite Spot**	Encourage your child to pick up the picture card when they hear it in the song and move it through the air.
Animals/Puppets **Hello Mr. Animal**	Let your child feel and explore puppet's features; encourage interaction with the puppet by pretending to kiss, nudge, and play with your child.
Books **Ten Little Monkeys** (Big Book)	Pat the beat on your child's knees or bounce your child to the beat in your lap.
Body Parts **My Hand on My Head**	Take your child's hands and touch each body part mentioned in the song, or have your child hold the mirror while you point to each body part.
Mirror Time **This is How I Look**	Have your child hold the mirror so you can see your face in the mirror, too. Make the different emotional faces in the mirror for your child to see.
Movement **Hot Air Balloon**	Face each other in a circle with children facing center of circle. Pick children up and fly them through the air to the center of the circle and back out.

Affection/Bonding **In My Own Little Way**	Show your child affection during this song by hugging, kissing, and rocking with your child. It is always good for your child to hear "I Love You."
Goodbye Song **It's Time to Go** (using sign language)	Take your child's hands and form the signs for your child.

Bright Start Music   12–18 Month Group Session Plan #11

*Throughout Session - Use verbal directions for activities for child to follow. Avoid giving gestural cues; give directions while pointing to objects.

SKILL AREAS & SONGS	PARENT INSTRUCTION
Hello Song **When I Meet a New Friend**	Encourage your child to greet their friends at music by going up to them to say hello, shake hands, or give a hug.
Sign Language Song **Birdie Beat** Signs: **Bird, Tree, Fly, Wind**	Take your child's hands and form the signs for your child. Find a routine time to sign with your child so you don't forget to do it at home. Examples of routine times include: meal times, bath time, play time, and bedtime.
Instruments- Rhythm Instruments **Click! Click! Click! Go the Castanets**	Have your child stand up and pick up an instrument off the floor from standing. Ask your child to hand you an instrument to play together. Ask your child, "What's this?" Play an instrument while moving around your child to follow and localize sound.
Movement **Tree Hugs**	Encourage your child to do the movements in the song. Model the movements for your child!
Visual- Picture Cards **My Favorite Spot**	Encourage your child to pick up the picture card when they hear it in the song and move it through the air.
Animals/Puppets **Animal Song**	Let your child feel and explore puppet's features, encourage interaction with the puppet by pretending to kiss, nudge, and play with your child.
Books **Mulberry Bush** (Big Book)	Pat the beat on your child's knees or bounce your child to the beat in your lap.
Body Parts **You Do the Same** Incorporate rolling and throwing small balls	Take your child's hands and touch each body part mentioned in the song, or have your child hold the mirror while you point to each body part.
Mirror Time **I Feel Silly**	Have your child hold the mirror so you can see your face in the mirror, too. Make the different emotional faces in the mirror for your child to see.
Movement **Hot Air Balloon**	Face each other in a circle with children facing center of circle. Pick children up and fly them through the air to the center of the circle and back out.

Affection/Bonding **In My Own Little Way**	Show your child affection during this song by hugging, kissing, and rocking with your child. It is always good for your child to hear "I Love You."
Goodbye Song **It's Time to Go** (using sign language)	Take your child's hands and form the signs for your child.

Bright Start Music   12–18 Month Group   Session Plan #12

*Throughout Session- Use verbal directions for activities for child to follow. Avoid giving gestural cues; give directions while pointing to objects.

SKILL AREAS & SONGS	PARENT INSTRUCTION
Hello Song **When I Meet a New Friend**	Encourage your child to greet their friends at music by going up to them to say hello, shake hands, or give a hug.
Sign Language Song **Birdie Beat** Signs: **Bird, Tree, Fly, Wind**	Take your child's hands and form the signs for your child. Find a routine time to sign with your child so you don't forget to do it at home. Examples of routine times include: meal times, bath time, play time, and bedtime.
Instruments- Rhythm Instruments **Click! Click! Click! Go the Castanets**	Have your child stand up and pick up an instrument off the floor from standing. Ask your child to hand you an instrument to play together. Ask your child, "What's this?" Play an instrument while moving around your child to follow and localize sound.
Movement **Flower Power**	Encourage your child to do the movements in the song. Model the movements for your child!
Visual- Picture Cards **My Favorite Spot**	Encourage your child to pick up the picture card when they hear it in the song and move it through the air.
Animals/Puppets **Monkey Hug**	Let your child feel and explore puppet's features, encourage interaction with the puppet by pretending to kiss, nudge, and play with your child.
Books **Farmer in the Dell** (Big Book)	Pat the beat on your child's knees or bounce your child to the beat in your lap.
Body Parts **My Hand on My Head**	Take your child's hands and touch each body part mentioned in the song, or have your child hold the mirror while you point to each body part.
Mirror Time **I Feel Silly**	Have your child hold the mirror so you can see your face in the mirror, too. Make the different emotional faces in the mirror for your child to see.
Movement **The Owl**	Pretend to fly like an owl as you walk with your child (holding hands if needed) - to the front, to the side, and backwards.

Affection/Bonding **Baby, Baby**	Show your child affection during this song by hugging, kissing, and rocking with your child. It is always good for your child to hear "I Love You."
Goodbye Song **It's Time to Go** (using sign language)	Take your child's hands and form the signs for your child.

Bright Start Music   18–24 Month Group   Session Plan #1

SKILL AREAS & SONGS	PARENT INSTRUCTION
Hello Song **How Do You Doodle**	*Ask parents to bring a picture of their child from home or take a Polaroid picture. Children's learning to identify themselves in a picture is a step forward in their abstract thinking skills!
Instruments- Tambourines and/or Drums **Listen to How I Beat My Drum** **Clean Up**	Have your child stand up and pick up an instrument off the floor from standing. Ask your child to hand you an instrument to play together. When children respond to your request to do an activity together they are choosing to engage in a social exchange. That is an important skill to develop for interacting later in life! Show your child where the instruments go when the song is over.
Movement **We're Gonna Dance, We're Gonna Wiggle**	Encourage your child to follow the movement directions in the song. Coordinating complex movements through space develops many skill areas at the same time. Cognitive processing and visual input are at work to analyze what motion they are observing and how to imitate it; kinesthetic skills are being developed as they try the new motion without falling over; social skills and emotional awareness are being developed as they watch other people's reactions to performing the movements; interpersonal awareness is developing as they form their own reaction to the activity! That's a lot going on!!
Body Parts/Gestures **Hello, Salutations**	Encourage your child to follow the "invisible" movements in the song- blink eyes, pat head, wrinkle nose, etc. Invisible gestures are ones they cannot see themselves perform with their eyes. That is hard to do and increases their self-awareness!

Animals/Picture Cards **Marty Monkey** **Clean Up**	Present the picture book upside down for your child to turn upright, and encourage them to turn the pages. Encourage your child to show you or point to the picture card of each animal when the animal sound is heard in the song. Encouraging early literacy skills impacts school readiness, language development and comprehension skills! Encourage your child to put the picture cards away when the song is over and show your child where the picture cards go if needed.
Body Parts **Tony Chestnut**	Encourage your child to point to each body part named in the song.
Emotions/Dramatic Play **Monkey Moves!**	Encourage your child to act out the emotions described in each verse. Dance during the chorus. Children figure out new information they are learning around them during dramatic play by reenacting their observations over and over again.
Multicultural- Rhythm Instruments **Pollito, Chicken** **Clean Up**	Encourage your child to dance and play their instrument with other children in the group! Help your child to put away their instrument.
Movement **The Owl**	Pretend to fly like an owl as you walk with your child (holding hands if needed) - to the front, to the side, and backwards. Movement through space provides opportunities for vestibular and kinesthetic development.
Affection/Bonding **La La La Lullaby**	Show your child affection during this song by hugging, kissing, and rocking with your child. It is always good for your child to hear "I Love You." Attachment and bonding is an important foundation for children to have. Feeling secure impacts social development later in life.
Goodbye Song **It's Time to Go** (using sign language)	Take your child's hands and form the signs for your child. As your child increases his/her independence, transitioning away from an activity they are enjoying can be difficult. Using this song can help!

Bright Start Music   18–24 Month Group   Session Plan #2

SKILL AREAS & SONGS	PARENT INSTRUCTION
Hello Song **How Do You Doodle**	*Ask parents to bring a picture of their child from home or take a Polaroid picture. Children's learning to identify themselves in a picture is a step forward in their abstract thinking skills!
Instruments- Rhythm Instruments **Leader of the Band** **Clean Up**	Have your child stand up and pick up an instrument off the floor from standing. Ask your child to hand you an instrument to play together. When children respond to your request to do an activity together they are choosing to engage in a social exchange. That is an important skill to develop for interacting later in life! Show your child where the instruments go when the song is over.
Movement **We're Gonna Dance, We're Gonna Wiggle**	Encourage your child to follow the movement directions in the song. Coordinating complex movements through space develops many skill areas at the same time. Cognitive processing and visual input are at work to analyze what motion they are observing and how to imitate it; kinesthetic skills are being developed as they try the new motion without falling over; social skills and emotional awareness are being developed as they watch other people's reactions to performing the movements; interpersonal awareness is developing as they form their own reaction to the activity! That's a lot going on!!
Body Parts/Gestures **Loop De Loop**	Encourage your child to follow the "invisible" movements in the song- blink eyes, pat head, wrinkle nose, etc. Invisible gestures are ones they can not see themselves perform with their eyes. That is hard to do and increases their self-awareness!

Animals/Picture Cards **Mouse in My House** **Clean Up**	Present the picture book upside down for your child to turn upright, and encourage them to turn the pages. Encourage your child to show you or point to the picture card of each animal when the animal sound is heard in the song. Encouraging early literacy skills impacts school readiness, language development and comprehension skills! Help your child to put the picture cards away when the song is over.
Body Parts **Tony Chestnut**	Encourage your child to point to each body part named in the song.
Emotions/Dramatic Play **I Feel Silly**	Encourage your child to act out the emotions described in each verse. Dance during the chorus. Children figure out new information they are learning by reenacting their observations over and over again.
Multicultural- Rhythm Instruments **Pollito, Chicken** **Clean Up**	Encourage your child to dance and play their instrument with other children in the group! Help your child to put away their instrument.
Movement **I Roll the Ball to You**	Form small circles with 1-2 other children/ parents and roll, bounce, toss the balls. Catching and throwing balls requires advanced hand/eye coordination as well as cognitive processing to know where the ball should go!
Affection/Bonding **La La La Lullaby**	Show your child affection during this song by hugging, kissing, and rocking with your child. It is always good for your child to hear "I Love You." Attachment and bonding is an important foundation for children to have. Feeling secure impacts social development later in life.
Goodbye Song **It's Time to Go** (using sign language)	As your child increases his/her independence, transitioning away from an activity they are enjoying can be difficult. Using this song can help!

Bright Start Music   18–24 Month Group   Session Plan #3

SKILL AREAS & SONGS	PARENT INSTRUCTION
Hello Song **How Do You Doodle**	*Ask parents to bring a picture of their child from home or take a Polaroid picture. Children's learning to identify themselves in a picture is a step forward in their abstract thinking skills!
Instruments- Rhythm Instruments **1,2,3, Play with Me** **Clean Up**	Have your child stand up and pick up an instrument off the floor from standing. Ask your child to hand you an instrument to play together. Give your child opportunities to ask you to play at home by placing favorite toys, books, or animals within view during your play time. Initiating social interactions is an important step in establishing relationships. Show your child where the instruments go when the song is over. Encourage your child to help clean up items around the house like shoes and toys that have a designated place to go.
Movement **It's Time for Parade**	Form a large circle or line and parade around the room, following the directions in the song. Organized group activities like parades promote community social rules and awareness.
Body Parts/Gestures **The Body Language Song**	Encourage your child to follow the "invisible" movements in the song- blink eyes, pat head, wrinkle nose, etc. Invisible gestures are ones they cannot see themselves perform with their eyes. That is hard to do and increases their self-awareness!
Animals/Puppets **Animal Parade** **Clean Up**	Encourage your child to act out what the animals do while you are making the animal sounds. The puppets can run, jump, lick, sleep, chase each other, etc. Encourage your child to put the puppets away when the song is over and show your child where the puppets go if needed.
Song Book **Mouse in My House**	Present the picture book upside down for your child to turn upright, and encourage them to turn the pages. Encourage your child to show you or point to the picture card of each animal when the animal sound is heard in the song. Encouraging early literacy skills impacts school readiness, language development and comprehension skills!

Body Parts **Tony Chestnut**	Encourage your child to point to each body part named in the song. Increasing body awareness is important!
Emotions/Dramatic Play **What's Your Name?**	Encourage your child to act out each place (walking down street, going to a party, etc.) described in each verse. Pretend play with your child after you have new experiences. For example, you can act out going to the grocery store, the zoo, the mall, etc.
Multicultural- Rhythm Instruments **Funga A La Feeya** **Clean Up**	Encourage your child to dance and play their instrument with other children in the group! Help your child to put away their instrument.
Movement **Monkey Moves!**	Encourage your child to act out the movements in each verse. Play imitation games at home! Instead of Simon Says, do a movement and encourage your child to copy you!
Affection/Bonding **Never Let Me Go**	Show your child affection during this song by hugging, kissing, and rocking with your child. It is always good to tell your child "I Love You."
Goodbye Song **It's Time to Go** (using sign language)	Take your child's hands and form the signs for your child. After repeated exposure to the time to go routine, your child may begin to prompt you when it is time to leave a place by trying to sing this song!

Bright Start Music   18–24 Month Group Session Plan #4

SKILL AREAS & SONGS	PARENT INSTRUCTION
Hello Song **How Do You Doodle**	*Ask parents to bring a picture of their child from home or take a Polaroid picture. Children's learning to identify themselves in a picture is a step forward in their abstract thinking skills!
Instruments- Rhythm Instruments **1,2,3, Play with Me** **Clean Up**	Have your child stand up and pick up an instrument off the floor from standing. Ask your child to hand you an instrument to play together. Give your child opportunities to ask you to play at home by placing favorite toys, books, or animals within view during your play time. Initiating social interactions is an important step in establishing relationships. Show your child where the instruments go when the song is over. Encourage your child to help clean up items around the house like shoes and toys that have a designated place to go.
Movement **It's Time for Parade**	Form a large circle or line and parade around the room, following the directions in the song. Parading around provides great opportunities for peer modeling of new behaviors!
Body Parts/Gestures **Hello, Salutations**	Encourage your child to follow the "invisible" movements in the song- blink eyes, pat head, wrinkle nose, etc. Encourage your child to practice this skill at home...after trying, let your child see themselves do the invisible gesture in front of a mirror!
Animals/Puppets **Animal Parade** **Clean Up**	Encourage your child to act out what the animals do while you are making the animal sounds. The puppets can run, jump, lick, sleep, chase each other, etc. Encourage your child to put the puppets away when the song is over and show your child where the puppets go if needed.

Song Book **Mouse in My House**	Present the picture book to your child upside down for your child to turn upright and encourage them to turn the pages. Read, read, read! Ask your child to point to the things they see in books.
Body Parts **Tony Chestnut**	Encourage your child to point to each body part named in the song.
Emotions/Dramatic Play **The Emotion Song**	Encourage your child to act out each place (walking down street, going to a party, etc.) described in each verse. Pretend play with your child after you have new experiences. For example, you can act out going to the grocery store, the zoo, the mall, etc.
Multicultural- Rhythm Instruments **Funga A La Feeya** **Clean Up**	Encourage your child to dance and play their instrument with other children in the group! Help your child to put away their instrument.
Movement **Dance to the Music**	Encourage your child to act out the movements in each verse. Moving to music is fun and develops skills in all domain areas!
Affection/Bonding **Never Let Me Go**	Show your child affection during this song by hugging, kissing, and rocking with your child. It is always good for your child to hear "I Love You."
Goodbye Song **It's Time to Go** (using sign language)	Take your child's hands and form the signs for your child. After repeated exposure to the time to go routine, your child may begin to prompt you when it is time to leave a place by trying to sing this song!

Bright Start Music   18–24 Month Group   Session Plan #5

SKILL AREAS & SONGS	PARENT INSTRUCTION
Hello Song **How Do You Doodle**	*Ask parents to bring a picture of their child from home or take a Polaroid picture. Children's learning to identify themselves in a picture is a step forward in their abstract thinking skills!
Instruments- Tambourines and/or Drums **Listen to How I Beat My Drum** **Clean Up**	Have your child stand up and pick up an instrument off the floor from standing. Ask your child to hand you an instrument to play together. Show your child where the instruments go when the song is over.
Movement **Dance to the Music**	Encourage your child to follow the movement directions in the song.
Body Parts/Gestures **Loop De Loop**	Encourage your child to follow the "invisible" movements in the song- blink eyes, pat head, wrinkle nose, etc.
Animals/Picture Cards **Marty Monkey** **Clean Up**	Present the picture book upside down for your child to turn upright, and encourage them to turn the pages. Encourage your child to show you or point to the picture card of each animal when the animal sound is heard in the song. Encouraging early literacy skills impacts school readiness, language development and comprehension skills! Encourage your child to put the picture cards away when the song is over and show your child where the picture cards go if needed.
Body Parts **When I Wake Up**	Encourage your child to point to each body part and article of clothing named in the song.
Emotions/Dramatic Play **Mood Groove**	Encourage your child to act out each place (walking down street, going to a party, etc.) described in each verse.

___Multicultural- Rhythm Instruments___ **We Circle Around,** and **Clean Up**	Encourage your child to dance and play their instrument with other children in the group! Help your child to put away their instrument.
___Movement___ **I Roll the Ball To You**	Form small circles with 1-2 other children/ parents and roll, bounce, toss the balls.
___Affection/Bonding___ **Do Wop Lullaby**	Show your child affection during this song by hugging, kissing, and rocking with your child. It is always good for your child to hear "I Love You."
___Goodbye Song___ **It's Time to Go** (using sign language)	Take your child's hands and form the signs for your child.

Bright Start Music   18–24 Month Group   Session Plan #6

SKILL AREAS & SONGS	PARENT INSTRUCTION
Hello Song **How Do You Doodle**	*Ask parents to bring a picture of their child from home or take a Polaroid picture. Children's learning to identify themselves in a picture is a step forward in their abstract thinking skills!
Instruments- Tambourines and/or Drums **Listen to How I Beat My Drum** **Clean Up**	Have your child stand up and pick up an instrument off the floor from standing. Ask your child to hand you an instrument to play together. Show your child where the instruments go when the song is over.
Movement **Dance to the Music**	Encourage your child to follow the movement directions in the song.
Body Parts/Gestures **The Body Language Song**	Encourage your child to follow the "invisible" movements in the song- blink eyes, pat head, wrinkle nose, etc.
Animals/Picture Cards **Marty Monkey** **Clean Up**	Present the picture book to your child upside down for your child to turn upright and encourage them to turn the pages. Encourage your child to show you or point to the picture card of each animal when the animal sound is heard in the song. Encourage your child to put the picture cards away when the song is over and show your child where the picture cards go if needed.
Body Parts **When I Wake Up**	Encourage your child to point to each body part and article of clothing named in the song.
Emotions/Dramatic Play **I Feel Silly**	Encourage your child to act out each place (walking down street, going to a party, etc.) described in each verse.
Multicultural- Rhythm Instruments **We Circle Around,** and **Clean Up**	Encourage your child to dance and play their instrument with other children in the group! Help your child to put away their instrument.
Movement **It's Time for Parade**	Form a large circle or line and parade around the room, following the directions in the song.

__Affection/Bonding__ **Do Wop Lullaby**	Show your child affection during this song by hugging, kissing, and rocking with your child. It is always good for your child to hear "I Love You."
__Goodbye Song__ **It's Time to Go** (using sign language)	Take your child's hands and form the signs for your child.

Bright Start Music   18–24 Month Group   Session Plan #7

SKILL AREAS & SONGS	PARENT INSTRUCTION
Hello Song **How Do You Doodle**	*Ask parents to bring a picture of their child from home or take a Polaroid picture. Children's learning to identify themselves in a picture is a step forward in their abstract thinking skills!
Instruments- Rhythm Instruments **Leader of the Band** **Clean Up**	Have your child stand up and pick up an instrument off the floor from standing. Ask your child to hand you an instrument to play together. Show your child where the instruments go when the song is over.
Movement **Monkey Moves!**	Encourage your child to follow the movement directions in the song.
Body Parts/Gestures **Hello, Salutations**	Encourage your child to follow the "invisible" movements in the song- blink eyes, pat head, wrinkle nose, etc.
Animals/Puppets **A Rustle in a Bush** **Clean Up**	Present the picture book to your child upside down for your child to turn upright and encourage them to turn the pages. Encourage your child to show you or point to the picture card of each animal when the animal sound is heard in the song. Encourage your child to put the picture cards away when the song is over and show your child where the picture cards go if needed.
Body Parts **When I Wake Up**	Encourage your child to point to each body part and article of clothing named in the song.
Emotions/Dramatic Play **What's Your Name?**	Encourage your child to act out the emotions in each verse.
Multicultural- Rhythm Instruments **Pajarito** **Clean Up**	Encourage your child to dance and play their instrument with other children in the group! Help your child to put away their instrument.
Movement **The Bicycle**	Encourage your child to follow the movement directions in the song.

Affection/Bonding **La La La Lullaby**	Show your child affection during this song by hugging, kissing, and rocking with your child. It is always good for your child to hear "I Love You."
Goodbye Song **It's Time to Go** (using sign language)	Take your child's hands and form the signs for your child.

Bright Start Music   18–24 Month Group   Session Plan #8

SKILL AREAS & SONGS	PARENT INSTRUCTION
Hello Song **How Do You Doodle**	*Ask parents to bring a picture of their child from home or take a Polaroid picture. Children's learning to identify themselves in a picture is a step forward in their abstract thinking skills!
Instruments- Rhythm Instruments **1,2,3, Play with Me** **Clean Up**	Have your child stand up and pick up an instrument off the floor from standing. Ask your child to hand you an instrument to play together. Show your child where the instruments go when the song is over.
Movement **Monkey Moves!**	Encourage your child to follow the movement directions in the song.
Body Parts/Gestures **Loop De Loop**	Encourage your child to follow the "invisible" movements in the song- blink eyes, pat head, wrinkle nose, etc.
Animals/Puppets **A Rustle in a Bush** **Clean Up**	Present the picture book upside down for your child to turn upright, and encourage them to turn the pages. Encourage your child to show you or point to the picture card of each animal when the animal sound is heard in the song. Encourage your child to put the picture cards away when the song is over and show your child where the picture cards go if needed.
Body Parts **When I Wake Up**	Encourage your child to point to each body part and article of clothing named in the song.
Emotions/Dramatic Play **The Emotion Song**	Encourage your child to act out the emotions in each verse.
Multicultural- Rhythm Instruments **Pajarito** **Clean Up**	Encourage your child to dance and play their instrument with other children in the group! Help your child to put away their instrument.
Movement **I Roll The Ball to You**	Form small circles with 1-2 other children/parents and roll, bounce, toss the balls.

Affection/Bonding **La La La Lullaby**	Show your child affection during this song by hugging, kissing, and rocking with your child. It is always good for your child to hear "I Love You."
Goodbye Song **It's Time to Go** (using sign language)	Take your child's hands and form the signs for your child.

Bright Start Music   18–24 Month Group   Session Plan #9

SKILL AREAS & SONGS	PARENT INSTRUCTION
Hello Song How Do You Doodle	*Ask parents to bring a picture of their child from home or take a Polaroid picture. Children's learning to identify themselves in a picture is a step forward in their abstract thinking skills!
Instruments- Rhythm Instruments 1,2,3, Play with Me Clean Up	Have your child stand up and pick up an instrument off the floor from standing. Ask your child to hand you an instrument to play together. Show your child where the instruments go when the song is over.
Movement The Bicycle	Encourage your child to follow the movement directions in the song.
Body Parts/Gestures The Body Language Song	Encourage your child to follow the "invisible" movements in the song- blink eyes, pat head, wrinkle nose, etc.
Animals/Puppets Animal Parade Clean Up	Encourage your child to show you or point to each animal when the animal sound is heard in the song. Also, ask them to say the name of the animal when shown the puppet. Encourage your child to put the puppets away when the song is over and show your child where the puppets go if needed.
Songbook Mouse in My House	Present the picture book to your child upside down for your child to turn upright and encourage them to turn the pages.
Body Parts If I Arr a Pirate	Encourage your child to point to each body part named in the song.
Emotions/Dramatic Play Mood Groove	Encourage your child to act out the emotions in each verse.
Multicultural- Rhythm Instruments Zum Gali Gali Clean Up	Encourage your child to dance and play their instrument with other children in the group! Help your child to put away their instrument.

Movement **We're Gonna Dance, We're Gonna Wiggle**	Encourage your child to follow the movement directions in the song.
Affection/Bonding **Never Let Me Go**	Show your child affection during this song by hugging, kissing, and rocking with your child. It is always good for your child to hear "I Love You."
Goodbye Song **It's Time to Go** (using sign language)	Take your child's hands and form the signs for your child.

Bright Start Music   18–24 Month Group   Session Plan #10

SKILL AREAS & SONGS	PARENT INSTRUCTION
Hello Song **How Do You Doodle**	*Ask parents to bring a picture of their child from home or take a Polaroid picture. Children's learning to identify themselves in a picture is a step forward in their abstract thinking skills!
Instruments- Rhythm Instruments **Leader of the Band** **Clean Up**	Have your child stand up and pick up an instrument off the floor from standing. Ask your child to hand you an instrument to play together. Show your child where the instruments go when the song is over.
Movement **It's Time for Parade**	Form a large circle or line and parade around the room, following the directions in the song.
Body Parts/Gestures **Hello, Salutations**	Encourage your child to follow the "invisible" movements in the song- blink eyes, pat head, wrinkle nose, etc.
Animals/Puppets **Animal Parade** **Clean Up**	Encourage your child to show you or point to each animal when the animal sound is heard in the song. Also, ask them to say the name of the animal when shown the puppet. Encourage your child to put the puppets away when the song is over and show your child where the puppets go if needed.
Songbook **Mouse in My House**	Present the picture book to your child upside down for your child to turn upright and encourage them to turn the pages.
Body Parts **If I Arr a Pirate**	Encourage your child to point to each body part named in the song.
Emotions/Dramatic Play **I Feel Silly**	Encourage your child to act out the emotions in each verse.
Multicultural- Rhythm Instruments **Zum Gali Gali** **Clean Up**	Encourage your child to dance and play their instrument with other children in the group! Help your child to put away their instrument.
Movement **The Bicycle**	Encourage your child to follow the movement directions in the song.

<u>Affection/Bonding</u> **Never Let Me Go**	Show your child affection during this song by hugging, kissing, and rocking with your child. It is always good for your child to hear "I Love You."
<u>Goodbye Song</u> **It's Time to Go** (using sign language)	Take your child's hands and form the signs for your child.

Bright Start Music   18–24 Month Group   Session Plan #11

SKILL AREAS & SONGS	PARENT INSTRUCTION
Hello Song **How Do You Doodle**	*Ask parents to bring a picture of their child from home or take a Polaroid picture. Children's learning to identify themselves in a picture is a step forward in their abstract thinking skills!
Instruments- Tambourines and/or Drums **Listen to How I Beat My Drum** **Clean Up**	Have your child stand up and pick up an instrument off the floor from standing. Ask your child to hand you an instrument to play together. Show your child where the instruments go when the song is over.
Movement **We're Gonna Dance, We're Gonna Wiggle**	Encourage your child to follow the movement directions in the song.
Body Parts/Gestures **Loop De Loop**	Encourage your child to follow the "invisible" movements in the song- blink eyes, pat head, wrinkle nose, etc.
Animals/Picture Cards **Marty Monkey** **Clean Up**	Present the picture book upside down for your child to turn upright, and encourage them to turn the pages. Encourage your child to show you or point to the picture card of each animal when the animal sound is heard in the song. Encourage your child to put the puppets away when the song is over and show your child where the puppets go if needed.
Body Parts **If I Arr a Pirate**	Encourage your child to point to each body part named in the song.
Emotions/Dramatic Play **What's Your Name?**	Encourage your child to act out each place (walking down street, going to a party, etc.) described in each verse.
Multicultural- Rhythm Instruments **Siyahamba** **Clean Up**	Encourage your child to dance and play their instrument with other children in the group! Help your child to put away their instrument.
Movement **I Roll the Ball to You**	Form small circles with 1-2 other children/parents and roll, bounce, toss the balls.

Affection/Bonding **Do Wop Lullaby**	Show your child affection during this song by hugging, kissing, and rocking with your child. It is always good for your child to hear "I Love You."
Goodbye Song **It's Time to Go** (using sign language)	Take your child's hands and form the signs for your child.

Bright Start Music   18–24 Month Group Session Plan #12

SKILL AREAS & SONGS	PARENT INSTRUCTION
Hello Song **How Do You Doodle**	*Ask parents to bring a picture of their child from home or take a Polaroid picture. Children's learning to identify themselves in a picture is a step forward in their abstract thinking skills!
Instruments- Tambourines and/or Drums **Listen to How I Beat My Drum** **Clean Up**	Have your child stand up and pick up an instrument off the floor from standing. Ask your child to hand you an instrument to play together. Show your child where the instruments go when the song is over.
Movement **Dance to the Music**	Encourage your child to follow the movement directions in the song.
Body Parts/Gestures **The Body Language Song**	Encourage your child to follow the "invisible" movements in the song- blink eyes, pat head, wrinkle nose, etc.
Animals/Puppets **A Rustle in a Bush** **Clean Up**	Present the picture book upside down for your child to turn upright, and encourage them to turn the pages. Encourage your child to show you or point to the picture card of each animal when the animal sound is heard in the song. Encourage your child to put the puppets away when the song is over and show your child where the puppets go if needed.
Body Parts **If I Arr a Pirate**	Encourage your child to point to each body part named in the song.
Emotions/Dramatic Play **The Emotion Song**	Encourage your child to act out the emotions in each verse.
Multicultural- Rhythm Instruments **Siyahamba** **Clean Up**	Encourage your child to dance and play their instrument with other children in the group! Help your child to put away their instrument.
Movement **The Bicycle**	Encourage your child to follow the movement directions in the song.

Affection/Bonding **Do Wop Lullaby**	Show your child affection during this song by hugging, kissing, and rocking with your child. It is always good for your child to hear "I Love You."
Goodbye Song **It's Time to Go** (using sign language)	Take your child's hands and form the signs for your child.

DEVELOPMENTAL MUSIC GROUPS WITHOUT PARENT INVOLVEMENT

INPATIENT AND OUTPATIENT HOSPITAL SETTINGS

This section of session plans for groups without caregivers present suggests ways to address developmental milestones for a group of children or individual child without a caregiver present. Music therapists providing services to children who are developmentally under 2 years old in inpatient and outpatient hospital settings do not always have the ability to incorporate caregivers during sessions due to parents' work schedules or the needs of other children who are at home. The session plans in this section recommend fewer songs and target domain areas for a 30-minute session due to the increased time needed to successfully model the behaviors or outcomes addressed in each activity. When a caregiver is present, he or she is cued by the music therapist to model the targeted intervention with the child. When the caregiver is not present, the music therapist needs extra time to model all the behaviors and actions for each song, which may require multiple breaks within songs. The stopping and starting of songs to demonstrate the interactive sections commonly results in repeating the song for continuity.

Chaining, where each step, word, or action serves as a cue for the next, is a common technique recommended for children with special needs in the hospital setting. When a song is implemented with the chaining technique, extra time will be required. Session plans can be adapted and modified any number of ways to fit the specific needs presented by an individual patient or group of patients. Once the music therapist is familiar with the content of this curriculum, identifying the specific goal areas and songs to best meet the needs of patients will become easier and will enable quick session planning.

Including older siblings visiting inpatients or accompanying outpatients is a wonderful way to provide peer modeling of appropriate behaviors and skills during the session. Children learn many new skills through the observation of peers in their environment. The original music in the curriculum has the potential to capture the interest of older siblings, due to either the intrinsic quality of the music composition or just the novelty of hearing songs for the first time. Another captivating component of the sessions for older siblings is the amount of manipulatives used throughout the curriculum. Most siblings enjoy the experience of interacting with the variety of instruments, puppets, and visual aids recommended for use during songs. If a sibling is old enough to play more of a teacher role as opposed to purely a participant role, he or she can be instructed to interact more directly with the patient through techniques such as hand-over-hand and verbal prompting. Using developmentally appropriate ways for older siblings to interact with their younger siblings is invaluable. After the patient is discharged, an older sibling may have the opportunity to continue the interactions learned during the music sessions. The continued interaction and peer modeling the patient experiences in the home environment will enhance his or her development and provide rich opportunities for learning new skills.

If you find yourself wanting to implement the more comprehensive session plans designed for caregiver involvement even though you do not have caregivers present, there are ways to make this more feasible. Leading the group without any other staff assistance is possible if the group size is limited to 2 or 3 high-functioning patients. For a larger group or a group involving patients with multiple needs, incorporating staff assistance will enable you to implement the comprehensive session plans. Other staff involved in the sessions could include:

- Music therapists

- Music therapy students or interns

- Child Life Specialists

- Physical therapists

- Speech therapists

- Hospital volunteers

If Child Life Specialists, physical therapists, and/or speech therapists are included, then you have successfully created a multidisciplinary treatment session! The specific developmental goals addressed in each session (which are listed on each session plan) provide a starting point for discussing common goals being addressed across disciplines. Staff members from other disciplines may not be aware of the very specific cross-domain learning occurring during music therapy sessions. This knowledge base will vary considerably and will largely depend on how closely each music therapist works with other disciplines.

Do not be surprised if staff members from other disciplines begin to show a preference for co-treatment with music therapy after being exposed to the specificity of what music therapists address in sessions. It is common for patients to meet cross-domain objectives and goals during music therapy with more ease than they typically demonstrate in other therapy sessions. This is understandable when the function of the music is taken into consideration. Music can act as a distractor from many negative or uncomfortable side effects of a particular action. For example, if a speech goal or objective is being addressed, a patient might show fatigue more quickly without music present because his or her focus of attention is on the repetition or motor movement of the speech task. When the same goal or objective is addressed within the structure of a music therapy activity, the patient's focus of attention is usually on the music stimulus. This shift in attention commonly extends the amount of time a patient is happily engaged in the activity before showing signs of fatigue or boredom.

The education of allied health disciplines that target the broad range of goals and objectives the music therapist is able to address within sessions can have a positive impact beyond the infant developmental population. Music therapists serve a variety of patient populations within medical environments and interact with many staff members from various units. Considering staff turnover rates and the opportunity to educate different staff units about the effectiveness of music therapy, a music therapist can feel overwhelmed with the task of education. The current curriculum, with its breadth of developmental objectives, provides a starting point to articulate the comprehensiveness of domain areas targeted by music therapy with infants and young children. Once staff members are oriented to this concept, conversation can naturally transition to related music therapy treatment objectives for patients in other population groups.

If staff members are not involved in the music therapy sessions, the dialogue can still be initiated concerning cross-domain goals and objectives addressed in this program. Most healthcare systems have adopted patient-centered multidisciplinary treatment approaches that enable the music therapist to know what goals and objectives are being addressed in other therapies. Finding the common treatment areas and documenting progress made within music therapy sessions will allow the music therapist to identify similarities seen between various therapies. Discussing the very specific skills targeted within music therapy sessions enables related therapists to see how music therapists can systematically address need areas for patients.

If you wish to have an individual session with a patient who does not have a caregiver visiting, this program can be adjusted to meet individual patient needs. If a patient has developmental needs in only one or two domain areas, the session plans can be modified to focus on those areas by combining activities from the various plans into one session. The session plans listed in the section titled "Domain Specific Sessions" are grouped by individual need area as well as combination need areas.

Music therapists are able to assess developmental changes and progress made over time by extracting the skills most often observed in sessions from the developmental checklists. For example, the excerpt on the following page is taken from a developmental documentation form created for use with this curriculum.

DEVELOPMENTAL PROGRESS					
	Date:	Date:	Date:	Date:	Date:
	Indiv. Group	Indiv. Group	Indiv. Group	Indiv. Group	Indiv. Group
Adult Participant					
EXPRESSIVE LANGUAGE					
Babbles hard/soft & short/long sounds					
Says 1 to 2 words: Dada/Mama/Bye-Bye					
Waves bye-bye					
Points to what he/she wants					
Shakes head yes/no					
Gestures					
RECEPTIVE LANGUAGE					
Turns head toward voice					
Moves eyes toward sound					
Attends to music					
Orients head toward sound					
Plays simple game (Peek-a-Boo)					
Understands "no"					
Follows 1-step command: with gesture/ without gesture					
Recognizes words for common items					
Looks at objects "Where is the ......?"					

The needs of the patient are easily identified by using the skills for the developmental age that is appropriate for the patient, resulting in a picture of the patient's current ability level. Creating an individualized session plan is then possible by referring to the developmental skills addressed in each song activity that match the need area of the child. For example, if a child is picking up an instrument consistently using his palm but is not yet releasing instruments by placing them on the ground first, then songs that incorporate the skill for releasing instruments can be grouped together to focus on fine motor development.

When approaching patient treatment from an interdisciplinary treatment approach, all team members will be informed of the goals others are addressing. The developmental checklist provided can be used to clearly communicate the specific objectives being targeted within music therapy sessions. It also can be used as a tool for identifying ability areas and areas of strength for each patient. Team members can benefit from knowing exactly which area of communication, motor, cognitive, or social-emotional development is being targeted within music therapy intervention sessions.

Early Intervention School Settings

When using this program for children with special needs, modifications can be made based on the number of staff members available to assist during the class time and the ability level of the student. For this reason, the music educator or therapist is encouraged to use this curriculum to create session plans that will best meet the needs of the students. In some groups, special education aides may be present, which will increase the number of music activities the music educator or therapist is able to complete within a class session.

Abbreviated session plans can be found in the section titled "Session Plans for Groups without Caregivers Present." These session plans can be combined or shortened based on the needs of each class. When hand-over-hand instruction is required for student participation and no aides are present, the number of activities the educator or therapist is able to complete will be fewer than when children are more independent or when aides are present.

If possible, incorporate peer models in the early intervention setting. The level of involvement in the sessions will depend on the age of the peers involved in the group. Young peers can model each behavior or targeted outcome by following cues given by the music educator or therapist leading the session. Older peers can assist in placing manipulatives and instruments in the students' hands, as well as offering assistance needed to engage in the activity.

A large body of research supports the inclusion of peer models, indicating benefits for both peers and students with special needs. Preschool-aged children with developmental delays can increase engaged and on-task behaviors; interactive social, communicative, and play behaviors; imitative, preacademic, and academic skills; and classroom transitions when peer mediators participate in intervention sessions (Harper & Maheady, 2007; Harris, Pretti-Frontczak, & Brown, 2009; Robertson, Green, Alper, Schloss, & Kohler, 2003). All the developmental checklist items can be included as documentation in the Individualized Education Plan/Individualized Family Service Plan (IEP/IFSP). Areas targeted as goals on the IEP/IFSP can be addressed in the music therapy sessions and documented as being included through the specific developmental skills addressed by each activity in this curriculum. An individualized session plan can be compiled for the specific need areas addressed for the children present in each group by using the section titled "Developmental Skills Addressed in Each Session." Or, if the targeted need areas are included in the "Domain Specific Session Plans," the session plans provided within this curriculum may be appropriate. The ability to create individualized sessions from the developmental checklist skills targeted in each song activity is especially useful for those who work with students who receive one-on-one interactions.

Child Development Center Educators

Many child development centers incorporate songs and chants throughout the day during circle time, by going to a special music area, or in singing songs during clean up. While some child development educators are comfortable singing, many are not and use only recorded music in their classroom. Although teachers may be embarrassed or uncomfortable singing in front of children, most children are able to immerse themselves in music activities and will not notice if their teacher isn't singing exactly the way the recording sounds. However, they will notice if the teacher is not singing along at all! Modeling how to interact with the music activity in the classroom increases the children's ability to successfully engage in the song and fosters a community of making music together.

Child development centers that are able to schedule 30-minute music sessions can use the full session plans formatted for use without caregivers present. With the many centers and outside play time structuring the day in child development centers, there may not be an entire 30 minutes to set aside for music circle time. The abbreviated session plans can be used in this situation as they are designed for 10- to 15-minute group interactions. With the shorter interaction time, more frequent sessions may be possible (e.g., three 10-minute times per week) to allow the same total amount of music interaction as one 30-minute session.

When providing music interaction for infants without parents or family members present, it may be necessary to limit the number of infants in each music circle time to enable the teachers to assist infants with the manipulatives assigned to each song. If a larger group of infants attends the music interaction and it is not possible for staff members and teachers to assist each infant, rotate the manipulatives throughout the music session, assisting each infant in the experience. Infants still learn through observing their environment and peers. Providing enough assistance with the manipulatives to keep the infant interested and engaged in the activities is the fundamental focus of the music time.

Inclusion of Children with Special Needs During Music Activities

Children with special needs are able to engage in music activities and benefit from the targeted music goals and peer interaction within each music session. The educator or therapist should first identify the developmental age of the child to facilitate participation at an appropriate developmental level. Many assessment tools can aid in this process. The Ages and Stages Questionnaire (Squires & Bricker, 2009) and the Developmental Assessment of Young Children (Voress & Maddox, 1998) are both comprehensive developmental assessments that require no formal training to use. Once the developmental level of the child is determined, the appropriate group for the child can be identified. If an aide or volunteer is present to assist a child with special needs during the session, the child will experience more meaningful participation. If the child development center has older children present who can participate in the music group, the older peer can help the child play instruments and use manipulatives during the music activities.

If the child development center is within the public school system, the child with special needs participating in the music session will have an Individualized Education Plan/Individualized Family Service Plan (IEP/IFSP). The developmental skills checklist provides specific developmental objectives to target during the music session and to report on the IEP/IFSP. This helps inform IEP/IFSP team members of areas of the IEP/IFSP that are to be addressed through music activities available in this curriculum.

REFERENCES

Harper, G. F., & Maheady, L. (2007). Peer-mediated teaching and students with learning disabilities. *Intervention in School and Clinic, 43*, 101–107.

Harris, K. I., Pretti-Frontczak, K., & Brown, T. (2009). Peer-mediated intervention: An effective inclusion strategy for all young children. *YC Young Children, 64*, 43–49.

Robertson, J., Green, K., Alper, S., Schloss, P., & Kohler, F. (2003). Using a peer-mediated intervention to facilitate children's participation in inclusive childcare activities. *Education and Treatment of Children, 26*(2),182–197.

Squires, J., & Bricker, D. (2009). *Ages and Stages Questionnaire: A parent-completed child-monitoring system*. Baltimore: Paul H. Brookes.

Voress, J. K., & Maddox, T. (1998). *Developmental Assessment of Young Children*. San Antonio, TX: Pearson Education.

SESSION PLANS FOR GROUPS WITHOUT CAREGIVERS PRESENT
(No Parent Instructions or Comments Included)
Darcy Walworth, PhD, MT-BC, and Judy Nguyen, MM, MT-BC

As noted in the prior section, this grouping of session plans is designed to address the full range of developmental skill areas in a 30- to 45-minute session time for infants. However, the following session plans do not include instructions for parents.

Bright Start Music   6–12 Month Group   Session Plan #1

SKILL AREAS	SONGS
Hello Song	**My Right Hand Says Hello**
Sing and Sign Song	**Clap Your Hands** (signs: more, music)
Instruments- Shakers	**Shake, Shake, Shake!**
Movement	**Pat a Cake** **Itsy Bitsy Spider** **Ten in the Bed**
Visual- Scarves	**Blow Me Some Bubbles** **I Can Name the Colors**
Animals/Puppets	**Old MacDonald** **Brown Bear, Brown Bear*** (with book) *Sung to tune of Twinkle, Twinkle, Little Star
Body Parts	**Head, Shoulders, Knees, and Toes**
Mirror Time	**If You're Happy and You Know It** (with different expressions)
Affection/Bonding	**Never Let Me Go**
Instruments- Ocean Drums/Rain Sticks	**Hush Little Baby**
Goodbye Song	**It's Time to Go** (using sign language)

Bright Start Music   6–12 Month Group   Session Plan #2

SKILL AREAS	SONGS
Hello Song	**My Right Hand Says Hello**
Sing and Sign Songs	**This is the Mommy Wiggle** (signs: mommy, daddy) Review: **Clap Your Hands** (signs: more, music)
Instruments- Shakers	**Shake, Shake, Shake!**
Movement	**Going Over the Sea** (MT use **ocean drum**)
Visual- Scarves	**Twinkle Twinkle**- with **bubbles** **Little Red Caboose**- with **train** moving
Animals/Puppets	**Old MacDonald** **Brown Bear, Brown Bear*** (with book) *Sung to tune of Twinkle, Twinkle, Little Star
Body Parts	**If I Arr a Pirate**
Mirror Time	**If You're Happy and You Know It** (with different expressions)
Affection/Bonding	**Never Let Me Go**
Instruments- Ocean Drums/Rain Sticks	**Hush Little Baby**
Goodbye Song	**It's Time to Go** (using sign language)

Bright Start Music   6–12 Month Group   Session Plan #3

SKILL AREAS	SONGS
Hello Song	My Right Hand Says Hello
Sing and Sign Songs	Mommy Go 'Round the Sun (signs: chair/sit, play/toy)
	Review: **This is the Mommy Wiggle** (signs: mommy, daddy)
	Review: **Clap Your Hands** (signs: more, music)
Instruments- Drums	Humpty Dumpty
	One, Two, Buckle My Shoe
	Two Little Blackbirds
Movement	Ten in the Bed
Visual- Scarves	I Can Name the Colors with scarves
	Little Red Caboose- with train moving
Animals/Puppets	Had a Little Rooster
Body Parts	Head, Shoulders, Knees, and Toes
Mirror Time	You Are My Sunshine (with different expressions)
Affection/Bonding	Never Let Me Go
Instruments- Ocean Drums/Rain Sticks	Soon the Moon Will Rise
Goodbye Song	It's Time to Go (using sign language)

Bright Start Music   6–12 Month Group   Session Plan #4

SKILL AREAS	SONGS
Hello Song	**My Right Hand Says Hello**
Sing and Sign Songs	**Doggie Doggie** (signs: dog, cat, ball) Review: **Mommy Go 'Round the Sun** (signs: chair/sit, play/toy) Review: **This is the Mommy Wiggle** (signs: mommy, daddy)
Instruments- Drums	**This Old Man** **One, Two, Buckle My Shoe**
Movement	**London Bridge** **Row, Row, Row Your Boat**
Visual- Scarves	**Twinkle Twinkle**- with **bubbles** **Little Red Caboose**- with **train** moving
Animals/Puppets	**Had a Little Rooster**
Body Parts	**If I Arr a Pirate**
Mirror Time	**You Are My Sunshine** (with different expressions)
Affection/Bonding	**Never Let Me Go**
Instruments- Ocean Drums/Rain Sticks	**Soon the Moon Will Rise**
Goodbye Song	**It's Time to Go** (using sign language)

Bright Start Music   **6–12 Month Group**   **Session Plan #5**

SKILL AREAS	SONGS
Hello Song	**My Right Hand Says Hello**
Sing and Sign Songs	**Roll the Ball** (signs: want, please, help, sorry) Review: **Doggie Doggie** (signs: dog, cat, ball) Review: **Mommy Go 'Round the Sun** (signs: chair/sit, play/toy)
Instruments- Shakers	**Mister Golden Sun** **Oh Where Has My Little Dog Gone?**
Movement	**London Bridge** **Row, Row, Row Your Boat**
Visual- Scarves	**Me Some Bubbles**- with **bubbles** **Little Red Caboose**- with **train** moving
Animals/Puppets	**Polar Bear, Polar Bear*** (with book) *Sung to tune of Twinkle, Twinkle, Little Star **Old MacDonald**- with puppets
Body Parts	**Head, Shoulders, Knees, and Toes**
Mirror Time	**If You're Happy and You Know It** (with different expressions)
Affection/Bonding	**Always in My Heart**
Instruments- Ocean Drums/Rain Sticks	**Big Bright Moon**
Goodbye Song	**It's Time to Go** (using sign language)

Bright Start Music   6–12 Month Group   Session Plan #6

SKILL AREAS	SONGS
Hello Song	**My Right Hand Says Hello**
Sing and Sign Songs	**The Walking Song** (signs: all-done, stop, ouch/hurt, hot) Review: **Roll the Ball** (signs: want, please, help, sorry) **Doggie Doggie** (signs: dog, cat, ball)
Instruments- Drums	**Click, Click, Click, Go the Castanets** **This Old Man**
Movement	**The Ants Go Marching**
Visual- Scarves	**Blow Me Some Bubbles**- with **bubbles** **Little Red Caboose**- with **train** moving **I Can Name the Colors**- with Color Circles
Animals/Puppets	**Polar Bear, Polar Bear*** (with book) *Sung to tune of Twinkle, Twinkle, Little Star **Old MacDonald**- with puppets
Body Parts	**If I Arr a Pirate**
Mirror Time	**You Are My Sunshine** (with different expressions)
Affection/Bonding	**How Will You Grow?**
Instruments- Ocean Drums/Rain Sticks	**Big Bright Moon**
Goodbye Song	**It's Time to Go** (using sign language)

Bright Start Music   6–12 Month Group   Session Plan #7

SKILL AREAS	SONGS
Hello Song	**My Right Hand Says Hello**
Sing and Sign Songs	**Where's Baby** (signs: eat/food/spoon, boy, girl) Review: **The Walking Song** (signs: all-done, stop, ouch/hurt, hot) Review: **Roll the Ball** (signs: want, please, help, sorry)
Instruments- Triangles/Wood Blocks	**The Alphabet Song** **My Favorite Spot**
Movement (for children who can walk, you can walk in a circle like a train)	**The Ants Go Marching** **I've Been Working on the Railroad**
Visual- Tracking Let child choose from instrument choices	**Skip to My Lou** **Mister Golden Sun** **Tingalayo**
Animals/Puppets Put puppets out in middle of circle out of reach for child to crawl/scoot/reach to get them	**Had a Little Rooster**
Body Parts	**Hokey Pokey**
Mirror Time	**The More We Get Together** (with different emotions written in song)
Affection/Bonding	**How Will You Grow?**
Instruments- Ocean Drums/Rain Sticks	**Big Bright Moon**
Goodbye Song	**It's Time to Go** (using sign language)

Bright Start Music   6–12 Month Group   Session Plan #8

SKILL AREAS	SONGS
Hello Song	**My Right Hand Says Hello**
Sing and Sign Songs	**Miss Mary Jane** (signs: car, airplane) Review: **Where's Baby** (signs: eat/food/spoon, boy, girl) Review: **The Walking Song** (signs: all-done, stop, ouch/hurt, hot)
Instruments- Triangles/Wood Blocks	**The Alphabet Song** **My Favorite Spot**
Movement (for children who can walk, you can walk in a circle like a train)	**The Ants Go Marching** **I've Been Working on the Railroad**
Visual- Tracking Let child choose from instrument choices	**Blow Me Some Bubbles** **Kookabura**
Animals/Puppets Put puppets out in middle of circle out of reach for child to crawl/scoot/reach to get them	**Animal Song**
Body Parts Ask: Where is your <u>hand</u>? (fill in blank with other body parts)	**My Hand on My Head**
Mirror Time	**Peek-A-Boo** (with different emotions written in song)
Affection/Bonding	**How Will You Grow?**
Instruments- Ocean Drums/Rain Sticks	**Big Bright Moon**
Goodbye Song	**It's Time to Go** (using sign language)

Bright Start Music   6–12 Month Group   Session Plan #9

SKILL AREAS	SONGS
Hello Song	**My Right Hand Says Hello**
Sing and Sign Songs	**The Little Cat Goes Creeping** (signs: sleep/bed, fish, thank you) Review: **Miss Mary Jane** (signs: car, airplane) Review: **Where's Baby** (signs: eat/food/spoon, boy, girl)
Instruments- Claves/Wood Blocks/Drums	**The Alphabet Song** **My Favorite Spot**
Movement	**Five Little Ducks**
Visual- Tracking Let child choose from instrument choices	**Kookabura** **Whack the Drum**
Animals/Puppets Put puppets out in middle of circle out of reach for child to crawl/scoot/reach to get them	**Had a Little Rooster**
Body Parts Ask: Where is your <u>hand</u>? (fill in blank with other body parts)	**If I Arr a Pirate**
Mirror Time	**Peek-A-Boo** (with different emotions written in song)
Affection/Bonding	**Always in My Heart**
Instruments- Ocean Drums/Rain Sticks	**Soon the Moon Will Rise**
Goodbye Song	**It's Time to Go** (using sign language)

Bright Start Music   6–12 Month Group   Session Plan #10

SKILL AREAS	SONGS
Hello Song	**My Right Hand Says Hello**
Sing and Sign Songs	**Bunny Boogie** (signs: bunny) Review: **The Little Cat Goes Creeping** (signs: sleep/bed, fish, thank you) Review: **Miss Mary Jane** (signs: car, airplane)
Instruments- Claves/Wood Blocks/Drums	**My Favorite Spot** **BINGO**
Movement *Roll balls from MT to each child/parent	**London Bridge** **Row, Row, Row Your Boat** **I Roll the Ball to You***
Visual- Tracking Create shaker instrument from beans in a can (let child put beans in can & take out when songs are done)	**Blow Me Some Bubbles** **Five Green and Speckled Frogs**
Animals/Puppets Put puppets out in middle of circle out of reach for child to crawl/scoot/reach to get them	**Animal Song**
Body Parts Ask: Where is your <u>hand</u>? (fill in blank with other body parts)	**My Hand on My Head**
Mirror Time	**Where is Thumbkin?** (with different emotions written in song)
Affection/Bonding	**Always in My Heart**
Instruments- Ocean Drums/Rain Sticks	**Soon the Moon Will Rise**
Goodbye Song	**It's Time to Go** (using sign language)

Bright Start Music   6–12 Month Group   Session Plan #11

SKILL AREAS	SONGS
Hello Song	**My Right Hand Says Hello**
Sing and Sign Songs	**Charlie Over the Water** (signs: water) Review: **Bunny Boogie** (signs: bunny) Review: **The Little Cat Goes Creeping** (signs: sleep/bed, fish, thank you)
Instruments- Triangles/Wood Blocks	**Twinkle Twinkle** **Itsy Bitsy Spider**
Movement *Roll balls from MT to each child/parent	**London Bridge** **Row, Row, Row Your Boat** **I Roll the Ball to You***
Visual- Tracking Create shaker instrument from beans in a can (let child put beans in can & take out when songs are done)	**Blow Me Some Bubbles** **Five Green and Speckled Frogs**
Animals/Puppets Use **Picture Cards** of birds or **Scarves** to mimic bird movement	**Birdie Beat** Allow children to explore activity circle freely during this activity
Body Parts Ask: Where is your <u>hand</u>? (fill in blank with other body parts)	**Loop De Loop**
Mirror Time Put mirror wrong side up to let child find functional side	**Where is Thumbkin?** (with different emotions written in song)
Affection/Bonding	**How You Will Grow?**
Instruments- Ocean Drums/Rain Sticks	**Goodnight, My Sweet One**
Goodbye Song	**It's Time to Go** (using sign language)

Bright Start Music   6–12 Month Group   Session Plan #12

SKILL AREAS	SONGS
Hello Song	**My Right Hand Says Hello**
Sing and Sign Songs	**My World** (signs: book)
	Review: **Charlie Over the Water** (signs: water)
	Review: **Bunny Boogie** (signs: bunny)
Instruments- Claves/Wood Blocks/Drums	**Skip to My Lou**
	Humpty Dumpty
Movement *Roll balls from MT to each child/parent	**Five Little Monkeys Jumping on the Bed** **I Roll the Ball to You***
Visual- Tracking Create shaker instrument from beans in a can (let child put beans in can & take out when songs are done)	**I'm a Little Teapot** **If All the Raindrops**
Animals/Puppets Use **Picture Cards** of birds or **Scarves** to mimic bird movement	**Birdie Beat** Allow children to explore activity circle freely during this activity
Body Parts Ask: Where is your <u>hand</u>? (fill in blank with other body parts)	**Loop De Loop**
Mirror Time Put mirror wrong side up to let child find functional side	**Where is Thumbkin?** (with different emotions written in song)
Affection/Bonding	**Always in My Heart**
Instruments- Ocean Drums/Rain Sticks	**Goodnight, My Sweet One**
Goodbye Song	**It's Time to Go** (using sign language)

Bright Start Music   12–18 Month Group Session Plan #1

*Throughout Session - Use verbal directions for activities for child to follow. Avoid giving gestural cues; give directions while pointing to objects.

SKILL AREAS	SONGS
Hello Song	**When I Meet a New Friend**
Sing and Sign Songs	**La La La Lullaby** Signs: Sleep/bed, I love you Review: **Skye Boat Song** Signs: stars, blanket, moon, I love you Review: **My World** Signs: book
Instruments- Rhythm Instruments Create shaker instrument from beans in a can (let child put beans in can and take out when songs are done)	**Playing Along**
Movement	**The Owl**
Visual- Scarves	**I Can Name the Color**
Animals/Puppets	**Hello Mr. Animal**
Books	**Ten Little Monkeys** (Big Book)
Body Parts	**If I Arr a Pirate**
Mirror Time	**Look in the Mirror**
Movement	**Hot Air Balloon**
Affection/Bonding	**In My Own Little Way**
Goodbye Song	**It's Time to Go** (using sign language)

Bright Start Music   12–18 Month Group Session Plan #2

*Throughout Session - Use verbal directions for activities for child to follow. Avoid giving gestural cues; give directions while pointing to objects.

SKILL AREAS	SONGS
Hello Song	**When I Meet a New Friend**
Sing and Sign Songs	**La La La Lullaby** Signs: Sleep/bed, I love you Review: **Skye Boat Song** Signs: stars, blanket, moon, I love you Review: **My World** Sign: book
Instruments- Rhythm Instruments	**Playing Along**
Movement	**The Owl**
Visual- Scarves	**I Can Name the Color**
Animals/Puppets	**Hello Mr. Animal**
Books	**Ten Little Monkeys** (Big Book)
Body Parts Incorporate rolling and throwing small balls	**You Do the Same**
Mirror Time	**Look in the Mirror**
Movement	**Hot Air Balloon**
Affection/Bonding	**In My Own Little Way**
Goodbye Song	**It's Time to Go** (using sign language)

Bright Start Music   12–18 Month Group   Session Plan #3

*Throughout Session - Use verbal directions for activities for child to follow. Avoid giving gestural cues; give directions while pointing to objects.

SKILL AREAS	SONGS
Hello Song	**When I Meet a New Friend**
Sing and Sign Songs	**La La La Lullaby** Signs: Sleep/bed, I love you Review: **Skye Boat Song** Signs: stars, blanket, moon, I love you
Instruments- Rhythm Instruments Create shaker instrument from beans in a can (let child put beans in can and take out when songs are done)	**Razzle Dazzle 'Em**
Movement	**The Owl**
Visual- Scarves	**I Can Name the Color**
Animals/Puppets	**Animal Song**
Books	**Mulberry Bush** (Big Book)
Body Parts	**Look in the Mirror**
Mirror Time	**This is How I Look**
Movement Can incorporate rain sticks or ocean drums	**Pitter Patter**
Affection/Bonding	**In My Own Little Way**
Goodbye Song	**It's Time to Go** (using sign language)

Bright Start Music   12–18 Month Group Session Plan #4

*Throughout Session - Use verbal directions for activities for child to follow. Avoid giving gestural cues; give directions while pointing to objects.

SKILL AREAS	SONGS
Hello Song	When I Meet a New Friend
Sign Language Song Choose any colors and animals signs in book	Brown Bear, Brown Bear Sing to the tune of Twinkle, Twinkle
Instruments- Rhythm Instruments	Playing Along
Movement	Let's Go for a Ride
Visual- Scarves	I Can Name the Color
Animals/Puppets	Monkey Hug
Books	Farmer in the Dell (Big Book)
Body Parts Incorporate rolling and throwing small balls	You Do the Same
Mirror Time	This is How I Look
Movement	There's a Tickle Under My Skin
Affection/Bonding	Doo Wop Love
Goodbye Song	It's Time to Go (using sign language)

Bright Start Music   12–18 Month Group   Session Plan #5

*Throughout Session - Use verbal directions for activities for child to follow. Avoid giving gestural cues; give directions while pointing to objects.

SKILL AREAS	SONGS
Hello Song	**When I Meet a New Friend**
Sign Language Song Choose any colors and animals signs in book	**Brown Bear, Brown Bear** Sing to the tune of Twinkle, Twinkle
Instruments- Rhythm Instruments Create shaker instrument from beans in a can (let child put beans in can & take out when songs are done)	**Razzle Dazzle 'Em**
Movement	**Let's Go for a Ride**
Visual- Scarves	**I Can Name the Color**
Animals/Puppets	**Animal Song** with **Picture Cards**
Books	**This Old Man** (Big Book)
Body Parts	**Look in the Mirror**
Mirror Time	**I Feel Silly**
Movement Can incorporate rain sticks or ocean drums	**Pitter Patter**
Affection/Bonding	**Baby Baby**
Goodbye Song	**It's Time to Go** (using sign language)

Bright Start Music   12–18 Month Group Session Plan #6

*Throughout Session - Use verbal directions for activities for child to follow. Avoid giving gestural cues; give directions while pointing to objects.

SKILL AREAS	SONGS
Hello Song	**When I Meet a New Friend**
Sign Language Song Choose any colors and animals signs in book	**Brown Bear, Brown Bear** Sing to the tune of Twinkle, Twinkle
Instruments- Rhythm Instruments	**Playing Along**
Movement	**Let's Go for a Ride**
Visual- Scarves	**I Can Name the Color**
Animals/Puppets	**Mr. Animal** with **Picture Cards**
Books	**Nine Ducks Nine** (Big Book)
Body Parts Incorporate rolling and throwing small balls	**You Do the Same**
Mirror Time	**I Feel Silly**
Movement	**There's a Tickle Under My Skin**
Affection/Bonding	**Baby Baby**
Goodbye Song	**It's Time to Go** (using sign language)

Bright Start Music   12–18 Month Group   Session Plan #7

*Throughout Session - Use verbal directions for activities for child to follow. Avoid giving gestural cues; give directions while pointing to objects.

SKILL AREAS	SONGS
Hello Song	When I Meet a New Friend
Sign Language Song Choose any animals signs in book	Polar Bear, Polar Bear (with Big Book)
Instruments- Rhythm Instruments	Whack That Drum
Movement	Tree Hugs
Visual- Picture Cards	My Favorite Spot
Animals/Puppets	Animal Song
Books	Walking Through the Jungle (Big Book)
Body Parts Incorporate rolling and throwing small balls	You Do the Same
Mirror Time	I Feel Silly
Movement Can incorporate rain sticks or ocean drums	Pitter Patter
Affection/Bonding	Baby Baby
Goodbye Song	It's Time to Go (using sign language)

Bright Start Music   12–18 Month Group Session Plan #8

*Throughout Session - Use verbal directions for activities for child to follow. Avoid giving gestural cues; give directions while pointing to objects.

SKILL AREAS	SONGS
Hello Song	When I Meet a New Friend
Sign Language Song Choose any animals signs in book	Polar Bear, Polar Bear (with Big Book)
Instruments- Rhythm Instruments	Whack That Drum
Movement	Flower Power
Visual- Picture Cards	My Favorite Spot
Animals/Puppets	Monkey Hug
Books	Panda Bear, Panda Bear, What Do You See? (Big Book)
Body Parts	My Hand on My Head
Mirror Time	Look in the Mirror
Movement	There's a Tickle Under My Skin
Affection/Bonding	Doo Wop Love
Goodbye Song	It's Time to Go (using sign language)

Bright Start Music   12–18 Month Group   Session Plan #9

*Throughout Session - Use verbal directions for activities for child to follow. Avoid giving gestural cues; give directions while pointing to objects.

SKILL AREAS	SONGS
Hello Song	**When I Meet a New Friend**
Sign Language Song Choose any animals signs in book	**Polar Bear, Polar Bear** (with Big Book)
Instruments- Rhythm Instruments	**I'm the Sun**
Movement	**Flower Power**
Visual- Picture Cards	**My Favorite Spot**
Animals/Puppets	**Animal Song**
Books	**Wheels on the Bus** (Big Book)
Body Parts Incorporate rolling and throwing small balls	**You Do the Same**
Mirror Time	**This is How I Look**
Movement	**Hot Air Balloon**
Affection/Bonding	**Doo Wop Love**
Goodbye Song	**It's Time to Go** (using sign language)

Bright Start Music   12–18 Month Group Session Plan #10

*Throughout Session - Use verbal directions for activities for child to follow. Avoid giving gestural cues; give directions while pointing to objects.

SKILL AREAS	SONGS
Hello Song	When I Meet a New Friend
Sign Language Song	Birdie Beat Signs: Bird, Tree, Fly, Wind
Instruments- Rhythm Instruments	I'm the Sun
Movement	Tree Hugs
Visual- Picture Cards	My Favorite Spot
Animals/Puppets	Hello Mr. Animal
Books	Ten Little Monkeys (Big Book)
Body Parts	My Hand on My Head
Mirror Time	This is How I Look
Movement	Hot Air Balloon
Affection/Bonding	In My Own Little Way
Goodbye Song	It's Time to Go (using sign language)

Bright Start Music   12–18 Month Group   Session Plan #11

*Throughout Session - Use verbal directions for activities for child to follow. Avoid giving gestural cues; give directions while pointing to objects.

SKILL AREAS	SONGS
Hello Song	**When I Meet a New Friend**
Sign Language Song	**Birdie Beat** Signs: Bird, Tree, Fly, Wind
Instruments- Rhythm Instruments	**Click! Click! Click! Go the Castanets**
Movement	**Tree Hugs**
Visual- Picture Cards	**My Favorite Spot**
Animals/Puppets	**Animal Song**
Books	**Mulberry Bush** (Big Book)
Body Parts Incorporate rolling and throwing small balls	**You Do the Same**
Mirror Time	**I Feel Silly**
Movement	**Hot Air Balloon**
Affection/Bonding	**In My Own Little Way**
Goodbye Song	**It's Time to Go** (using sign language)

Bright Start Music   12–18 Month Group Session Plan #12

*Throughout Session - Use verbal directions for activities for child to follow. Avoid giving gestural cues; give directions while pointing to objects.

SKILL AREAS	SONGS
Hello Song	**When I Meet a New Friend**
Sign Language Song	**Birdie Beat** Signs: Bird, Tree, Fly, Wind
Instruments- Rhythm Instruments	**Click! Click! Click! Go the Castanets**
Movement	**Flower Power**
Visual- Picture Cards	**My Favorite Spot**
Animals/Puppets	**Monkey Hug**
Books	**Farmer in The Dell** (Big Book)
Body Parts	**My Hand on My Head**
Mirror Time	**I Feel Silly**
Movement	**The Owl**
Affection/Bonding	**Baby, Baby**
Goodbye Song	**It's Time to Go** (using sign language)

Bright Start Music   18–24 Month Group Session Plan #1

SKILL AREAS	SONGS
Hello Song	How Do You Doodle
Instruments- Tambourines and/or Drums	Listen to How I Beat My Drum Clean Up
Movement	We're Gonna Dance, We're Gonna Wiggle
Body Parts/Gestures	Hello, Salutations
Animals/Picture Cards	Marty Monkey Clean Up
Body Parts	Tony Chestnut
Emotions/Dramatic Play	Monkey Moves!
Multicultural- Rhythm Instruments	Pollito, Chicken Clean Up
Movement	The Owl
Affection/Bonding	La La La Lullaby
Goodbye Song	It's Time to Go (using sign language)

Bright Start Music   18–24 Month Group   Session Plan #2

SKILL AREAS	SONGS
Hello Song	How Do You Doodle
Instruments- Rhythm Instruments	Leader of the Band Clean Up
Movement	We're Gonna Dance, We're Gonna Wiggle
Body Parts/Gestures	Loop De Loop
Animals/Picture Cards	Mouse in My House Clean Up
Body Parts	Tony Chestnut
Emotions/Dramatic Play	I Feel Silly
Multicultural- Rhythm Instruments	Pollito, Chicken Clean Up
Movement	I Roll the Ball to You
Affection/Bonding	La La La Lullaby
Goodbye Song	It's Time to Go (using sign language)

Bright Start Music   18–24 Month Group   Session Plan #3

SKILL AREAS	SONGS
Hello Song	How Do You Doodle
Instruments- Rhythm Instruments	1,2,3, Play with Me Clean Up
Movement	It's Time for Parade
Body Parts/Gestures	The Body Language Song
Animals/Puppets	Animal Parade Clean Up
Song Book	Mouse in My House
Body Parts	Tony Chestnut
Emotions/Dramatic Play	What's Your Name?
Multicultural- Rhythm Instruments	Funga A La Feeya Clean Up
Movement	Monkey Moves!
Affection/Bonding	Never Let Me Go
Goodbye Song	It's Time to Go (using sign language)

Bright Start Music   18–24 Month Group Session Plan #4

SKILL AREAS	SONGS
Hello Song	How Do You Doodle
Instruments- Rhythm Instruments	1,2,3, Play with Me Clean Up
Movement	It's Time for Parade
Body Parts/Gestures	Hello, Salutations
Animals/Puppets	Animal Parade Clean Up
Song Book	Mouse in My House
Body Parts	Tony Chestnut
Emotions/Dramatic Play	I Feel Silly
Multicultural- Rhythm Instruments	Funga A La Feeya Clean Up
Movement	Dance to the Music
Affection/Bonding	Never Let Me Go
Goodbye Song	It's Time to Go (using sign language)

Bright Start Music   18–24 Month Group   Session Plan #5

SKILL AREAS	SONGS
Hello Song	How Do You Doodle
Instruments- Tambourines and/or Drums	Listen to How I Beat My Drum Clean Up
Movement	Dance to the Music
Body Parts/Gestures	Loop De Loop
Animals/Picture Cards	Marty Monkey Clean Up
Body Parts	When I Wake Up
Emotions/Dramatic Play	Mood Groove
Multicultural- Rhythm Instruments	We Circle Around Clean Up
Movement	I Roll the Ball To You
Affection/Bonding	Do Wop Lullaby
Goodbye Song	It's Time to Go (using sign language)

Bright Start Music   18–24 Month Group Session Plan #6

SKILL AREAS	SONGS
Hello Song	How Do You Doodle
Instruments- Tambourines and/or Drums	Listen to How I Beat My Drum Clean Up
Movement	Dance to the Music
Body Parts/Gestures	The Body Language Song
Animals/Picture Cards	Marty Monkey Clean Up
Body Parts	When I Wake Up
Emotions/Dramatic Play	I Feel Silly
Multicultural- Rhythm Instruments	We Circle Around Clean Up
Movement	It's Time for Parade
Affection/Bonding	Do Wop Lullaby
Goodbye Song	It's Time to Go (using sign language)

Bright Start Music   18–24 Month Group   Session Plan #7

SKILL AREAS	SONGS
Hello Song	How Do You Doodle
Instruments- Rhythm Instruments	Leader of the Band
	Clean Up
Movement	Monkey Moves!
Body Parts/Gestures	Hello, Salutations
Animals/Puppets	A Rustle in a Bush
	Clean Up
Body Parts	When I Wake Up
Emotions/Dramatic Play	What's Your Name?
Multicultural- Rhythm Instruments	Pajarito
	Clean Up
Movement	The Bicycle
Affection/Bonding	La La La Lullaby
Goodbye Song	It's Time to Go (using sign language)

Bright Start Music   18–24 Month Group   Session Plan #8

SKILL AREAS	SONGS
Hello Song	How Do You Doodle
Instruments- Rhythm Instruments	1,2,3, Play with Me Clean Up
Movement	Monkey Moves!
Body Parts/Gestures	Loop De Loop
Animals/Puppets	A Rustle in a Bush Clean Up
Body Parts	When I Wake Up
Emotions/Dramatic Play	I Feel Silly
Multicultural- Rhythm Instruments	Pajarito Clean Up
Movement	I Roll the Ball To You
Affection/Bonding	La La La Lullaby
Goodbye Song	It's Time to Go (using sign language)

Bright Start Music   **18–24 Month Group** **Session Plan #9**

SKILL AREAS	SONGS
Hello Song	How Do You Doodle
Instruments- Rhythm Instruments	1,2,3, Play with Me Clean Up
Movement	The Bicycle
Body Parts/Gestures	The Body Language Song
Animals/Puppets	Animal Parade Clean Up
Songbook	Mouse in My House
Body Parts	If I Arr a Pirate
Emotions/Dramatic Play	Mood Groove
Multicultural- Rhythm Instruments	Zum Gali Gali Clean Up
Movement	We're Gonna Dance, We're Gonna Wiggle
Affection/Bonding	Never Let Me Go
Goodbye Song	It's Time to Go (using sign language)

Bright Start Music   18–24 Month Group   Session Plan #10

SKILL AREAS	SONGS
Hello Song	How Do You Doodle
Instruments- Rhythm Instruments	Leader of the Band Clean Up
Movement	It's Time for Parade
Body Parts/Gestures	Hello, Salutations
Animals/Puppets	Animal Parade Clean Up
Songbook	Mouse in My House
Body Parts	If I Arr a Pirate
Emotions/Dramatic Play	I Feel Silly
Multicultural- Rhythm Instruments	Zum Gali Gali Clean Up
Movement	The Bicycle
Affection/Bonding	Never Let Me Go
Goodbye Song	It's Time to Go (using sign language)

Bright Start Music   18–24 Month Group   Session Plan #11

SKILL AREAS	SONGS
Hello Song	How Do You Doodle
Instruments- Tambourines and/or Drums	Listen to How I Beat My Drum Clean Up
Movement	We're Gonna Dance, We're Gonna Wiggle
Body Parts/Gestures	Loop De Loop
Animals/Picture Cards	Marty Monkey Clean Up
Body Parts	If I Arr a Pirate
Emotions/Dramatic Play	What's Your Name?
Multicultural- Rhythm Instruments	Siyahamba Clean Up
Movement	I Roll the Ball to You
Affection/Bonding	Do Wop Lullaby
Goodbye Song	It's Time to Go (using sign language)

Bright Start Music   18–24 Month Group   Session Plan #12

SKILL AREAS	SONGS
Hello Song	How Do You Doodle
Instruments- Tambourines and/or Drums	Listen to How I Beat My Drum Clean Up
Movement	Dance to the Music
Body Parts/Gestures	The Body Language Song
Animals/Puppets	A Rustle in a Bush Clean Up
Body Parts	If I Arr a Pirate
Emotions/Dramatic Play	I Feel Silly
Multicultural- Rhythm Instruments	Siyahamba Clean Up
Movement	The Bicycle
Affection/Bonding	Do Wop Lullaby
Goodbye Song	It's Time to Go (using sign language)

ABBREVIATED SESSION PLANS FOR USE IN CIRCLE TIME

Circle time session plans are provided for times and situations when a full 30- to 45- minute session is not ideal. All developmental skill areas are covered in a more concentrated format, although the amount of exposure to specific skills is decreased in comparison to the full session plan format. The circle time session plans are designed for situations when 10- to 15- minutes of music interactions are desired.

Bright Start Music   6–12 Month Group   Session Plan #1

SKILL AREAS	SONGS
Instruments- Shakers	Shake, Shake, Shake!
Movement	Pat a Cake Itsy Bitsy Spider Ten in the Bed
Visual- Scarves	Blow Me Some Bubbles I Can Name the Colors
Animals/Puppets	Old MacDonald Brown Bear, Brown Bear* (with **book**) *Sung to tune of Twinkle, Twinkle, Little Star
Body Parts	Head, Shoulders, Knees, and Toes
Instruments- Ocean Drums/Rain Sticks	Hush Little Baby

Bright Start Music   6–12 Month Group   Session Plan #2

SKILL AREAS	SONGS
Instruments- Shakers	Shake, Shake, Shake!
Movement	Going Over the Sea (MT use **ocean drum**)
Visual- Scarves	Twinkle Twinkle- with **bubbles** Little Red Caboose- with **train** moving
Animals/Puppets	Old MacDonald Brown Bear, Brown Bear* (with **book**) *Sung to tune of Twinkle, Twinkle, Little Star
Body Parts	If I Arr a Pirate
Instruments- Ocean Drums/Rain Sticks	Hush Little Baby

Bright Start Music   6–12 Month Group   Session Plan #3

SKILL AREAS	SONGS
Instruments- Drums	Humpty Dumpty One, Two, Buckle My Shoe Two Little Blackbirds
Movement	Ten in the Bed
Visual- Scarves	I Can Name the Colors with **scarves** Little Red Caboose- with **train** moving
Animals/Puppets	Had a Little Rooster
Body Parts	Head, Shoulders, Knees, and Toes
Instruments- Ocean Drums/Rain Sticks	Soon the Moon Will Rise

Bright Start Music   6–12 Month Group   Session Plan #4

SKILL AREAS	SONGS
Instruments- Drums	This Old Man One, Two, Buckle My Shoe
Movement	London Bridge Row, Row, Row Your Boat
Visual- Scarves	Twinkle Twinkle- with **bubbles** Little Red Caboose- with **train** moving
Animals/Puppets	Had a Little Rooster
Body Parts	If I Arr a Pirate
Instruments- Ocean Drums/Rain Sticks	Soon the Moon Will Rise

Bright Start Music   6–12 Month Group   Session Plan #5

SKILL AREAS	SONGS
Instruments- Shakers	Mister Golden Sun Oh Where Has My Little Dog Gone?
Movement	London Bridge Row, Row, Row Your Boat
Visual- Scarves	Blow Me Some Bubbles- with **bubbles** Little Red Caboose- with **train** moving
Animals/Puppets	Polar Bear, Polar Bear* (with **book**) *Sung to tune of Twinkle, Twinkle, Little Star Old MacDonald- with **puppets**
Body Parts	Head, Shoulders, Knees, and Toes
Instruments- Ocean Drums/Rain Sticks	Big Bright Moon

Bright Start Music   6–12 Month Group   Session Plan #6

SKILL AREAS	SONGS
Sing and Sign Songs	**The Walking Song** (signs: all-done, stop, ouch/hurt, hot) Review: **Roll the Ball** (signs: want, please, help, sorry) **Doggie Doggie** (signs: dog, cat, ball)
Instruments- Drums	**Click, Click, Click, Go the Castanets** **This Old Man**
Movement	**The Ants Go Marching**
Visual- Scarves	**Blow Me Some Bubbles** -with **bubbles** **Little Red Caboose**- with **train** moving **I Can Name the Colors** - with **Color Circles**
Animals/Puppets	**Polar Bear, Polar Bear*** (with **book**) *Sung to tune of Twinkle, Twinkle, Little Star **Old MacDonald**- with **puppets**
Mirror Time	**You Are My Sunshine** (with different expressions)

Bright Start Music   6–12 Month Group   Session Plan #7

SKILL AREAS	SONGS
Sing and Sign Songs	**Where's Baby** (signs: eat/food/spoon, boy, girl) Review: **The Walking Song** (signs: all-done, stop, ouch/hurt, hot) Review: **Roll the Ball** (signs: want, please, help, sorry)
Movement (for children who can walk, you can walk in a circle like a train)	**The Ants Go Marching** **I've Been Working on the Railroad**
Visual- Tracking Let child choose from instrument choices	**Skip to My Lou** **Mister Golden Sun** **Tingalayo**
Animals/Puppets Put puppets out in middle of circle out of reach for child to crawl/scoot/reach to get them	**Had a Little Rooster**
Body Parts	**Hokey Pokey**
Mirror Time	**The More We Get Together** (with different emotions written in song)

Bright Start Music   6–12 Month Group   Session Plan #8

SKILL AREAS	SONGS
Sing and Sign Songs	**Miss Mary Jane** (signs: car, airplane) Review: **Where's Baby** (signs: eat/food/spoon, boy, girl) Review: **The Walking Song** (signs: all-done, stop, ouch/hurt, hot)
Movement (for children who can walk, you can walk in a circle like a train)	**The Ants Go Marching** **I've Been Working on the Railroad**
Visual- Tracking Let child choose from instrument choices	**Blow Me Some Bubbles** **Kookabura**
Animals/Puppets Put puppets out in middle of circle out of reach for child to crawl/scoot/reach to get them	**Animal Song**
Body Parts Ask: Where is your <u>hand</u>? (fill in blank with other body parts)	**My Hand on My Head**
Mirror Time	**Peek-A-Boo** (with different emotions written in song)

Bright Start Music   6–12 Month Group   Session Plan #9

SKILL AREAS	SONGS
Sing and Sign Songs	**The Little Cat Goes Creeping** (signs: sleep/bed, fish, thank you) Review: **Miss Mary Jane** (signs: car, airplane) Review: **Where's Baby** (signs: eat/food/spoon, boy, girl)
Instruments- Claves/Wood Blocks/Drums	**The Alphabet Song** **My Favorite Spot**
Visual- Tracking Let child choose from instrument choices	**Kookabura** **Whack the Drum**
Animals/Puppets Put puppets out in middle of circle out of reach for child to crawl/scoot/reach to get them	**Had a Little Rooster**
Body Parts Ask: Where is your <u>hand</u>? (fill in blank with other body parts)	**If I Arr a Pirate**
Mirror Time	**Peek-A-Boo** (with different emotions written in song)

Bright Start Music   6–12 Month Group   Session Plan #10

SKILL AREAS	SONGS
Sing and Sign Songs	**Bunny Boogie** (signs: bunny) Review: **The Little Cat Goes Creeping** (signs: sleep/bed, fish, thank you) Review: **Miss Mary Jane** (signs: car, airplane)
Movement *Roll balls from MT to each child/parent	**London Bridge** **Row, Row, Row Your Boat** **I Roll the Ball to You***
Visual- Tracking Create shaker instrument from beans in a can (let child put beans in can and take out when songs are done)	**Blow Me Some Bubbles** **Five Green and Speckled Frogs**
Animals/Puppets Put puppets out in middle of circle out of reach for child to crawl/scoot/reach to get it	**Animal Song**
Body Parts Ask: Where is your <u>hand</u>? (fill in blank with other body parts)	**My Hand on My Head**
Mirror Time	**Where is Thumbkin?** (with different emotions written in song)

Bright Start Music   6–12 Month Group   Session Plan #11

SKILL AREAS	SONGS
Sing and Sign Songs	**Charlie Over the Water** (signs: water) Review: **Bunny Boogie** (signs: bunny) Review: **The Little Cat Goes Creeping** (signs: sleep/bed, fish, thank you)
Movement *Roll balls from MT to each child/parent	**London Bridge** **Row, Row, Row Your Boat** **I Roll the Ball to You***
Visual- Tracking Create shaker instrument from beans in a can (let child put beans in can and take out when songs are done)	**Blow Me Some Bubbles** **Five Green and Speckled Frogs**
Animals/Puppets Use **Picture Cards** of birds or **Scarves** to mimic bird movement	**Birdie Beat** Allow children to explore activity circle freely during this activity
Body Parts Ask: Where is your <u>hand</u>? (fill in blank with other body parts)	**Loop De Loop**
Mirror Time Put mirror wrong side up to let child find functional side	**Where is Thumbkin?** (with different emotions written in song)

Bright Start Music   6–12 Month Group   Session Plan #12

SKILL AREAS	SONGS
Sing and Sign Songs	**My World** (signs: book) Review: **Charlie Over the Water** (signs: water) Review: **Bunny Boogie** (signs: bunny)
Movement *Roll balls from MT to each child/parent	**Five Little Monkeys Jumping on the Bed** **I Roll the Ball to You***
Visual- Tracking Create shaker instrument from beans in a can (let child put beans in can & take out when songs are done)	**I'm a Little Teapot** **If All the Raindrops**
Animals/Puppets Use **Picture Cards** of birds or **Scarves** to mimic bird movement	**Birdie Beat** Allow children to explore activity circle freely during this activity
Body Parts Ask: Where is your <u>hand</u>? (fill in blank with other body parts)	**Loop De Loop**
Mirror Time Put mirror wrong side up to let child find functional side	**Where is Thumbkin?** (with different emotions written in song)

Bright Start Music   12–18 Month Group   Session Plan #1

*Throughout Session - Use verbal directions for activities for child to follow. Avoid giving gestural cues; give directions while pointing to objects.

SKILL AREAS	SONGS
Sing and Sign Songs	**La La La Lullaby** (signs: sleep/bed, I love you) Review: **Skye Boat Song** (signs: stars, blanket, moon, I love you) Review: **My World** (signs: book)
Instruments- Rhythm Instruments Create shaker instrument from beans in a can (let child put beans in can & take out when songs are done)	**Playing Along**
Movement	**The Owl**
Animals/Puppets	**Hello Mr. Animal**
Body Parts	**If I Arr a Pirate**
Movement	**Hot Air Balloon**

Bright Start Music   12–18 Month Group Session Plan #2

*Throughout Session - Use verbal directions for activities for child to follow. Avoid giving gestural cues; give directions while pointing to objects.

SKILL AREAS	SONGS
Sing and Sign Songs	**La La La Lullaby** (signs: Sleep/bed, I love you) Review: **Skye Boat Song** (signs: stars, blanket, moon, I love you) Review: **My World** (signs: book)
Instruments- Rhythm Instruments	**Playing Along**
Visual- Scarves	**I Can Name the Color**
Books	**Ten Little Monkeys** (Big Book)
Body Parts Incorporate rolling and throwing small balls	**You Do the Same**
Mirror Time	**Look in the Mirror**

Bright Start Music   12–18 Month Group   Session Plan #3

*Throughout Session - Use verbal directions for activities for child to follow. Avoid giving gestural cues; give directions while pointing to objects.

SKILL AREAS	SONGS
Sing and Sign Songs	**La La La Lullaby** (signs: sleep/bed, I love you) Review: **Skye Boat Song** (signs: stars, blanket, moon, I love you)
Movement	**The Owl**
Visual- Scarves	**I Can Name the Color**
Body Parts	**Look in the Mirror**
Mirror Time	**This is How I Look**
Movement Can incorporate rain sticks or ocean drums	**Pitter Patter**

Bright Start Music   12–18 Month Group   Session Plan #4

*Throughout Session - Use verbal directions for activities for child to follow. Avoid giving gestural cues; give directions while pointing to objects.

SKILL AREAS	SONGS
Sign Language Song Choose any colors and animals signs in book	**Brown Bear, Brown Bear** Sing to the tune of Twinkle, Twinkle
Instruments- Rhythm Instruments	**Playing Along**
Animals/Puppets	**Monkey Hug**
Body Parts Incorporate rolling and throwing small balls	**You Do the Same**
Mirror Time	**This is How I Look**
Movement	**There's a Tickle Under My Skin**

Bright Start Music   12–18 Month Group Session Plan #5

*Throughout Session - Use verbal directions for activities for child to follow. Avoid giving gestural cues; give directions while pointing to objects.

SKILL AREAS	SONGS
Sign Language Song Choose any colors and animals signs in book	**Brown Bear, Brown Bear** Sing to the tune of Twinkle, Twinkle
Animals/Puppets	**Animal Song** with **Picture Cards**
Books	**This Old Man** (Big Book)
Body Parts	**Look in the Mirror**
Mirror Time	**I Feel Silly**
Movement Can incorporate rain sticks or ocean drums	**Pitter Patter**

Bright Start Music   12–18 Month Group Session Plan #6

*Throughout Session - Use verbal directions for activities for child to follow. Avoid giving gestural cues; give directions while pointing to objects.

SKILL AREAS	SONGS
Sign Language Song Choose any colors and animals signs in book	**Brown Bear, Brown Bear** Sing to the tune of Twinkle, Twinkle
Instruments- Rhythm Instruments	**Playing Along**
Movement	**Let's Go for a Ride**
Body Parts Incorporate rolling and throwing small balls	**You Do the Same**
Mirror Time	**I Feel Silly**
Movement	**There's a Tickle Under My Skin**

Bright Start Music   12–18 Month Group   Session Plan #7

*Throughout Session - Use verbal directions for activities for child to follow. Avoid giving gestural cues; give directions while pointing to objects.

SKILL AREAS	SONGS
Sign Language Song Choose any animals signs in book	**Polar Bear, Polar Bear** (with Big Book)
Instruments- Rhythm Instruments	**Click! Click! Click! Go the Castanets**
Animals/Puppets	**Animal Song**
Body Parts Incorporate rolling and throwing small balls	**You Do the Same**
Mirror Time	**I Feel Silly**
Movement Can incorporate rain sticks or ocean drums	**Pitter Patter**

Bright Start Music   12–18 Month Group   Session Plan #8

*Throughout Session - Use verbal directions for activities for child to follow. Avoid giving gestural cues; give directions while pointing to objects.

SKILL AREAS	SONGS
Sign Language Song Choose any animals signs in book	**Polar Bear, Polar Bear** (with Big Book)
Instruments- Rhythm Instruments	**Click! Click! Click! Go the Castanets**
Books	**Panda Bear, Panda Bear, What Do You See?** (Big Book)
Body Parts	**My Hand on My Head**
Mirror Time	**Look in the Mirror**
Movement	**There's a Tickle Under My Skin**

Bright Start Music   12–18 Month Group   Session Plan #9

*Throughout Session - Use verbal directions for activities for child to follow. Avoid giving gestural cues; give directions while pointing to objects.

SKILL AREAS	SONGS
Sign Language Song Choose any animals signs in book	**Polar Bear, Polar Bear** (with Big Book)
Animals/Puppets	**Animal Song**
Books	**Wheels on the Bus** (Big Book)
Body Parts Incorporate rolling and throwing small balls	**You Do the Same**
Mirror Time	**This is How I Look**
Movement	**Hot Air Balloon**

Bright Start Music   12–18 Month Group   Session Plan #10

*Throughout Session - Use verbal directions for activities for child to follow. Avoid giving gestural cues; give directions while pointing to objects.

SKILL AREAS	SONGS
Sign Language Song	**Birdie Beat** (signs: bird, tree, fly, wind)
Animals/Puppets	**Hello Mr. Animal**
Books	**Ten Little Monkeys** (Big Book)
Body Parts	**My Hand on My Head**
Mirror Time	**This is How I Look**
Movement	**Hot Air Balloon**

Bright Start Music   12–18 Month Group   Session Plan #11

*Throughout Session - Use verbal directions for activities for child to follow. Avoid giving gestural cues; give directions while pointing to objects.

SKILL AREAS	SONGS
Sign Language Song	**Birdie Beat** (signs: bird, tree, fly, wind)
Instruments- Rhythm Instruments	**Click! Click! Click! Go the Castanets**
Movement	**Tree Hugs**
Body Parts Incorporate rolling and throwing small balls	**You Do the Same**
Mirror Time	**I Feel Silly**
Movement	**Hot Air Balloon**

Bright Start Music   12–18 Month Group   Session Plan #12

*Throughout Session - Use verbal directions for activities for child to follow. Avoid giving gestural cues; give directions while pointing to objects.

SKILL AREAS	SONGS
Sign Language Song	**Birdie Beat** (signs: bird, tree, fly, wind)
Instruments- Rhythm Instruments	**Click! Click! Click! Go the Castanets**
Movement	**Flower Power**
Visual- Picture Cards	**My Favorite Spot**
Body Parts	**My Hand on My Head**
Mirror Time	**I Feel Silly**

Bright Start Music   18–24 Month Group   Session Plan #1

SKILL AREAS	SONGS
Instruments- Tambourines and/or Drums	Listen to How I Beat My Drum
	Clean Up
Movement	We're Gonna Dance, We're Gonna Wiggle
Body Parts/Gestures	Hello, Salutations
Animals/Picture Cards	Marty Monkey
	Clean Up
Body Parts	Tony Chestnut
Multicultural- Rhythm Instruments	Pollito, Chicken
	Clean Up
Movement	The Owl

Bright Start Music   18–24 Month Group   Session Plan #2

SKILL AREAS	SONGS
Movement	We're Gonna Dance, We're Gonna Wiggle
Animals/Picture Cards	Mouse in My House
	Clean Up
Body Parts	Tony Chestnut
Emotions/Dramatic Play	I Feel Silly
Multicultural- Rhythm Instruments	Pollito, Chicken
	Clean Up
Movement	I Roll the Ball to You

Bright Start Music   18–24 Month Group   Session Plan #3

SKILL AREAS	SONGS
Instruments- Rhythm Instruments	1,2,3, Play with Me Clean Up
Movement	It's Time for Parade
Body Parts/Gestures	The Body Language Song
Emotions/Dramatic Play	What's Your Name?
Multicultural- Rhythm Instruments	Funga A La Feeya Clean Up
Movement	Monkey Moves!

Bright Start Music   18–24 Month Group   Session Plan #4

SKILL AREAS	SONGS
Movement	It's Time for Parade
Body Parts/Gestures	Hello, Salutations
Song Book	Mouse in My House
Body Parts	Tony Chestnut
Emotions/Dramatic Play	I Feel Silly
Multicultural- Rhythm Instruments	Funga A La Feeya Clean Up
Movement	Dance to the Music

Bright Start Music   18–24 Month Group Session Plan #5

SKILL AREAS	SONGS
Instruments- Tambourines and/or Drums	Listen to How I Beat My Drum Clean Up
Movement	Dance to the Music
Animals/Picture Cards	Marty Monkey Clean Up
Body Parts	When I Wake Up
Multicultural- Rhythm Instruments	We Circle Around Clean Up
Movement	I Roll the Ball To You

Bright Start Music   18–24 Month Group Session Plan #6

SKILL AREAS	SONGS
Movement	Dance to the Music
Body Parts/Gestures	The Body Language Song
Animals/Picture Cards	Marty Monkey Clean Up
Emotions/Dramatic Play	I Feel Silly
Multicultural- Rhythm Instruments	We Circle Around Clean Up
Movement	It's Time for Parade

Bright Start Music   18–24 Month Group   Session Plan #7

SKILL AREAS	SONGS
Instruments- Rhythm Instruments	**Leader of the Band** **Clean Up**
Animals/Puppets	**A Rustle in a Bush** **Clean Up**
Body Parts	**When I Wake Up**
Emotions/Dramatic Play	**What's Your Name?**
Multicultural- Rhythm Instruments	**Pajarito** **Clean Up**
Movement	**The Bicycle**

Bright Start Music   18–24 Month Group   Session Plan #8

SKILL AREAS	SONGS
Instruments- Rhythm Instruments	**1,2,3, Play with Me** **Clean Up**
Movement	**Monkey Moves!**
Body Parts	**When I Wake Up**
Emotions/Dramatic Play	**I Feel Silly**
Multicultural- Rhythm Instruments	**Pajarito** **Clean Up**
Movement	**I Roll the Ball To You**

Bright Start Music   18–24 Month Group   Session Plan #9

SKILL AREAS	SONGS
Instruments- Rhythm Instruments	1,2,3, Play with Me Clean Up
Animals/Puppets	Animal Parade Clean Up
Songbook	Mouse in My House
Body Parts	If I Arr a Pirate
Multicultural- Rhythm Instruments	Zum Gali Gali Clean Up
Movement	We're Gonna Dance, We're Gonna Wiggle

Bright Start Music   18–24 Month Group   Session Plan #10

SKILL AREAS	SONGS
Movement	It's Time for Parade
Animals/Puppets	Animal Parade Clean Up
Songbook	Mouse in My House
Body Parts	If I Arr a Pirate
Emotions/Dramatic Play	I Feel Silly
Multicultural- Rhythm Instruments	Zum Gali Gali Clean Up

Bright Start Music   18–24 Month Group   Session Plan #11

SKILL AREAS	SONGS
Instruments- Tambourines and/or Drums	Listen to How I Beat My Drum Clean Up
Movement	We're Gonna Dance, We're Gonna Wiggle
Animals/Picture Cards	Marty Monkey Clean Up
Body Parts	If I Arr a Pirate
Multicultural- Rhythm Instruments	Siyahamba Clean Up
Movement	I Roll the Ball to You

Bright Start Music   18–24 Month Group   Session Plan #12

SKILL AREAS	SONGS
Movement	Dance to the Music
Animals/Puppets	A Rustle in a Bush Clean Up
Body Parts	If I Arr a Pirate
Emotions/Dramatic Play	I Feel Silly
Multicultural- Rhythm Instruments	Siyahamba Clean Up
Movement	The Bicycle

SKILL AREA/DOMAIN-SPECIFIC SESSION PLANS
TARGETING MOTOR OR COMMUNICATION/LANGUAGE

The following groups of session plans target communication- and motor-specific skill areas. These skill areas were chosen due to the increased number of songs in the curriculum that have the ability to target either motor or communication domains. As music interventions are typically a shared and cognitive experience, all sessions will naturally provide cognitive stimulation and social interactions for skill development. Therefore, social and cognition are not separated out in skill-specific session plan groupings.

MOTOR SKILL-SPECIFIC SESSION PLANS

The following grouping of session plans is designed to address motor skills. These session plans provide an increased exposure to songs for children needing targeted motor skill interventions.

Bright Start Music   6–12 Month Group   Motor Session Plan #1

SKILL AREAS	SONGS
Hello Song	My Right Hand Says Hello
Sing and Sign Song	Clap Your Hands (signs: more, music)
Instruments- Shakers	Shake, Shake, Shake!
Movement	Pat a Cake Itsy Bitsy Spider Ten in the Bed
Body Parts	Head, Shoulders, Knees, and Toes
Instruments- Ocean Drums/Rain Sticks	Hush Little Baby
Goodbye Song	It's Time to Go (using sign language)

Bright Start Music   6–12 Month Group   Motor Session Plan #2

SKILL AREAS	SONGS
Hello Song	**My Right Hand Says Hello**
Sing and Sign Songs	**This is the Mommy Wiggle** (signs: mommy, daddy) Review: **Clap Your Hands** (signs: more, music)
Instruments- Shakers	**Shake, Shake, Shake!**
Movement	**Going Over the Sea** (MT use **ocean drum**)
Body Parts	**If I Arr a Pirate**
Instruments- Ocean Drums/Rain Sticks	**Hush Little Baby**
Goodbye Song	**It's Time to Go** (using sign language)

Bright Start Music   6–12 Month Group   Motor Session Plan #3

SKILL AREAS	SONGS
Hello Song	**My Right Hand Says Hello**
Sing and Sign Songs	**Mommy Go 'Round the Sun** (signs: chair/sit, play/toy) Review: **This is the Mommy Wiggle** (signs: mommy, daddy) Review: **Clap Your Hands** (signs: more, music)
Instruments- Drums	**Humpty Dumpty** **One, Two, Buckle My Shoe** **Two Little Blackbirds**
Movement	**Ten in the Bed**
Body Parts	**Head, Shoulders, Knees, and Toes**
Mirror Time	**You Are My Sunshine** (with different expressions)
Instruments- Ocean Drums/Rain Sticks	**Soon the Moon Will Rise**
Goodbye Song	**It's Time to Go** (using sign language)

Bright Start Music   6–12 Month Group   Motor Session Plan #4

SKILL AREAS	SONGS
Hello Song	**My Right Hand Says Hello**
Sing and Sign Songs	**Doggie Doggie** (signs: dog, cat, ball) Review: **Mommy Go 'Round the Sun** (signs: chair/sit, play/toy) Review: **This is the Mommy Wiggle** (signs: mommy, daddy)
Instruments- Drums	**This Old Man** **One, Two, Buckle My Shoe**
Movement	**London Bridge** **Row, Row, Row Your Boat**
Body Parts	**If I Arr a Pirate**
Instruments- Ocean Drums/Rain Sticks	**Soon the Moon Will Rise**
Goodbye Song	**It's Time to Go** (using sign language)

Bright Start Music   6–12 Month Group   Motor Session Plan #5

SKILL AREAS	SONGS
Hello Song	**My Right Hand Says Hello**
Sing and Sign Songs	**Roll the Ball** (signs: want, please, help, sorry) Review: **Doggie Doggie** (signs: dog, cat, ball) Review: **Mommy Go 'Round the Sun** (signs: chair/sit, play/toy)
Instruments- Shakers	**Mister Golden Sun** **Oh Where Has My Little Dog Gone?**
Movement	**London Bridge** **Row, Row, Row Your Boat**
Body Parts	**Head, Shoulders, Knees, and Toes**
Instruments- Ocean Drums/Rain Sticks	**Big Bright Moon**
Goodbye Song	**It's Time to Go** (using sign language)

Bright Start Music   6–12 Month Group   Motor Session Plan #6

SKILL AREAS	SONGS
Hello Song	**My Right Hand Says Hello**
Sing and Sign Songs	**The Walking Song** (signs: all-done, stop, ouch/hurt, hot) Review: **Roll the Ball** (signs: want, please, help, sorry) **Doggie Doggie** (signs: dog, cat, ball)
Instruments- Drums	**Click, Click, Click, Go the Castanets** **This Old Man**
Movement	**The Ants Go Marching**
Body Parts	**If I Arr a Pirate**
Instruments- Ocean Drums/Rain Sticks	**Big Bright Moon**
Goodbye Song	**It's Time to Go** (using sign language)

Bright Start Music   6–12 Month Group   Motor Session Plan #7

SKILL AREAS	SONGS
Hello Song	**My Right Hand Says Hello**
Sing and Sign Songs	**Where's Baby** (signs: eat/food/spoon, boy, girl) Review: **The Walking Song** (signs: all-done, stop, ouch/hurt, hot) Review: **Roll the Ball** (signs: want, please, help, sorry)
Instruments- Triangles/Wood Blocks	**The Alphabet Song** **My Favorite Spot**
Movement (for children who can walk, you can walk in a circle like a train)	**The Ants Go Marching** **I've Been Working on the Railroad**
Body Parts	**Hokey Pokey**
Instruments- Ocean Drums/Rain Sticks	**Big Bright Moon**
Goodbye Song	**It's Time to Go** (using sign language)

Bright Start Music   6–12 Month Group   Motor Session Plan #8

SKILL AREAS	SONGS
Hello Song	**My Right Hand Says Hello**
Sing and Sign Songs	**Miss Mary Jane** (signs: car, airplane) Review: **Where's Baby** (signs: eat/food/spoon, boy, girl) Review: **The Walking Song** (signs: all-done, stop, ouch/hurt, hot)
Instruments- Triangles/Wood Blocks	**The Alphabet Song** **My Favorite Spot**
Movement (for children who can walk, you can walk in a circle like a train)	**The Ants Go Marching** **I've Been Working on the Railroad**
Body Parts Ask: Where is your <u>hand</u>? (fill in blank with other body parts)	**My Hand on My Head**
Instruments- Ocean Drums/Rain Sticks	**Big Bright Moon**
Goodbye Song	**It's Time to Go** (using sign language)

Bright Start Music   6–12 Month Group   Motor Session Plan #9

SKILL AREAS	SONGS
Hello Song	**My Right Hand Says Hello**
Sing and Sign Songs	**The Little Cat Goes Creeping** (signs: sleep/bed, fish, thank you) Review: **Miss Mary Jane** (signs: car, airplane) Review: **Where's Baby** (signs: eat/food/spoon, boy, girl)
Instruments- Claves/Wood Blocks/Drums	**The Alphabet Song** **My Favorite Spot**
Movement	**Five Little Ducks**
Body Parts Ask: Where is your <u>hand</u>? (fill in blank with other body parts)	**If I Arr a Pirate**
Instruments- Ocean Drums/Rain Sticks	**Soon the Moon Will Rise**
Goodbye Song	**It's Time to Go** (using sign language)

Bright Start Music   6–12 Month Group   Motor Session Plan #10

SKILL AREAS	SONGS
Hello Song	**My Right Hand Says Hello**
Sing and Sign Songs	**Bunny Boogie** (signs: bunny) Review: **The Little Cat Goes Creeping** (signs: sleep/bed, fish, thank you) Review: **Miss Mary Jane** (signs: car, airplane)
Instruments- Claves/Wood Blocks/Drums	**My Favorite Spot** **BINGO**
Movement *Roll balls from MT to each child/parent	**London Bridge** **Row, Row, Row Your Boat** **I Roll the Ball to You***
Body Parts Ask: Where is your <u>hand</u>? (fill in blank with other body parts)	**My Hand on My Head**
Instruments- Ocean Drums/Rain Sticks	**Soon the Moon Will Rise**
Goodbye Song	**It's Time to Go** (using sign language)

Bright Start Music   6–12 Month Group   Motor Session Plan #11

SKILL AREAS	SONGS
Hello Song	**My Right Hand Says Hello**
Sing and Sign Songs	**Charlie Over the Water** (signs: water) Review: **Bunny Boogie** (signs: bunny) Review: **The Little Cat Goes Creeping** (signs: sleep/bed, fish, thank you)
Instruments- Triangles/Wood Blocks	**Twinkle Twinkle** **Itsy Bitsy Spider**
Movement *Roll balls from MT to each child/parent	**London Bridge** **Row, Row, Row Your Boat** **I Roll the Ball to You***
Body Parts Ask: Where is your <u>hand</u>? (fill in blank with other body parts)	**Loop De Loop**
Instruments- Ocean Drums/Rain Sticks	**Goodnight, My Sweet One**
Goodbye Song	**It's Time to Go** (using sign language)

Bright Start Music   6–12 Month Group   Motor Session Plan #12

SKILL AREAS	SONGS
Hello Song	**My Right Hand Says Hello**
Sing and Sign Songs	**My World** (signs: book) Review: **Charlie Over the Water** (signs: water) Review: **Bunny Boogie** (signs: bunny)
Instruments- Claves/Wood Blocks/Drums	**Skip to My Lou** **Humpty Dumpty**
Movement *Roll balls from MT to each child/parent	**Five Little Monkeys Jumping on the Bed** **I Roll the Ball to You***
Body Parts Ask: Where is your <u>hand</u>? (fill in blank with other body parts)	**Loop De Loop**
Instruments- Ocean Drums/Rain Sticks	**Goodnight, My Sweet One**
Goodbye Song	**It's Time to Go** (using sign language)

Bright Start Music   12–18 Month Group Motor Session Plan #1

*Throughout Session - Use verbal directions for activities for child to follow. Avoid giving gestural cues; give directions while pointing to objects.

SKILL AREAS	SONGS
Hello Song	**When I Meet a New Friend**
Sing and Sign Songs	**La La La Lullaby** (signs: sleep/bed, I love you) Review: **Skye Boat Song** (signs: stars, blanket, moon, I love you) Review: **My World** (signs: book)
Instruments- Rhythm Instruments Create shaker instrument from beans in a can (let child put beans in can and take out when songs are done)	**Playing Along**
Movement	**The Owl**
Body Parts	**If I Arr a Pirate**
Movement	**Hot Air Balloon**
Goodbye Song	**It's Time to Go** (using sign language)

Bright Start Music   12–18 Month Group   Motor Session Plan #2

*Throughout Session - Use verbal directions for activities for child to follow. Avoid giving gestural cues; give directions while pointing to objects.

SKILL AREAS	SONGS
Hello Song	**When I Meet a New Friend**
Sing and Sign Songs	**La La La Lullaby** (signs: sleep/bed, I love you) Review: **Skye Boat Song** (signs: stars, blanket, moon, I love you) Review: **My World** (signs: book)
Instruments- Rhythm Instruments	**Playing Along**
Movement	**The Owl**
Body Parts Incorporate rolling and throwing small balls	**You Do the Same**
Movement	**Hot Air Balloon**
Goodbye Song	**It's Time to Go** (using sign language)

Bright Start Music   12–18 Month Group   Motor Session Plan #3

*Throughout Session - Use verbal directions for activities for child to follow. Avoid giving gestural cues; give directions while pointing to objects.

SKILL AREAS	SONGS
Hello Song	**When I Meet a New Friend**
Sing and Sign Songs	**La La La Lullaby** (signs: sleep/bed, I love you) Review: **Skye Boat Song** (signs: stars, blanket, moon, I love you)
Instruments- Rhythm Instruments Create shaker instrument from beans in a can (let child put beans in can and take out when songs are done)	**Razzle Dazzle 'Em**
Movement	**The Owl**
Body Parts	**Look in the Mirror**
Movement Can incorporate rain sticks or ocean drums	**Pitter Patter**
Goodbye Song	**It's Time to Go** (using sign language)

Bright Start Music   12–18 Month Group   Motor Session Plan #4

*Throughout Session - Use verbal directions for activities for child to follow. Avoid giving gestural cues; give directions while pointing to objects.

SKILL AREAS	SONGS
Hello Song	**When I Meet a New Friend**
Sign Language Song Choose any colors and animals signs in book	**Brown Bear, Brown Bear** Sing to the tune of Twinkle, Twinkle
Instruments- Rhythm Instruments	**Playing Along**
Movement	**Let's Go for a Ride**
Body Parts Incorporate rolling and throwing small balls	**You Do the Same**
Movement	**There's a Tickle Under My Skin**
Goodbye Song	**It's Time to Go** (using sign language)

Bright Start Music   12–18 Month Group   Motor Session Plan #5

*Throughout Session - Use verbal directions for activities for child to follow. Avoid giving gestural cues; give directions while pointing to objects.

SKILL AREAS	SONGS
Hello Song	**When I Meet a New Friend**
Sign Language Song Choose any colors and animals signs in book	**Brown Bear, Brown Bear** Sing to the tune of Twinkle, Twinkle
Instruments- Rhythm Instruments Create shaker instrument from beans in a can (let child put beans in can and take out when songs are done)	**Razzle Dazzle 'Em**
Movement	**Let's Go for a Ride**
Body Parts	**Look in the Mirror**
Movement Can incorporate rain sticks or ocean drums	**Pitter Patter**
Goodbye Song	**It's Time to Go** (using sign language)

Bright Start Music   12–18 Month Group   Motor Session Plan #6

*Throughout Session - Use verbal directions for activities for child to follow. Avoid giving gestural cues; give directions while pointing to objects.

SKILL AREAS	SONGS
Hello Song	**When I Meet a New Friend**
Sign Language Song Choose any colors and animals signs in book	**Brown Bear, Brown Bear** Sing to the tune of Twinkle, Twinkle
Instruments- Rhythm Instruments	**Playing Along**
Movement	**Let's Go for a Ride**
Body Parts Incorporate rolling and throwing small balls	**You Do the Same**
Movement	**There's a Tickle Under My Skin**
Goodbye Song	**It's Time to Go** (using sign language)

Bright Start Music   12–18 Month Group   Motor Session Plan #7

*Throughout Session - Use verbal directions for activities for child to follow. Avoid giving gestural cues; give directions while pointing to objects.

SKILL AREAS	SONGS
Hello Song	**When I Meet a New Friend**
Sign Language Song Choose any animals signs in book	**Polar Bear, Polar Bear** (with Big Book)
Instruments- Rhythm Instruments	**Click! Click! Click! Go the Castanets**
Movement	**Tree Hugs**
Body Parts Incorporate rolling and throwing small balls	**You Do the Same**
Movement Can incorporate rain sticks or ocean drums.	**Pitter Patter**
Goodbye Song	**It's Time to Go** (using sign language)

Bright Start Music   12–18 Month Group   Motor Session Plan #8

*Throughout Session - Use verbal directions for activities for child to follow. Avoid giving gestural cues; give directions while pointing to objects.

SKILL AREAS	SONGS
Hello Song	When I Meet a New Friend
Sign Language Song Choose any animals signs in book	Polar Bear, Polar Bear (with Big Book)
Instruments- Rhythm Instruments	Click! Click! Click! Go the Castanets
Movement	Flower Power
Body Parts	My Hand on My Head
Movement	There's a Tickle Under My Skin
Goodbye Song	It's Time to Go (using sign language)

Bright Start Music   12–18 Month Group Motor Session Plan #9

*Throughout Session - Use verbal directions for activities for child to follow. Avoid giving gestural cues; give directions while pointing to objects.

SKILL AREAS	SONGS
Hello Song	**When I Meet a New Friend**
Sign Language Song Choose any animals signs in book	**Polar Bear, Polar Bear** (with Big Book)
Instruments- Rhythm Instruments	**I'm the Sun**
Movement	**Flower Power**
Body Parts Incorporate rolling and throwing small balls	**You Do the Same**
Movement	**Hot Air Balloon**
Goodbye Song	**It's Time to Go** (using sign language)

Bright Start Music   12–18 Month Group   Motor Session Plan #10

*Throughout Session - Use verbal directions for activities for child to follow. Avoid giving gestural cues; give directions while pointing to objects.

SKILL AREAS	SONGS
Hello Song	When I Meet a New Friend
Sign Language Song	Birdie Beat (signs: bird, tree, fly, wind)
Instruments- Rhythm Instruments	I'm the Sun
Movement	Tree Hugs
Body Parts	My Hand on My Head
Movement	Hot Air Balloon
Goodbye Song	It's Time to Go (using sign language)

Bright Start Music   12–18 Month Group Motor Session Plan #11

*Throughout Session - Use verbal directions for activities for child to follow. Avoid giving gestural cues; give directions while pointing to objects.

SKILL AREAS	SONGS
Hello Song	**When I Meet a New Friend**
Sign Language Song	**Birdie Beat** (signs: bird, tree, fly, wind)
Instruments- Rhythm Instruments	**Click! Click! Click! Go the Castanets**
Movement	**Tree Hugs**
Body Parts Incorporate rolling and throwing small balls	**You Do the Same**
Movement	**Hot Air Balloon**
Goodbye Song	**It's Time to Go** (using sign language)

Bright Start Music   12–18 Month Group Motor Session Plan #12

*Throughout Session - Use verbal directions for activities for child to follow. Avoid giving gestural cues; give directions while pointing to objects.

SKILL AREAS	SONGS
Hello Song	When I Meet a New Friend
Sign Language Song	Birdie Beat (signs: bird, tree, fly, wind
Instruments- Rhythm Instruments	Click! Click! Click! Go the Castanets
Movement	Flower Power
Body Parts	My Hand on My Head
Movement	The Owl
Goodbye Song	It's Time to Go (using sign language)

Bright Start Music   18–24 Month Group   Motor Session Plan #1

SKILL AREAS	SONGS
Hello Song	How Do You Doodle
Instruments- Tambourines and/or Drums	Listen to How I Beat My Drum Clean Up
Movement	We're Gonna Dance, We're Gonna Wiggle
Body Parts/Gestures	Hello, Salutations
Multicultural- Rhythm Instruments	Pollito, Chicken Clean Up
Movement	The Owl
Goodbye Song	It's Time to Go (using sign language)

Bright Start Music   18–24 Month Group   Motor Session Plan #2

SKILL AREAS	SONGS
Hello Song	How Do You Doodle
Instruments- Rhythm Instruments	Leader of the Band Clean Up
Movement	We're Gonna Dance, We're Gonna Wiggle
Body Parts/Gestures	Loop De Loop
Body Parts	Tony Chestnut
Multicultural- Rhythm Instruments	Pollito, Chicken Clean Up
Movement	I Roll the Ball to You
Goodbye Song	It's Time to Go (using sign language)

Bright Start Music   18–24 Month Group   Motor Session Plan #3

SKILL AREAS	SONGS
Hello Song	How Do You Doodle
Instruments- Rhythm Instruments	1,2,3, Play with Me Clean Up
Movement	It's Time for Parade
Body Parts/Gestures	The Body Language Song
Body Parts	Tony Chestnut
Multicultural- Rhythm Instruments	Funga A La Feeya Clean Up
Movement	Monkey Moves!
Goodbye Song	It's Time to Go (using sign language)

Bright Start Music   18–24 Month Group   Motor Session Plan #4

SKILL AREAS	SONGS
Hello Song	How Do You Doodle
Instruments- Rhythm Instruments	1,2,3, Play with Me Clean Up
Movement	It's Time for Parade
Body Parts/Gestures	Hello, Salutations
Body Parts	Tony Chestnut
Multicultural- Rhythm Instruments	Funga A La Feeya Clean Up
Movement	Dance to the Music
Goodbye Song	It's Time to Go (using sign language)

Bright Start Music   18–24 Month Group   Motor Session Plan #5

SKILL AREAS	SONGS
Hello Song	How Do You Doodle
Instruments- Tambourines and/or Drums	Listen to How I Beat My Drum Clean Up
Movement	Dance to the Music
Body Parts/Gestures	Loop De Loop
Body Parts	When I Wake Up
Multicultural- Rhythm Instruments	We Circle Around Clean Up
Movement	I Roll the Ball To You
Goodbye Song	It's Time to Go (using sign language)

Bright Start Music   18–24 Month Group   Motor Session Plan #6

SKILL AREAS	SONGS
Hello Song	How Do You Doodle
Instruments- Tambourines and/or Drums	Listen to How I Beat My Drum Clean Up
Movement	Dance to the Music
Body Parts/Gestures	The Body Language Song
Body Parts	When I Wake Up
Multicultural- Rhythm Instruments	We Circle Around Clean Up
Movement	It's Time for Parade
Goodbye Song	It's Time to Go (using sign language)

Bright Start Music   18–24 Month Group   Motor Session Plan #7

SKILL AREAS	SONGS
Hello Song	How Do You Doodle
Instruments- Rhythm Instruments	Leader of the Band Clean Up
Movement	Monkey Moves!
Body Parts/Gestures	Hello, Salutations
Body Parts	When I Wake Up
Multicultural- Rhythm Instruments	Pajarito Clean Up
Movement	The Bicycle
Goodbye Song	It's Time to Go (using sign language)

Bright Start Music   18–24 Month Group   Motor Session Plan #8

SKILL AREAS	SONGS
Hello Song	How Do You Doodle
Instruments- Rhythm Instruments	1,2,3, Play with Me Clean Up
Movement	Monkey Moves!
Body Parts/Gestures	Loop De Loop
Body Parts	When I Wake Up
Multicultural- Rhythm Instruments	Pajarito Clean Up
Movement	I Roll the Ball To You
Goodbye Song	It's Time to Go (using sign language)

Bright Start Music   18–24 Month Group Motor Session Plan #9

SKILL AREAS	SONGS
Hello Song	How Do You Doodle
Instruments- Rhythm Instruments	1,2,3, Play with Me Clean Up
Movement	The Bicycle
Body Parts/Gestures	The Body Language Song
Body Parts	If I Arr a Pirate
Multicultural- Rhythm Instruments	Zum Gali Gali Clean Up
Movement	We're Gonna Dance, We're Gonna Wiggle
Goodbye Song	It's Time to Go (using sign language)

Bright Start Music   18–24 Month Group   Motor Session Plan #10

SKILL AREAS	SONGS
Hello Song	How Do You Doodle
Instruments- Rhythm Instruments	Leader of the Band Clean Up
Movement	It's Time for Parade
Body Parts/Gestures	Hello, Salutations
Body Parts	If I Arr a Pirate
Multicultural- Rhythm Instruments	Zum Gali Gali Clean Up
Movement	The Bicycle
Goodbye Song	It's Time to Go (using sign language)

Bright Start Music   18–24 Month Group Motor Session Plan #11

SKILL AREAS	SONGS
Hello Song	How Do You Doodle
Instruments- Tambourines and/or Drums	Listen to How I Beat My Drum Clean Up
Movement	We're Gonna Dance, We're Gonna Wiggle
Body Parts/Gestures	Loop De Loop
Body Parts	If I Arr a Pirate
Multicultural- Rhythm Instruments	Siyahamba Clean Up
Movement	I Roll the Ball to You
Goodbye Song	It's Time to Go (using sign language)

Bright Start Music   18–24 Month Group   Motor Session Plan #12

SKILL AREAS	SONGS
Hello Song	How Do You Doodle
Instruments- Tambourines and/or Drums	Listen to How I Beat My Drum Clean Up
Movement	Dance to the Music
Body Parts/Gestures	The Body Language Song
Body Parts	If I Arr a Pirate
Multicultural- Rhythm Instruments	Siyahamba Clean Up
Movement	The Bicycle
Goodbye Song	It's Time to Go (using sign language)

COMMUNICATION/LANGUAGE SKILL-SPECIFIC SESSION PLANS

The following grouping of session plans is designed to address communication/language skills. *Communication* is inclusive of all communication component areas. The language developmental skills charts can be referenced for these session plans. These session plans provide an increased exposure to songs for children needing targeted communication/language skill interventions.

Bright Start Music   6–12 Month Group   Communication Session Plan #1

SKILL AREAS	SONGS
Hello Song	My Right Hand Says Hello
Sing and Sign Song	Clap Your Hands (signs: more, music)
Visual- Scarves	Blow Me Some Bubbles I Can Name the Colors
Animals/Puppets	Old MacDonald Brown Bear, Brown Bear* (with book) *Sung to tune of Twinkle, Twinkle, Little Star
Mirror Time	If You're Happy and You Know It (with different expressions)
Affection/Bonding	Never Let Me Go
Goodbye Song	It's Time to Go (using sign language)

Bright Start Music   6–12 Month Group   Communication Session Plan #2

SKILL AREAS	SONGS
Hello Song	**My Right Hand Says Hello**
Sing and Sign Songs	**This is the Mommy Wiggle** (signs: mommy, daddy) Review: **Clap Your Hands** (signs: more, music)
Visual- Scarves	**Twinkle, Twinkle**- with **bubbles** **Little Red Caboose**- with **train** moving
Animals/Puppets	**Old MacDonald** **Brown Bear, Brown Bear*** (with book) *Sung to tune of Twinkle, Twinkle, Little Star
Mirror Time	**If You're Happy and You Know It** (with different expressions)
Affection/Bonding	**Never Let Me Go**
Goodbye Song	**It's Time to Go** (using sign language)

Bright Start Music   6–12 Month Group   Communication Session Plan #3

SKILL AREAS	SONGS
Hello Song	**My Right Hand Says Hello**
Sing and Sign Songs	**Mommy Go 'Round the Sun** (signs: chair/sit, play/toy) Review: **This is the Mommy Wiggle** (signs: mommy, daddy) Review: **Clap Your Hands** (signs: more, music)
Visual- Scarves	**I Can Name the Colors** with **scarves** **Little Red Caboose**- with **train** moving
Animals/Puppets	**Had a Little Rooster**
Mirror Time	**You Are My Sunshine** (with different expressions)
Affection/Bonding	**Never Let Me Go**
Goodbye Song	**It's Time to Go** (using sign language)

Bright Start Music   6–12 Month Group   Communication Session Plan #4

SKILL AREAS	SONGS
Hello Song	**My Right Hand Says Hello**
Sing and Sign Songs	**Doggie Doggie** (signs: dog, cat, ball) Review: **Mommy Go 'Round the Sun** (signs: chair/sit, play/toy) Review: **This is the Mommy Wiggle** (signs: mommy, daddy)
Visual- Scarves	**Twinkle, Twinkle**- with **bubbles** **Little Red Caboose**- with **train** moving
Animals/Puppets	**Had a Little Rooster**
Mirror Time	**You Are My Sunshine** (with different expressions)
Affection/Bonding	**Never Let Me Go**
Goodbye Song	**It's Time to Go** (using sign language)

Bright Start Music   6–12 Month Group   Communication Session Plan #5

SKILL AREAS	SONGS
Hello Song	**My Right Hand Says Hello**
Sing and Sign Songs	**Roll the Ball** (signs: want, please, help, sorry) Review: **Doggie Doggie** (signs: dog, cat, ball) Review: **Mommy Go 'Round the Sun** (signs: chair/sit, play/toy)
Visual- Scarves	**Blow Me Some Bubbles**- with **bubbles** **Little Red Caboose**- with **train** moving
Animals/Puppets	**Polar Bear, Polar Bear*** (with book) *Sung to tune of Twinkle, Twinkle, Little Star **Old MacDonald-** with puppets
Mirror Time	**If You're Happy and You Know It** (with different expressions)
Affection/Bonding	**Always in My Heart**
Goodbye Song	**It's Time to Go** (using sign language)

Bright Start Music   6–12 Month Group   Communication Session Plan #6

SKILL AREAS	SONGS
Hello Song	**My Right Hand Says Hello**
Sing and Sign Songs	**The Walking Song** (signs: all-done, stop, ouch/hurt, hot) Review: **Roll the Ball** (signs: want, please, help, sorry) **Doggie Doggie** (signs: dog, cat, ball)
Visual- Scarves	**Blow Me Some Bubbles**- with **bubbles** **Little Red Caboose**- with **train** moving **I Can Name the Colors**- with **Color Circles**
Animals/Puppets	**Polar Bear, Polar Bear*** (with book) *Sung to tune of Twinkle, Twinkle, Little Star **Old MacDonald**- with puppets
Mirror Time	**You Are My Sunshine** (with different expressions)
Affection/Bonding	**How Will You Grow?**
Goodbye Song	**It's Time to Go** (using sign language)

Bright Start Music   6–12 Month Group   Communication Session Plan #7

SKILL AREAS	SONGS
Hello Song	**My Right Hand Says Hello**
Sing and Sign Songs	**Where's Baby** (signs: eat/food/spoon, boy, girl) Review: **The Walking Song** (signs: all-done, stop, ouch/hurt, hot) Review: **Roll the Ball** (signs: want, please, help, sorry)
Visual- Tracking Let child choose from instrument choices	**Skip to My Lou** **Mister Golden Sun** **Tingalayo**
Animals/Puppets Put puppets out in middle of circle out of reach for child to crawl/scoot/reach to get them	**Had a Little Rooster**
Mirror Time	**The More We Get Together** (with different emotions written in song)
Affection/Bonding	**How Will You Grow?**
Goodbye Song	**It's Time to Go** (using sign language)

Bright Start Music   6–12 Month Group   Communication Session Plan #8

SKILL AREAS	SONGS
Hello Song	**My Right Hand Says Hello**
Sing and Sign Songs	**Miss Mary Jane** (signs: car, airplane) Review: **Where's Baby** (signs: eat/food/spoon, boy, girl) Review: **The Walking Song** (signs: all-done, stop, ouch/hurt, hot)
Visual- Tracking Let child choose from instrument choices	**Blow Me Some Bubbles** **Kookabura**
Animals/Puppets Put puppets out in middle of circle out of reach for child to crawl/scoot/reach to get them	**Animal Song**
Mirror Time	**Peek-A-Boo** (with different emotions written in song)
Affection/Bonding	**How Will You Grow?**
Goodbye Song	**It's Time to Go** (using sign language)

Bright Start Music   6–12 Month Group   Communication Session Plan #9

SKILL AREAS	SONGS
Hello Song	**My Right Hand Says Hello**
Sing and Sign Songs	**The Little Cat Goes Creeping** (signs: sleep/bed, fish, thank you) Review: **Miss Mary Jane** (signs: car, airplane) Review: **Where's Baby** (signs: eat/food/spoon, boy, girl)
Visual- Tracking Let child choose from instrument choices	**Kookabura** **Whack the Drum**
Animals/Puppets Put puppets out in middle of circle out of reach for child to crawl/scoot/reach to get them	**Had a Little Rooster**
Mirror Time	**Peek-A-Boo** (with different emotions written in song)
Affection/Bonding	**Always in My Heart**
Goodbye Song	**It's Time to Go** (using sign language)

Bright Start Music   6–12 Month Group   Communication Session Plan #10

SKILL AREAS	SONGS
Hello Song	**My Right Hand Says Hello**
Sing and Sign Songs	**Bunny Boogie** (signs: bunny) Review: **The Little Cat Goes Creeping** (signs: sleep/bed, fish, thank you) Review: **Miss Mary Jane** (signs: car, airplane)
Visual- Tracking Create shaker instrument from beans in a can (let child put beans in can and take out when songs are done)	**Blow Me Some Bubbles** **Five Green and Speckled Frogs**
Animals/Puppets Put puppets out in middle of circle out of reach for child to crawl/scoot/reach to get them	**Animal Song**
Mirror Time	**Where is Thumbkin?** (with different emotions written in song)
Affection/Bonding	**Always in My Heart**
Goodbye Song	**It's Time to Go** (using sign language)

Bright Start Music   6–12 Month Group   Communication Session Plan #11

SKILL AREAS	SONGS
Hello Song	**My Right Hand Says Hello**
Sing and Sign Songs	**Charlie Over the Water** (signs: water) Review: **Bunny Boogie** (signs: bunny) Review: **The Little Cat Goes Creeping** (signs: sleep/bed, fish, thank you)
Visual- Tracking Create shaker instrument from beans in a can (let child put beans in can and take out when songs are done)	**Blow Me Some Bubbles** **Five Green and Speckled Frogs**
Animals/Puppets Use **Picture Cards** of birds or **Scarves** to mimic bird movement	**Birdie Beat** Allow children to explore activity circle freely during this activity
Mirror Time Put mirror wrong side up to let child find functional side	**Where is Thumbkin?** (with different emotions written in song)
Affection/Bonding	**How You Will Grow?**
Goodbye Song	**It's Time to Go** (using sign language)

Bright Start Music   6–12 Month Group   Communication Session Plan #12

SKILL AREAS	SONGS
Hello Song	**My Right Hand Says Hello**
Sing and Sign Songs	**My World** (signs: book) Review: **Charlie Over the Water** (signs: water) Review: **Bunny Boogie** (signs: bunny)
Visual- Tracking Create shaker instrument from beans in a can (let child put beans in can and take out when songs are done)	**I'm a Little Teapot** **If All the Raindrops**
Animals/Puppets Use **Picture Cards** of birds or **Scarves** to mimic bird movement	**Birdie Beat** Allow children to explore activity circle freely during this activity
Mirror Time Put mirror wrong side up to let child find functional side	**Where is Thumbkin?** (with different emotions written in song)
Affection/Bonding	**Always in My Heart**
Goodbye Song	**It's Time to Go** (using sign language)

Bright Start Music   12–18 Month Group Communication Session Plan #1

*Throughout Session - Use verbal directions for activities for child to follow. Avoid giving gestural cues; give directions while pointing to objects.

SKILL AREAS	SONGS
Hello Song	**When I Meet a New Friend**
Sing and Sign Songs	**La La La Lullaby** (signs: sleep/bed, I love you) Review: **Skye Boat Song** (signs: stars, blanket, moon, I love you) Review: **My World** (signs: book)
Visual- Scarves	**I Can Name The Color**
Animals/Puppets	**Hello Mr. Animal**
Books	**Ten Little Monkeys** (Big Book)
Mirror Time	**Look in the Mirror**
Affection/Bonding	**In My Own Little Way**
Goodbye Song	**It's Time to Go** (using sign language)

Bright Start Music   12–18 Month Group Communication Session Plan #2

*Throughout Session - Use verbal directions for activities for child to follow. Avoid giving gestural cues; give directions while pointing to objects.

SKILL AREAS	SONGS
Hello Song	**When I Meet a New Friend**
Sing and Sign Songs	**La La La Lullaby** (signs: sleep/bed, I love you) Review: **Skye Boat Song** (signs: stars, blanket, moon, I love you) Review: **My World** (signs: book)
Visual- Scarves	**I Can Name The Color**
Animals/Puppets	**Hello Mr. Animal**
Books	**Ten Little Monkeys** (Big Book)
Mirror Time	**Look in the Mirror**
Affection/Bonding	**In My Own Little Way**
Goodbye Song	**It's Time to Go** (using sign language)

Bright Start Music   12–18 Month Group Communication Session Plan #3

*Throughout Session - Use verbal directions for activities for child to follow. Avoid giving gestural cues; give directions while pointing to objects.

SKILL AREAS	SONGS
Hello Song	**When I Meet a New Friend**
Sing and Sign Songs	**La La La Lullaby** (signs: sleep/bed, I love you) Review: **Skye Boat Song** (signs: stars, blanket, moon, I love you)
Visual- Scarves	**I Can Name The Color**
Animals/Puppets	**Animal Song**
Books	**Mulberry Bush** (Big Book)
Mirror Time	**This is How I Look**
Affection/Bonding	**In My Own Little Way**
Goodbye Song	**It's Time to Go** (using sign language)

Bright Start Music   12–18 Month Group Communication Session Plan #4

*Throughout Session - Use verbal directions for activities for child to follow. Avoid giving gestural cues; give directions while pointing to objects.

SKILL AREAS	SONGS
Hello Song	When I Meet a New Friend
Sign Language Song Choose any colors and animals signs in book	Brown Bear, Brown Bear Sing to the tune of Twinkle, Twinkle
Visual- Scarves	I Can Name the Color
Animals/Puppets	Monkey Hug
Books	Farmer in the Dell (Big Book)
Mirror Time	This is How I Look
Affection/Bonding	Doo Wop Love
Goodbye Song	It's Time to Go (using sign language)

Bright Start Music   12–18 Month Group Communication Session Plan #5

*Throughout Session - Use verbal directions for activities for child to follow. Avoid giving gestural cues; give directions while pointing to objects.

SKILL AREAS	SONGS
Hello Song	**When I Meet a New Friend**
Sign Language Song Choose any colors and animals signs in book	**Brown Bear, Brown Bear** Sing to the tune of Twinkle, Twinkle
Visual- Scarves	**I Can Name the Color**
Animals/Puppets	**Animal Song** with **Picture Cards**
Books	**This Old Man** (Big Book)
Mirror Time	**I Feel Silly**
Affection/Bonding	**Baby, Baby**
Goodbye Song	**It's Time to Go** (using sign language)

Bright Start Music   12–18 Month Group Communication Session Plan #6

*Throughout Session - Use verbal directions for activities for child to follow. Avoid giving gestural cues; give directions while pointing to objects.

SKILL AREAS	SONGS
Hello Song	**When I Meet a New Friend**
Sign Language Song Choose any colors and animals signs in book	**Brown Bear, Brown Bear** Sing to the tune of Twinkle, Twinkle
Visual- Scarves	**I Can Name the Color**
Animals/Puppets	**Mr. Animal** with **Picture Cards**
Books	**Nine Ducks Nine** (Big Book)
Mirror Time	**I Feel Silly**
Affection/Bonding	**Baby, Baby**
Goodbye Song	**It's Time to Go** (using sign language)

Bright Start Music   12–18 Month Group   Communication Session Plan #7

*Throughout Session - Use verbal directions for activities for child to follow. Avoid giving gestural cues; give directions while pointing to objects.

SKILL AREAS	SONGS
Hello Song	When I Meet a New Friend
Sign Language Song Choose any animals signs in book	Polar Bear, Polar Bear (with Big Book)
Visual- Picture Cards	My Favorite Spot
Animals/Puppets	Animal Song
Books	Walking Through the Jungle (Big Book)
Mirror Time	I Feel Silly
Affection/Bonding	Baby, Baby
Goodbye Song	It's Time to Go (using sign language)

Bright Start Music   12–18 Month Group Communication Session Plan #8

*Throughout Session - Use verbal directions for activities for child to follow. Avoid giving gestural cues; give directions while pointing to objects.

SKILL AREAS	SONGS
Hello Song	**When I Meet a New Friend**
Sign Language Song Choose any animals signs in book	**Polar Bear, Polar Bear** (with Big Book)
Visual- Picture Cards	**My Favorite Spot**
Animals/Puppets	**Monkey Hug**
Books	**Panda Bear, Panda Bear, What Do You See?** (Big Book)
Mirror Time	**Look in the Mirror**
Affection/Bonding	**Doo Wop Love**
Goodbye Song	**It's Time to Go** (using sign language)

Bright Start Music   12–18 Month Group   Communication Session Plan #9

*Throughout Session - Use verbal directions for activities for child to follow. Avoid giving gestural cues; give directions while pointing to objects.

SKILL AREAS	SONGS
Hello Song	When I Meet a New Friend
Sign Language Song Choose any animals signs in book	Polar Bear, Polar Bear (with Big Book)
Visual- Picture Cards	My Favorite Spot
Animals/Puppets	Animal Song
Books	Wheels on the Bus (Big Book)
Mirror Time	This is How I Look
Affection/Bonding	Doo Wop Love
Goodbye Song	It's Time to Go (using sign language)

Bright Start Music   12–18 Month Group   Communication Session Plan #10

*Throughout Session - Use verbal directions for activities for child to follow. Avoid giving gestural cues; give directions while pointing to objects.

SKILL AREAS	SONGS
Hello Song	**When I Meet a New Friend**
Sign Language Song	**Birdie Beat** (signs: bird, tree, fly, wind)
Visual- Picture Cards	**My Favorite Spot**
Animals/Puppets	**Hello Mr. Animal**
Books	**Ten Little Monkeys** (Big Book)
Mirror Time	**This is How I Look**
Affection/Bonding	**In My Own Little Way**
Goodbye Song	**It's Time to Go** (using sign language)

Bright Start Music   12–18 Month Group Communication Session Plan #11

*Throughout Session - Use verbal directions for activities for child to follow. Avoid giving gestural cues; give directions while pointing to objects.

SKILL AREAS	SONGS
Hello Song	**When I Meet a New Friend**
Sign Language Song	**Birdie Beat** (signs: bird, tree, fly, wind)
Visual- Picture Cards	**My Favorite Spot**
Animals/Puppets	**Animal Song**
Books	**Mulberry Bush** (Big Book)
Mirror Time	**I Feel Silly**
Affection/Bonding	**In My Own Little Way**
Goodbye Song	**It's Time to Go** (using sign language)

Bright Start Music   12–18 Month Group   Communication Session Plan #12

*Throughout Session - Use verbal directions for activities for child to follow. Avoid giving gestural cues; give directions while pointing to objects.

SKILL AREAS	SONGS
Hello Song	**When I Meet a New Friend**
Sign Language Song	**Birdie Beat** (signs: bird, tree, fly, wind)
Visual- Picture Cards	**My Favorite Spot**
Animals/Puppets	**Monkey Hug**
Books	**Farmer in the Dell** (Big Book)
Mirror Time	**I Feel Silly**
Affection/Bonding	**Baby, Baby**
Goodbye Song	**It's Time to Go** (using sign language)

Bright Start Music   18–24 Month Group   Communication Session Plan #1

SKILL AREAS	SONGS
Hello Song	How Do You Doodle
Body Parts/Gestures	Hello, Salutations
Animals/Picture Cards	Marty Monkey Clean Up
Body Parts	Tony Chestnut
Affection/Bonding	La La La Lullaby
Goodbye Song	It's Time to Go (using sign language)

Bright Start Music   18–24 Month Group   Communication Session Plan #2

SKILL AREAS	SONGS
Hello Song	How Do You Doodle
Body Parts/Gestures	Loop De Loop
Animals/Picture Cards	Mouse in My House Clean Up
Body Parts	Tony Chestnut
Affection/Bonding	La La La Lullaby
Goodbye Song	It's Time to Go (using sign language)

Bright Start Music   18–24 Month Group   Communication Session Plan #3

SKILL AREAS	SONGS
Hello Song	How Do You Doodle
Body Parts/Gestures	The Body Language Song
Animals/Puppets	Animal Parade
	Clean Up
Song Book	Mouse in My House
Body Parts	Tony Chestnut
Affection/Bonding	Never Let Me Go
Goodbye Song	It's Time to Go (using sign language)

Bright Start Music   18–24 Month Group   Communication Session Plan #4

SKILL AREAS	SONGS
Hello Song	How Do You Doodle
Body Parts/Gestures	Hello, Salutations
Animals/Puppets	Animal Parade
	Clean Up
Song Book	Mouse in My House
Body Parts	Tony Chestnut
Affection/Bonding	Never Let Me Go
Goodbye Song	It's Time to Go (using sign language)

Bright Start Music   18–24 Month Group   Communication Session Plan #5

SKILL AREAS	SONGS
Hello Song	How Do You Doodle
Body Parts/Gestures	Loop De Loop
Animals/Picture Cards	Marty Monkey
	Clean Up
Body Parts	When I Wake Up
Affection/Bonding	Do Wop Lullaby
Goodbye Song	It's Time to Go (using sign language)

Bright Start Music   18–24 Month Group   Communication Session Plan #6

SKILL AREAS	SONGS
Hello Song	How Do You Doodle
Body Parts/Gestures	The Body Language Song
Animals/Picture Cards	Marty Monkey
	Clean Up
Body Parts	When I Wake Up
Affection/Bonding	Do Wop Lullaby
Goodbye Song	It's Time to Go (using sign language)

Bright Start Music   18–24 Month Group   Communication Session Plan #7

SKILL AREAS	SONGS
Hello Song	How Do You Doodle
Body Parts/Gestures	Hello, Salutations
Animals/Puppets	A Rustle in a Bush Clean Up
Body Parts	When I Wake Up
Affection/Bonding	La La La Lullaby
Goodbye Song	It's Time to Go (using sign language)

Bright Start Music   18–24 Month Group   Communication Session Plan #8

SKILL AREAS	SONGS
Hello Song	How Do You Doodle
Body Parts/Gestures	Loop De Loop
Animals/Puppets	A Rustle in a Bush Clean Up
Body Parts	When I Wake Up
Affection/Bonding	La La La Lullaby
Goodbye Song	It's Time to Go (using sign language)

Bright Start Music   18–24 Month Group   Communication Session Plan #9

SKILL AREAS	SONGS
Hello Song	How Do You Doodle
Body Parts/Gestures	The Body Language Song
Animals/Puppets	Animal Parade
	Clean Up
Songbook	Mouse in My House
Body Parts	If I Arr a Pirate
Affection/Bonding	Never Let Me Go
Goodbye Song	It's Time to Go (using sign language)

Bright Start Music   18–24 Month Group   Communication Session Plan #10

SKILL AREAS	SONGS
Hello Song	How Do You Doodle
Body Parts/Gestures	Hello, Salutations
Animals/Puppets	Animal Parade
	Clean Up
Songbook	Mouse in My House
Body Parts	If I Arr a Pirate
Affection/Bonding	Never Let Me Go
Goodbye Song	It's Time to Go (using sign language)

Bright Start Music   18–24 Month Group   Communication Session Plan #11

SKILL AREAS	SONGS
Hello Song	How Do You Doodle
Body Parts/Gestures	Loop De Loop
Animals/Picture Cards	Marty Monkey
	Clean Up
Body Parts	If I Arr a Pirate
Affection/Bonding	Do Wop Lullaby
Goodbye Song	It's Time to Go (using sign language)

Bright Start Music   18–24 Month Group   Communication Session Plan #12

SKILL AREAS	SONGS
Hello Song	How Do You Doodle
Body Parts/Gestures	The Body Language Song
Animals/Puppets	A Rustle in a Bush
	Clean Up
Body Parts	If I Arr a Pirate
Affection/Bonding	Do Wop Lullaby
Goodbye Song	It's Time to Go (using sign language)

SUPPLEMENTAL MATERIALS
AND RESOURCES

DEVELOPMENTAL SKILL CHARTS GROUPED BY AGES [1]

6–12 Months Cognitive Developmental Skills

Skill Number	Skill Description
C1	Looks for dropped object by turning his/her head (e.g., spoon dropped from high chair, toy dropped when lying on back)
C2	Grasps toy with both hands voluntarily to obtain a desired toy (▶M18)
C3	Attempts to retrieve a toy that has been dropped (e.g., toy dropped when lying on back) (▶SE7)
C4	Explores objects by picking up toys and putting in mouth
C5	Tracks a moving object by moving eyes and head and/or entire body to follow moving object that has grabbed his/her attention
C6	Explores objects by transferring toys from one hand to the other
C7	Investigates cause and effect by banging toy up and down on the floor or table while playing
C8	Investigates cause and effect by shaking toy or object when he/she picks it up
C9	Investigates cause and effect by banging toy against another toy on the floor or other flat surface
C10	Knows familiar toys or other personal objects (e.g., blanket, stuffed animals)
C11	When holding an object, turns the object upside down to explore other side/view of object
C12	Looks for toys that are out of sight or hidden (after watching adult hide them)
C13	Watches and observes action in environment (attends to activity)
C14	Claps objects together when one object is held in each hand to explore sound produced
C15	Pushes an undesired object away from body (▶SE12)
C16	Puts small toys/objects into a large box (after watching adult do the same)

---

[1] All reported skills are based on traditional developmental milestones (CDC, 2012).

6–12 Months Language Developmental Skills

Skill Number	Skill Description
	Expressive Language
L1	Laughs when happy
L2	Babbles using different sounds including *p*, *b*, and *m* consonants
L3	Makes high pitched squeals when excited
L4	Makes deep tones sounds or grunts when displeased
L5	Makes a "razzing" sound with lips (like a "wet" raspberry)
L6	Makes a gurgling sound (both when alone and when playing with adult)
L7	Says one or two words such as Dada, Mama, Bye-bye (uses Dada/Mama nonspecifically)
L8	Babbles using both long and short sound groups (such as bibibi, gaga, tata)
L9	Begins using protowords (vocalizations used at appropriate times and with consistent structures that do not resemble the adult model)
L10	Gets and keeps attention using non-crying sounds
L11	Imitates by repeating back to you different speech sounds
L12	Uses Dada/Mama appropriately
L13	Waves bye-bye appropriately
L14	Says at least one word other than Mama/Dada
L15	Points to something he/she wants
L16	Begins to shake head to communicate "no" or "yes"
L17	Imitates a gesture other than a finger pointing (such as a sign language gesture or waving hand)
L18	Looks at adult or peer while making a gesture (such as a sign language gesture or waving hand)
L19	Waves to communicate when a new person is noticed
	Receptive Language
L20	Turns head to hear voice
L21	Attempts to locate sounds by moving eyes in the direction of sounds
L22	Respond to a change in adult voice with a change in behavior (▶ SE11)
L23	Attends to music played
L24	Orients head upward to locate source of sound
L25	Plays a simple game with you (such as So Big!, Peek-A-Boo, Clap Your Hands)
L26	Understands "no"
L27	Follows a one-step command when command is accompanied with a gesture
L28	Follow a simple command without adult using a gestures
L29	Recognizes words for common items (such as shoe, ball, cup)
L30	Looks at objects present if asked, "Where is the (ball, book, cat, etc.)?"

6–12 Months Motor Developmental Skills

Skill Number	Skill Description
	Gross Motor
M1	Rolls back to front (when lying on his/her back)
M2	Sits with support (from own hands or parent support)
M3	Pushes chest off of floor when on tummy (using hands with arms extended)
M4	Bears almost all weight on legs as pillars (while arms are supported)
M5	Lifts into a crawling position onto hands and knees when on the floor
M6	Sits without support
M7	Scoots/creeps on tummy
M8	Crawls with body off of the floor using hands and knees
M9	Stands holding onto support (like furniture or parent)
M10	Pulls self to a standing position
M11	Crawls quickly or "cruises"
M12	Performs other movements while sitting without support (e.g., moving hands, playing with toy)
M13	Lowers self down with control from standing to sitting with assistance
M14	Lifts one foot off of the ground
M15	Walks several steps without tripping with adult assistance for balance (holding hands)
M16	Walks with steps of uneven directions/lengths (without adult assistance)
M17	Dances or bounces to music
	Fine Motor
M18	Grasps toy with both hands voluntarily (e.g., when adult hands the toy to him/her)(▶C2)
M19	Grabs a toy offered by someone and looks at it
M20	Reaches and touches small items like Cheerios with finger
M21	Picks up a toy with one hand primarily using palm (e.g., toy placed near him/her)
M22	Picks up a toy with the tips of fingers (not grabbing with palm)
M23	Voluntarily releases toy by placing object down before releasing
M24	Picks up small object with fingers and thumb (pincer grasp)

6–12 Months Social-Emotional Developmental Skills

Skill Number	Skill Description
SE1	Recognizes familiar people
SE2	Explores body by grabbing feet when lying on his/her back
SE3	Settles and calms self when comforted by adult (e.g., shushing and talking calmly)
SE4	Smiles and coos at self reflection in a mirror
SE5	Pats mirror when seeing self reflection
SE6	Enjoys being tickled
SE7	Attempts to get a toy that is out of reach (▶C3)
SE8	Enjoys being held and cuddled
SE9	Raises arms to communicate wanting to be held
SE10	Plays games with people he/she knows
SE11	Understands differences in adult tone of voice (▶L22)
SE12	Pushes an undesired object away from body (▶C15)
SE13	Shows attachment for favorite toy or object
SE14	Gives objects to other people and wants them to be given immediately back
SE15	Shows affection when playing with toys by hugging stuffed animals/dolls
SE16	Wants caregiver to be within sight at all times
SE17	Plays by him/herself for short periods of time if caregiver is within sight or nearby

12–18 Months Cognitive Developmental Skills

Skill Number	Skill Description
C15	Pushes an undesired object away from body
C16	Puts small toys/objects into a large box (after watching adult do the same thing)
C17	Releases objects into a small container with precision (▶ M36)
C18	Pushes, dumps, and/or pulls to manipulate objects (exploring cause/effect)
C19	Explores environment and objects freely (▶ SE33)
C20	Reaches to try and touch most objects in environment

12–18 Months Language Developmental Skills

Skill Number	Skill Description
	Expressive Language
L10	Gets and keeps attention using non-crying sounds
L11	Imitates by repeating back to you different speech sounds
L12	Uses Dada/Mama appropriately
L13	Waves bye-bye appropriately
L14	Says at least one word other than Mama/Dada
L15	Points to something he/she wants
L16	Begins to shake head to communicate "no" or "yes"
L17	Imitates a gesture other than a finger pointing (such as a sign language gesture)
L18	Looks at adult or peer while making a gesture (such as a sign language gesture)
L19	Waves to communicate when a new person is noticed
L31	Points to body parts
L32	Uses immature jargoning ("words" have intonation, inflection, and rhythm of speech but is completely unintelligible)
L33	Says three different words other than Mama/Dada
L34	Uses many different consonant sounds to begin words
L35	Imitates 2-word sentences (e.g., repeats back "Mama drink," "Kitty home")
L36	Uses mature jargoning ("words" have intonation, inflection, and rhythm of speech and some words are intelligible)
L37	Uses more words in his/her vocabulary each month
L38	Uses 7-9 words in his/her vocabulary in addition to Mama/Dada
L39	Combines 2 or 3 words that have different meanings (e.g., "Doggie come home," "Mommy gone?")
	Receptive Language
L25	Plays a simple game with you (such as So Big!, Peek-A-Boo, Clap Your Hands)
L26	Understands "no"
L27	Follows a one-step command when command is accompanied by a gesture
L28	Follows a simple command without adult's gesture (e.g., Bring me a book)
L29	Recognizes words for common items (such as shoe, ball, cup)
L30	Looks at objects present if asked "Where is the (ball, book, cat, etc.)?
L40	Listens to simple songs, rhymes, and stories
L41	Points to or pats a picture in a book when named

12–18 Months Motor Developmental Skills

Skill Number	Skill Description
	Gross Motor
M15	Walks several steps without tripping with adult assistance for balance (holding hands)
M16	Walks with steps of uneven directions/lengths (without adult assistance)
M25	Pivots while sitting to pick up objects (twists around)
M26	Rolls a ball to an adult on request
M27	Runs independently
M28	Walks quickly without falling
M29	Squats to pick up an item off the floor and stands back up without assistance
M30	Jumps with both feet simultaneously
M31	Bends over to look through legs
M32	Carries large toy while walking
M33	Throws a ball forward with one hand
M34	Tries to kick a ball by walking into it or moving leg forward
	Fine Motor
M23	Voluntarily releases toy by placing down before releasing
M24	Picks up small object with fingers and thumb (pincer grasp)
M35	Helps with dressing self
M36	Releases objects into a small container with precision (▶C17)
M37	Uses a forward arm movement to throw a small ball
M38	Attempts to help turn pages of a book with assistance
M39	Imitates actions modeled by parent (housework, etc.) (▶C23, ▶SE31, ▶SE36)
M40	Turns pages of a book (usually 2-3 at a time)
M41	Uses both hands in midline with one hand holding, the other manipulating (e.g., one hand is holding a teething ring and the other hand is banging it)

12–18 Months Social-Emotional Developmental Skills

Skill Number	Skill Description
SE18	Gives objects to other people and wants them to be given immediately back
SE19	Shows affection when playing with toys by hugging stuffed animals/dolls
SE20	Wants caregiver to be within sight at all times
SE21	Plays by him/herself for short periods of time if caregiver is within sight or nearby
SE22	Enjoys adult reading stories to him/her
SE23	Pulls on adult clothes or hand to secure attention to self
SE24	Enjoys "performing" for an audience (likes applause) and adult attention
SE25	Imitates sounds others make (e.g., animal sounds, coughing)
SE26	Plays alone with toys on the floor
SE27	Offers a toy to own image in a mirror
SE28	Recognizes him/herself in pictures or in the mirror
SE29	Resists sharing toys or objects with other people
SE30	Approaches adult for help with toys (e.g., doesn't fit, can't open)
SE31	Imitates actions modeled by parent (e.g., sweeping the floor, talking on phone) (▶M39, ▶C23)

18–24 Months Cognitive Developmental Skills

Skill Number	Skill Description
C19	Explores environment and objects freely
C20	Reaches to try and touch most objects in environment
C21	Chooses between 2 objects to show preference of toys
C22	Enjoys singing familiar songs (▶L48)
C23	Imitates actions modeled by parent (e.g., sweeping the floor with a stick, talking on phone with a cup) (▶M39, ▶SE31, ▶SE36)
C24	Responds to correction with behavior or verbalizations
C25	Turns objects right side up to be able to use correctly (when adult hands object oriented upside down)
C26	Imitates "invisible" gestures (e.g., patting head, wrinkling nose, etc.) (▶SE48)
C27	Removes obstacles in the way of desired object
C28	Puts objects away where they belong (e.g., shakers in a bag, drum in a bin)

18–24 Months Language Developmental Skills

Skill Number	Skill Description
	Expressive Language
L31	Points to body parts (increases number of body parts he/she can point to each month)
L36	Uses mature jargoning ("words" have intonation, inflection, and rhythm of speech and some words are intelligible)
L38	Uses 7-9 words in his/her vocabulary (in addition to Mama/Dada)
L39	Combines 2 or 3 words that have different meanings (e.g., "Doggie come home," "Mommy gone?")
L42	Names at least one object when adult points to picture of the object and asks: "What is this?" (e.g., dog, kitty, cup)
L43	Uses 10-20 words in his/her vocabulary
L44	Uses 2-word sentences (e.g., "more milk," "mommy doll," "more book")
L45	Uses 1-2 word questions (e.g., "Go bye-bye?" "Where shoe?")
L46	Uses pronouns inappropriately
L47	Begins to use at least 2 pronouns appropriately (e.g., "me", "I", "you") (▶SE46)
L48	Sings familiar songs (using mature jargoning) (▶C22)
	Receptive Language
L26	Understands "no"
L28	Follows a simple command without adult using a gesture (e.g., Bring me a book)
L49	Points to or pats a picture in a book when object is named (without adult prompt)
L50	Follows a 2-step command (e.g., "Pick up the ball and roll it to me")

18–24 Months Motor Developmental Skills

Skill Number	Skill Description
	Gross Motor
M27	Runs independently
M30	Jumps with both feet simultaneously
M42	Tosses a ball with both hands
M43	Bends over to pick up toys from a standing position without falling
M44	Stands on one foot unsteadily
M45	Kicks ball forward with foot in a swinging motion
	Fine Motor
M39	Imitates actions modeled by parent (housework, etc.)
M40	Turns pages of a book (usually 2-3 at a time)
M41	Uses both hands in midline with one hand holding, the other manipulating (e.g., one hand is holding a teething ring and the other hand is banging it)
M46	Helps with undressing
M47	Turn pages of a book one at a time

18–24 Months Social-Emotional Developmental Skills

Skill Number	Skill Description
SE32	Enjoys "performing" for an audience (likes applause) and adult attention
SE33	Explores environment and objects freely (▶C19)
SE34	Avoids sharing toys or objects with other people
SE35	Approaches adult for help with toys (e.g., doesn't fit, can't open)
SE36	Imitates actions modeled by parent while engaged in pretend play (e.g., sweeping the floor, talking on phone) (▶M39, ▶C23)
SE37	Expects immediate gratification/action (has difficulty waiting)
SE38	Gets angry when upset and/or has a temper tantrum
SE39	Acts shy around strangers
SE40	Begins to show signs of independence
SE41	Attempts to complete tasks by self without help from adult
SE42	Shows affection with other by returning hugs or kisses
SE43	Shows sympathy to peers if others are upset
SE44	Shows attachment to favorite objects (e.g., toy or blanket)
SE45	Enjoys looking at pictures in books
SE46	Begins to use at least 2 pronouns appropriately (e.g., "me", "I", "you") (▶L47)
SE47	Engages in pretend play with toys (e.g., feeding a baby, putting stuffed animal to bed)
SE48	Imitates "invisible" gestures (e.g., patting head, wrinkling nose, etc.) (▶C26)

DEVELOPMENTAL SKILL CHARTS GROUPED BY DOMAINS

6–12 Months Cognitive Developmental Skills

Skill Number	Skill Description
C1	Looks for dropped object by turning his/her head (e.g., spoon dropped from high chair, toy dropped when lying on back)
C2	Grasps toy with both hands voluntarily to obtain a desired toy (▶M18)
C3	Attempts to retrieve a toy that has been dropped (e.g., toy dropped when lying on back) (▶SE7)
C4	Explores objects by picking up toys and putting in mouth
C5	Tracks a moving object by moving eyes and head and/or entire body to follow moving object that has grabbed his/her attention
C6	Explores objects by transferring toys from one hand to the other
C7	Investigates cause and effect by banging toy up and down on the floor or table while playing
C8	Investigates cause and effect by shaking toy or object when he/she picks it up
C9	Investigates cause and effect by banging toy against another toy on the floor or other flat surface
C10	Knows familiar toys or other personal objects (e.g., blanket, stuffed animals)
C11	When holding an object, turns the object upside down to explore other side/view of object
C12	Looks for toys that are out of sight or hidden (after watching adult hide them) toy)
C13	Watches and observes action in environment (attends to activity)
C14	Claps objects together when one object is held in each hand to explore sound produced
C15	Pushes an undesired object away from body (▶SE12)
C16	Puts small toys/objects into a large box (after watching adult do the same) thing)

12–18 Months Cognitive Developmental Skills

Skill Number	Skill Description
C15	Pushes an undesired object away from body
C16	Puts small toys/objects into a large box (after watching adult do the same) thing)
C17	Releases objects into a small container with precision (▶M36)
C18	Pushes, dumps, and/or pulls to manipulate objects (exploring cause/effect) and effect)
C19	Explores environment and objects freely (▶SE33)
C20	Reaches to try and touch most objects in environment

18–24 Months Cognitive Developmental Skills

Skill Number	Skill Description
C19	Explores environment and objects freely
C20	Reaches to try and touch most objects in environment
C21	Chooses between 2 objects to show preference of toys
C22	Enjoys singing familiar songs (▶L48)
C23	Imitates actions modeled by parent (e.g., sweeping the floor with a stick, talking on phone with a cup) (▶M39, ▶SE31, ▶SE36)
C24	Responds to correction with behavior or verbalizations
C25	Turns objects right side up to be able to use correctly (when adult hands object oriented upside down)
C26	Imitates "invisible" gestures (e.g., patting head, wrinkling nose, etc.) (▶SE48)
C27	Removes obstacles in the way of desired object
C28	Puts objects away where they belong

6–12 Months Language Developmental Skills

Skill Number	Skill Description
	Expressive Language
L1	Laughs when happy
L2	Babbles using different sounds including *p*, *b*, and *m* consonants
L3	Makes high pitched squeals when excited
L4	Makes deep tones sounds or grunts when displeased
L5	Makes a "razzing" sound with lips (like a "wet" raspberry)
L6	Makes a gurgling sound (both when alone and when playing with adult)
L7	Says one or two words such as Dada, Mama, Bye-bye (uses Dada/Mama nonspecifically)
L8	Babbles using both long and short sound groups (such as bibibi, gaga, tata)
L9	Begins using protowords (vocalizations used at appropriate times and with consistent structures that do not resemble the adult model)
L10	Gets and keeps attention using non-crying sounds
L11	Imitates by repeating back to you different speech sounds
L12	Uses Dada/Mama appropriately
L13	Waves bye-bye appropriately
L14	Says at least one word other than Mama/Dada
L15	Will point to something he/she wants
L16	Begins to shake head to communicate "no" or "yes"
L17	Imitates a gesture other than a finger pointing (such as a sign language gesture or waving hand)
L18	Looks at adult or peer while making a gesture (such as a sign language gesture or waving hand)
L19	Waves to communicate when a new person is noticed
	Receptive Language
L20	Turns head to hear voice
L21	Attempts to locate sounds by moving eyes in the direction of sounds
L22	Will respond to a change in adult voice with a change in behavior (▶ SE11)
L23	Attends to music played
L24	Orients head upward to locate source of sound
L25	Plays a simple game with you (such as So Big!, Peek-A-Boo, Clap Your Hands)
L26	Understands "no"
L27	Follows a one-step command when accompanied by a gesture gesturesgesture
L28	Follows a simple command without adult using a gesture
L29	Recognizes words for common items (such as shoe, ball, cup)
L30	Looks at objects present if asked "Where is the (ball, book, cat, etc.)?"

12–18 Months Language Developmental Skills

Skill Number	Skill Description
	Expressive Language
L10	Gets and keeps attention using non-crying sounds
L11	Imitates by repeating back to you different speech sounds
L12	Uses Dada/Mama appropriately
L13	Waves bye-bye appropriately
L14	Says at least one word other than Mama/Dada
L15	Points to something he/she wants
L16	Begins to shake head to communicate "no" or "yes"
L17	Imitates a gesture other than a finger pointing (such as a sign language gesture)
L18	Looks at adult or peer while making a gesture (such as a sign language gesture)
L19	Waves to communicate when a new person is noticed
L31	Points to body parts
L32	Uses immature jargoning ("words" have intonation, inflection, and rhythm of speech but are completely unintelligible)
L33	Says three different words other than Mama/Dada
L34	Uses many different consonant sounds to begin words
L35	Imitates 2-word sentences (e.g., repeats back "Mama drink," "Kitty home")
L36	Uses mature jargoning ("words" have intonation, inflection, and rhythm of speech and some words are intelligible)
L37	Uses more words each month
L38	Uses 7-9 words in his/her vocabulary in addition to Mama/Dada
L39	Combines 2 or 3 words that have different meanings (e.g., "Doggie come home," "Mommy gone?")
	Receptive Language
L25	Plays a simple game with you (such as So Big!, Peek-A-Boo, Clap Your Hands)
L26	Understands "no"
L27	Follows a one-step command when command is accompanied with a gesture
L28	Follows a simple command without adult gesture (e.g., Bring me a book)
L29	Recognizes words for common items (such as shoe, ball, cup)
L30	Looks at objects present if asked "Where is the (ball, book, cat, etc.)?"
L40	Listens to simple songs, rhymes, and stories
L41	Points to or pats a picture in a book when named

18–24 Months Language Developmental Skills

Skill Number	Skill Description
	Expressive Language
L31	Points to body parts (number of body parts he/she can point to increases each month)
L36	Uses mature jargoning ("words" have intonation, inflection, and rhythm of speech and some words are intelligible)
L38	Has 7-9 words in his/her vocabulary in addition to Mama/Dada
L39	Combines 2 or 3 words that have different meanings (e.g., "Doggie come home," "Mommy gone?")
L42	Names at least one object when adult points to picture of the object and asks: "What is this?" (e.g., dog, kitty, cup)
L43	Uses 10-20 words in his/her vocabulary
L44	Uses 2-word sentences (e.g., "more milk," "mommy doll," "more book")
L45	Uses 1-2 word questions (e.g., "Go bye-bye?" "Where shoe?")
L46	Uses pronouns inappropriately
L47	Begins to use at least 2 pronouns appropriately (e.g., "me", "I", "you") (▶SE46)
L48	Sings familiar songs (using mature jargoning) (▶C22)
	Receptive Language
L26	Understands "no"
L28	Follows a simple command without adult using a gesture (e.g., Bring me a book)
L49	Points to or pats a picture in a book when object is named, without adult showing them the picture to point to
L50	Follows a 2-step command (e.g., "Pick up the ball and roll it to me")

6–12 Months Motor Developmental Skills

Skill Number	Skill Description
	Gross Motor
M1	Rolls back to front (when lying on his/her back)
M2	Sits with support (from own hands or parent support)
M3	Pushes chest off of floor when on tummy (using hands with arms extended)
M4	Bears almost all weight on legs as pillars (while arms are supported)
M5	Lifts into a crawling position onto hands and knees when on the floor
M6	Sits without support
M7	Scoots/creeps on tummy
M8	Crawls with body off of the floor using hands and knees
M9	Stands holding onto support (like furniture or parent)
M10	Pulls self to a standing position
M11	Crawls quickly or "cruises"
M12	Performs other movements while sitting without support (e.g., moving hands, playing with toy)
M13	Lowers self down with control from standing to sitting with assistance
M14	Lifts one foot off of the ground
M15	Walks several steps without tripping with adult assistance for balance (holding hands)
M16	Walks with steps of uneven directions/lengths (without adult assistance)
M17	Dances or bounces to music
	Fine Motor
M18	Grasps toy with both hands voluntarily (e.g., when adult hands the toy to him/her) (▶C2)
M19	Grabs a toy offered by someone and looks at it
M20	Reaches and touches small items like Cheerios with finger
M21	Picks up a toy with one hand primarily using palm (e.g., toy placed near him/her)
M22	Picks up a toy with the tips of fingers (not grabbing with palm)
M23	Voluntarily releases toy by placing object down before releasing
M24	Picks up small object with fingers and thumb (pincer grasp)

12–18 Months Motor Developmental Skills

Skill Number	Skill Description
	Gross Motor
M15	Walks several steps without tripping with adult assistance for balance (holding hands)
M16	Walks with steps of uneven directions/lengths (without adult assistance)
M25	Pivots while sitting to pick up objects (twists around)
M26	Rolls a ball to an adult on request
M27	Runs independently
M28	Walks quickly without falling
M29	Squats to pick up an item off the floor and stands back up without assistance
M30	Jumps with both feet simultaneously
M31	Bends over to look through legs
M32	Carries large toy while walking
M33	Throws a ball forward with one hand
M34	Tries to kick a ball by walking into it or moving leg forward
	Fine Motor
M23	Voluntarily releases toy by placing down before releasing
M24	Picks small object with fingers and thumb (pincer grasp)
M35	Helps with dressing self
M36	Releases objects into a small container with precision (▶C17)
M37	Uses a forward arm movement to throw a small ball
M38	Attempts to help turn pages of a book with assistance
M39	Imitates actions modeled by parent (housework, etc.) (▶C23, ▶SE31, ▶SE36)
M40	Turns pages of a book (usually 2-3 at a time)
M41	Uses both hands in midline with one hand holding, the other manipulating (e.g., one hand is holding a teething ring and the other hand is banging it)

18–24 Months Motor Developmental Skills

Skill Number	Skill Description
	Gross Motor
M27	Runs independently
M30	Jumps with both feet simultaneously
M42	Tosses a ball with both hands
M43	Bends over to pick up toys from a standing position without falling
M44	Stands on one foot unsteadily
M45	Kicks ball forward with foot in a swinging motion
	Fine Motor
M39	Imitates actions modeled by parent (housework, etc.)
M40	Turns pages of a book (usually 2-3 at a time)
M41	Uses both hands in midline with one hand holding, the other manipulating (e.g., one hand is holding a teething ring and the other hand is banging it)
M46	Helps with undressing
M47	Turns pages of a book one at a time

6–12 Months Social-Emotional Developmental Skills

Skill Number	Skill Description
SE1	Recognizes familiar people
SE2	Explores body by grabbing feet when lying on his/her back
SE3	Settles and calms self when comforted by adult (e.g., shushing and talking calmly)
SE4	Smiles and coos at self reflection in a mirror
SE5	Pats mirror when seeing self reflection
SE6	Enjoys being tickled
SE7	Attempts to get a toy that is out of reach (▶C3)
SE8	Enjoys being held and cuddled
SE9	Raises arms to communicate wanting to be held
SE10	Plays games with people he/she knows
SE11	Understands differences in adult tone of voice (▶L22)
SE12	Pushes an undesired object away from body (▶C15)
SE13	Shows attachment for favorite toy or object
SE14	Gives objects to other people and wants them to be given immediately back
SE15	Shows affection when playing with toys by hugging stuffed animals/dolls
SE16	Wants caregiver to be within sight at all times
SE17	Plays by him/herself for short periods of time if caregiver is within sight or nearby

12–18 Months Social-Emotional Developmental Skills

Skill Number	Skill Description
SE18	Gives objects to other people and wants them to be given immediately back
SE19	Shows affection when playing with toys by hugging stuffed animals/dolls
SE20	Wants caregiver to be within sight at all times
SE21	Plays by him/herself for short periods of time if caregiver is within sight or nearby
SE22	Enjoys adult reading stories to him/her
SE23	Pulls on adult clothes or hand to secure attention to self
SE24	Enjoys "performing" for an audience (likes applause) and adult attention
SE25	Imitates sounds others make (e.g., animal sounds, coughing)
SE26	Plays alone with toys on the floor
SE27	Offers a toy to own image in a mirror
SE28	Recognizes him/herself in pictures or in the mirror
SE29	Resists sharing toys or objects with other people
SE30	Approaches adult for help with toys (e.g., doesn't fit, can't open)
SE31	Imitates actions modeled by parent (e.g., sweeping the floor, talking on phone) (▶M39, ▶C23)

18–24 Months Social-Emotional Developmental Skills

Skill Number	Skill Description
SE32	Enjoys "performing" for an audience (likes applause and adult attention)
SE33	Explores environment and objects freely (▶C19)
SE34	Resists sharing toys or objects with other people
SE35	Approaches adult for help with toys (e.g., doesn't fit, can't open)
SE36	Imitates actions modeled by parent while engaged in pretend play (e.g., sweeping the floor, talking on phone) (▶M39, ▶C23)
SE37	Wants immediate gratification or action (has difficulty waiting)
SE38	Gets angry when upset (has temper tantrums)
SE39	Acts shy around strangers
SE40	Begins to show signs of independence
SE41	Attempts to complete tasks by self without help from adult
SE42	Shows affection with other by returning hugs or kisses
SE43	Shows sympathy to peers if others are upset
SE44	Shows attachment to favorite objects (e.g., toy or blanket)
SE45	Enjoys looking at pictures in books
SE46	Begins to use at least 2 pronouns appropriately (e.g., "me", "I", "you") (▶L47)
SE47	Engages in pretend play with toys (e.g., feeding a baby, putting toy to bed)
SE48	Imitates "invisible" gestures (e.g., patting head, wrinkling nose, etc.) (▶C26)

DEVELOPMENTAL SKILLS ADDRESSED IN EACH SESSION

The following developmental skills are addressed or can be seen in all sessions and all songs for ages 6–12 months:

C13

L1

L2

L3

L4

L5

L6

L7

L8

L9

L10

L11

L12

L14

L16

L20

L21

L23

L26

M12

M17

SE1

SE3

SE12

SE16

SE17

Bright Start Music   6–12 Month Group   Session Plan #1

SKILL AREAS & SONGS	DEVELOPMENTAL SKILLS ADDRESSED
Hello Song **My Right Hand Says Hello**	L17, L18, L19, L27, M12
Sing and Sign Song **Clap Your Hands**	L17, L18, L19, L27
Instruments- Shakers **Shake, Shake, Shake!**	C1, C2, C3, C4, C6, C7, C8, C9, C10, C11, C12, C14,C15, L15, L24, L27, L28, L29, M18, M19, M21, M22, M23, SE7, SE13, SE14
Movement **Pat a Cake** **Itsy Bitsy Spider** **Ten in the Bed**	L25, L27, L28, M1, M2, M3, M4, M5, M6, M7, M8, M9, M10, M11, M13, M14, M15, M16, SE2
Visual- Scarves **Blow Me Some Bubbles** **I Can Name the Colors**	C5, L15, L25, L27, L28, L29
Animals/Puppets **Old MacDonald** **Brown Bear, Brown Bear** (with book)	C1, C2, C3, C4, C6, C7, C8, C9, C10, C11, C12, C14,C15, L15, L28, L29, M18, M19, M21, M22, M23, SE7, SE13, SE14, SE15
Body Parts **Head, Shoulders, Knees, and Toes**	L27, SE10
Mirror Time **If You're Happy and You Know It**	L15, L22, L25, L27, M18, M19, M21, M22, M23, SE4, SE5, SE7, SE10, SE11, SE14

Affection/Bonding **Hello, Baby**	SE6, SE8, SE9
Massage/Bedtime Routine **Hush Little Baby**	L15, L24, L29, M18, M19, M21, M22, M23, SE7, SE13, SE14
Goodbye Song **It's Time to Go** (using sign language)	L13, L17, L18, L27

Bright Start Music   6–12 Month Group   Session Plan #2

SKILL AREAS & SONGS	DEVELOPMENTAL SKILLS ADDRESSED
Hello Song **My Right Hand Says Hello**	L17, L18, L19, L27, M12
Sing and Sign Songs **This is the Mommy Wiggle** **Clap Your Hands**	L17, L18, L19, L27
Instruments- Shakers **Shake, Shake, Shake!**	C1, C2, C3, C4, C6, C7, C8, C9, C10, C11, C12, C14,C15, L15, L24, L27, L28, L29, M18, M19, M21, M22, M23, SE7, SE13, SE14
Movement **Going Over the Sea** (MT use **ocean drum**)	L25, L27, L28, M1, M2, M3, M4, M5, M6, M7, M8, M9, M10, M11, M13, M14, M15, M16, SE2
Visual- Scarves **Twinkle Twinkle**- with **bubbles** **Little Red Caboose**- with **train** moving	C5, L15, L25, L27, L28, L29
Animals/Puppets **Old MacDonald** **Brown Bear, Brown Bear** (with book)	C1, C2, C3, C4, C6, C7, C8, C9, C10, C11, C12, C14,C15, L15, L28, L29, M18, M19, M21, M22, M23, SE7, SE13, SE14, SE15
Body Parts **If I Arr a Pirate**	L27, SE10
Mirror Time **If You're Happy and You Know It**	L15, L22, L25, L27, M18, M19, M21, M22, M23, SE4, SE5, SE7, SE10, SE11, SE14

Affection/Bonding **Never Let Me Go**	SE6, SE8, SE9
Massage/Bedtime Routine **Hush Little Baby**	L15, L24, L29, M18, M19, M21, M22, M23, SE7, SE13, SE14
Goodbye Song **It's Time to Go** (using sign language)	L13, L17, L18, L27

Bright Start Music   6–12 Month Group   Session Plan #3

SKILL AREAS & SONGS	DEVELOPMENTAL SKILLS ADDRESSED
Hello Song **My Right Hand Says Hello**	L17, L18, L19, L27, M12
Sing and Sign Songs **Mommy Go 'Round the Sun** **This is the Mommy Wiggle** **Clap Your Hands**	L17, L18, L19, L27
Instruments- Drums **Humpty Dumpty** **One, Two, Buckle My Shoe** **Here We Go Round the Mulberry Bush**	C1, C2, C3, C4, C6, C7, C8, C9, C10, C11, C12, C14, C15, L15, L24, L27, L28, L29, M18, M19, M21, M22, M23, SE7, SE13, SE14
Movement **Ten in the Bed**	L25, L27, L28, M1, M2, M3, M4, M5, M6, M7, M8, M9, M10, M11, M13, M14, M15, M16, SE2
Visual- Scarves **I Can Name the Colors**- with **scarves** **Little Red Caboose**- with **train** moving	C5, L15, L25, L27, L28, L29
Animals/Puppets **Had a Little Rooster**	C1, C2, C3, C4, C6, C7, C8, C9, C10, C11, C12, C14, C15, L15, L28, L29, M18, M19, M21, M22, M23, SE7, SE13, SE14, SE15
Body Parts **Head, Shoulders, Knees, and Toes**	L27, SE10
Mirror Time **You Are My Sunshine**	L15, L22, L25, L27, M18, M19, M21, M22, M23, SE4, SE5, SE7, SE10, SE11, SE14

Affection/Bonding **Never Let Me Go**	SE6, SE8, SE9
Massage/Bedtime Routine **Soon the Moon Will Rise**	L15, L24, L29, M18, M19, M21, M22, M23, SE7, SE13, SE14
Goodbye Song **It's Time to Go** (using sign language)	L13, L17, L18, L27

Bright Start Music   6–12 Month Group   Session Plan #4

SKILL AREAS & SONGS	DEVELOPMENTAL SKILLS ADDRESSED
Hello Song **My Right Hand Says Hello**	L17, L18, L19, L27, M12
Sing and Sign Songs **Doggie Doggie** **Mommy Go 'Round the Sun** **This is the Mommy Wiggle**	L17, L18, L19, L27
Instruments- Drums **This Old Man** **One, Two, Buckle My Shoe**	C1, C2, C3, C4, C6, C7, C8, C9, C10, C11, C12, C14,C15, L15, L24, L27, L28, L29, M18, M19, M21, M22, M23, SE7, SE13, SE14
Movement **London Bridge** **Row, Row, Row Your Boat**	L25, L27, L28, M1, M2, M3, M4, M5, M6, M7, M8, M9, M10, M11, M13, M14, M15, M16, SE2
Visual- Scarves **Twinkle, Twinkle**- with **bubbles** **Little Red Caboose**- with **train** moving	C5, L15, L25, L27, L28, L29
Animals/Puppets **Had a Little Rooster**	C1, C2, C3, C4, C6, C7, C8, C9, C10, C11, C12, C14,C15, L15, L28, L29, M18, M19, M21, M22, M23, SE7, SE13, SE14, SE15
Body Parts **If I Arr a Pirate**	L27, SE10
Mirror Time **You Are My Sunshine**	L15, L22, L25, L27, M18, M19, M21, M22, M23, SE4, SE5, SE7, SE10, SE11, SE14

Affection/Bonding **Never Let Me Go**	SE6, SE8, SE9
Massage/Bedtime Routine **Soon the Moon Will Rise**	L15, L24, L29, M18, M19, M21, M22, M23, SE7, SE13, SE14
Goodbye Song **It's Time to Go** (using sign language)	L13, L17, L18, L27

Bright Start Music   6–12 Month Group   Session Plan #5

SKILL AREAS & SONGS	DEVELOPMENTAL SKILLS ADDRESSED
Hello Song **My Right Hand Says Hello**	L17, L18, L19, L27, M12
Sing and Sign Songs **Roll the Ball** **Doggie Doggie** **Mommy Go 'Round the Sun**	L17, L18, L19, L27
Instruments- Shakers **Mister Golden Sun** **Oh Where Has My Little Dog Gone?**	C1, C2, C3, C4, C6, C7, C8, C9, C10, C11, C12, C14,C15, L15, L24, L27, L28, L29, M18, M19, M21, M22, M23, SE7, SE13, SE14
Movement **London Bridge** **Row, Row, Row Your Boat**	L25, L27, L28, M1, M2, M3, M4, M5, M6, M7, M8, M9, M10, M11, M13, M14, M15, M16, SE2
Visual- Scarves **Blow Me Some Bubbles**- with **bubbles** **Little Red Caboose**- with **train** moving	C5, L15, L25, L27, L28, L29
Animals/Puppets **Polar Bear, Polar Bear**- with book **Old MacDonald**- with puppets	C1, C2, C3, C4, C6, C7, C8, C9, C10, C11, C12, C14,C15, L15, L28, L29, M18, M19, M21, M22, M23, SE7, SE13, SE14, SE15
Body Parts **Head, Shoulders, Knees, and Toes**	L27, SE10
Mirror Time **If You're Happy and You Know It**	L15, L22, L25, L27, M18, M19, M21, M22, M23, SE4, SE5, SE7, SE10, SE11, SE14

Affection/Bonding **Always in My Heart**	SE6, SE8, SE9
Massage/Bedtime Routine **Big Bright Moon**	L15, L24, L29, M18, M19, M21, M22, M23, SE7, SE13, SE14
Goodbye Song **It's Time to Go**	L13, L17, L18, L27

Bright Start Music   6–12 Month Group   Session Plan #6

SKILL AREAS & SONGS	DEVELOPMENTAL SKILLS ADDRESSED
Hello Song **My Right Hand Says Hello**	L17, L18, L19, L27, M12
Sing and Sign Songs **The Walking Song** **Roll the Ball** **Doggie Doggie**	L17, L18, L19, L27
Instruments- Drums **Click! Click! Click! Go the Castanets** **This Old Man**	C1, C2, C3, C4, C6, C7, C8, C9, C10, C11, C12, C14,C15, L15, L24, L27, L28, L29, M18, M19, M21, M22, M23, SE7, SE13, SE14
Movement **The Ants Go Marching**	L25, L27, L28, M1, M2, M3, M4, M5, M6, M7, M8, M9, M10, M11, M13, M14, M15, M16, SE2
Visual- Scarves **Blow Me Some Bubbles** **Little Red Caboose** **I Can Name the Colors**	C5, L15, L25, L27, L28, L29
Animals/Puppets **Polar Bear, Polar Bear**- with book **Old MacDonald**- with puppets	C1, C2, C3, C4, C6, C7, C8, C9, C10, C11, C12, C14,C15, L15, L28, L29, M18, M19, M21, M22, M23, SE7, SE13, SE14, SE15
Body Parts **If I Arr a Pirate**	L27, SE10
Mirror Time **You Are My Sunshine**	L15, L22, L25, L27, M18, M19, M21, M22, M23, SE4, SE5, SE7, SE10, SE11, SE14

Affection/Bonding	SE6, SE8, SE9
How Will You Grow?	
Massage/Bedtime Routine	L15, L24, L29, M18, M19, M21, M22, M23, SE7, SE13, SE14
Big Bright Moon	
Goodbye Song	L13, L17, L18, L27
It's Time to Go	

Bright Start Music   6–12 Month Group   Session Plan #7

SKILL AREAS & SONGS	DEVELOPMENTAL SKILLS ADDRESSED
Hello Song **My Right Hand Says Hello**	L17, L18, L19, L27, M12
Sing and Sign Songs **Where's Baby** **The Walking Song** **Roll the Ball**	L17, L18, L19, L27
Instruments- Triangles/Wood Blocks **The Alphabet Song** **My Favorite Spot**	C1, C2, C3, C4, C6, C7, C8, C9, C10, C11, C12, C14,C15, L15, L24, L27, L28, L29, M18, M19, M21, M22, M23, SE7, SE13, SE14
Movement **The Ants Go Marching** **I've Been Working on the Railroad**	L25, L27, L28, M1, M2, M3, M4, M5, M6, M7, M8, M9, M10, M11, M13, M14, M15, M16, SE2
Visual- Tracking **Skip to My Lou** **Mister Golden Sun** **Tingalayo**	C5, L15, L25, L27, L28, L29
Animals/Puppets **Had a Little Rooster**	C1, C2, C3, C4, C6, C7, C8, C9, C10, C11, C12, C14,C15, L15, L28, L29, M18, M19, M21, M22, M23, SE7, SE13, SE14, SE15
Body Parts **Hokey Pokey**	L27, SE10
Mirror Time **The More We Get Together**	L15, L22, L25, L27, M18, M19, M21, M22, M23, SE4, SE5, SE7, SE10, SE11, SE14

Affection/Bonding **How Will You Grow?**	SE6, SE8, SE9
Massage/Bedtime Routine **Big Bright Moon**	L15, L24, L29, M18, M19, M21, M22, M23, SE7, SE13, SE14
Goodbye Song **It's Time to Go** (using sign language)	L13, L17, L18, L27

Bright Start Music   6–12 Month Group   Session Plan #8

SKILL AREAS & SONGS	DEVELOPMENTAL SKILLS ADDRESSED
Hello Song **My Right Hand Says Hello**	L17, L18, L19, L27, M12
Sing and Sign Songs **Miss Mary Jane** **Where's Baby** **The Walking Song**	L17, L18, L19, L27
Instruments- Triangles/Wood Blocks **The Alphabet Song** **My Favorite Spot**	C1, C2, C3, C4, C6, C7, C8, C9, C10, C11, C12, C14,C15, L15, L24, L27, L28, L29, M18, M19, M21, M22, M23, SE7, SE13, SE14
Movement **The Ants Go Marching** **I've Been Working on the Railroad**	L25, L27, L28, M1, M2, M3, M4, M5, M6, M7, M8, M9, M10, M11, M13, M14, M15, M16, SE2
Visual- Tracking **Blow Me Some Bubbles** **Kookabura**	C5, L15, L25, L27, L28, L29
Animals/Puppets Put puppets out in middle of circle out of reach for child to crawl/scoot/reach to get them **Animal Song**	C1, C2, C3, C4, C6, C7, C8, C9, C10, C11, C12, C14,C15, L15, L28, L29, M18, M19, M21, M22, M23, SE7, SE13, SE14, SE15
Body Parts **My Hand on My Head** Ask: Where is your <u>hand</u>?	L27, SE10

Mirror Time **Peek-A-Boo**	L15, L22, L25, L27, M18, M19, M21, M22, M23, SE4, SE5, SE7, SE10, SE11, SE14
Affection/Bonding **How Will You Grow?**	SE6, SE8, SE9
Massage/Bedtime Routine **Big Bright Moon**	L15, L24, L29, M18, M19, M21, M22, M23, SE7, SE13, SE14
Goodbye Song **It's Time to Go** (using sign language)	L13, L17, L18, L27

Bright Start Music   6–12 Month Group   Session Plan #9

SKILL AREAS & SONGS	DEVELOPMENTAL SKILLS ADDRESSED
Hello Song **My Right Hand Says Hello**	L17, L18, L19, L27, M12
Sing and Sign Songs **The Little Cat Goes Creeping** **Miss Mary Jane** **Where's Baby**	L17, L18, L19, L27
Instruments- Claves/Wood Blocks/Drums **The Alphabet Song** **My Favorite Spot**	C1, C2, C3, C4, C6, C7, C8, C9, C10, C11, C12, C14,C15, L15, L24, L27, L28, L29, M18, M19, M21, M22, M23, SE7, SE13, SE14
Movement **Five Little Ducks**	L25, L27, L28, M1, M2, M3, M4, M5, M6, M7, M8, M9, M10, M11, M13, M14, M15, M16, SE2
Visual- Tracking **Kookabura** **Whack the Drum**	C5, L15, L25, L27, L28, L29
Animals/Puppets Put puppets out in middle of circle out of reach for child to crawl/scoot/reach to get them **Had a Little Rooster**	C1, C2, C3, C4, C6, C7, C8, C9, C10, C11, C12, C14,C15, L15, L28, L29, M18, M19, M21, M22, M23, SE7, SE13, SE14, SE15
Body Parts **If I Arr a Pirate**	L27, SE10
Mirror Time **Peek-A-Boo**	L15, L22, L25, L27, M18, M19, M21, M22, M23, SE4, SE5, SE7, SE10, SE11, SE14

Affection/Bonding **Always in My Heart**	SE6, SE8, SE9
Massage/Bedtime Routine **Soon the Moon Will Rise**	L15, L24, L29, M18, M19, M21, M22, M23, SE7, SE13, SE14
Goodbye Song **It's Time to Go** (using sign language)	L13, L17, L18, L27

Bright Start Music   6–12 Month Group   Session Plan #10

SKILL AREAS & SONGS	DEVELOPMENTAL SKILLS ADDRESSED
Hello Song **My Right Hand Says Hello**	L17, L18, L19, L27, M12
Sing and Sign Songs **Bunny Boogie** **The Little Cat Goes Creeping** **Miss Mary Jane**	L17, L18, L19, L27
Instruments- Claves/Wood Blocks/Drums **My Favorite Spot** **BINGO**	C1, C2, C3, C4, C6, C7, C8, C9, C10, C11, C12, C14,C15, L15, L24, L27, L28, L29, M18, M19, M21, M22, M23, SE7, SE13, SE14
Movement **London Bridge** **Row, Row, Row Your Boat** **I Roll the Ball to You Song**	L25, L27, L28, M1, M2, M3, M4, M5, M6, M7, M8, M9, M10, M11, M13, M14, M15, M16, SE2
Visual- Tracking (Let child put beans in can and take out when songs are done) **Blow Me Some Bubbles** **Five Green and Speckled Frogs**	C5, L15, L25, L27, L28, L29, M20, M22, M23, M24
Animals/Puppets Child to crawl/scoot/reach to get puppets **Animal Song**	C1, C2, C3, C4, C6, C7, C8, C9, C10, C11, C12, C14,C15, L15, L28, L29, M18, M19, M21, M22, M23, SE7, SE13, SE14, SE15
Body Parts **My Hand on My Head**	L27, SE10

Mirror Time **Where is Thumbkin?**	L15, L22, L25, L27, M18, M19, M21, M22, M23, SE4, SE5, SE7, SE10, SE11, SE14
Affection/Bonding **Always in My Heart**	SE6, SE8, SE9
Massage/Bedtime Routine **Soon the Moon Will Rise**	L15, L24, L29, M18, M19, M21, M22, M23, SE7, SE13, SE14
Goodbye Song **It's Time to Go**	L13, L17, L18, L27

Bright Start Music   6–12 Month Group   Session Plan #11

SKILL AREAS & SONGS	DEVELOPMENTAL SKILLS ADDRESSED
Hello Song **My Right Hand Says Hello**	L17, L18, L19, L27, M12
Sing and Sign Songs **Charlie Over the Water** **Bunny Boogie** **The Little Cat Goes Creeping**	L17, L18, L19, L27
Instruments- Triangles/Wood Blocks **Twinkle Twinkle** **Itsy Bitsy Spider**	C1, C2, C3, C4, C6, C7, C8, C9, C10, C11, C12, C14,C15, L15, L24, L27, L28, L29, M18, M19, M21, M22, M23, SE7, SE13, SE14
Movement **London Bridge** **Row, Row, Row Your Boat** **I Roll the Ball to You**	L25, L27, L28, M1, M2, M3, M4, M5, M6, M7, M8, M9, M10, M11, M13, M14, M15, M16, SE2
Visual- Tracking **Blow Me Some Bubbles** **Five Green and Speckled Frogs**	C5, L15, L25, L27, L28, L29, M20, M22, M23, M24
Animals/Puppets Use **Picture Cards** of birds or **Scarves** to mimic bird movement **Birdie Beat**	C1, C2, C3, C4, C6, C7, C8, C9, C10, C11, C12, C14,C15, L15, L28, L29, M18, M19, M21, M22, M23, SE7, SE13, SE14, SE15
Body Parts **Loop De Loop**	L27, SE10
Mirror Time **Where is Thumbkin?**	L15, L22, L25, L27, M18, M19, M21, M22, M23, SE4, SE5, SE7, SE10, SE11, SE14

Affection/Bonding **How You Will Grow?**	SE6, SE8, SE9
Massage/Bedtime Routine **Goodnight, My Sweet One**	L15, L24, L29, M18, M19, M21, M22, M23, SE7, SE13, SE14
Goodbye Song **It's Time to Go** (using sign language)	L13, L17, L18, L27

Bright Start Music   6–12 Month Group   Session Plan #12

SKILL AREAS & SONGS	DEVELOPMENTAL SKILLS ADDRESSED
Hello Song **My Right Hand Says Hello**	L17, L18, L19, L27, M12
Sing and Sign Songs **My World** **Charlie Over the Water** **Bunny Boogie**	L17, L18, L19, L27
Instruments- Claves/Wood Blocks/Drums **Baa, Baa, Black Sheep** **Humpty Dumpty**	C1, C2, C3, C4, C6, C7, C8, C9, C10, C11, C12, C14, C15, L15, L24, L27, L28, L29, M18, M19, M21, M22, M23, SE7, SE13, SE14
Movement **Five Little Monkeys Jumping on the Bed** **I Roll the Ball to You**	L25, L27, L28, M1, M2, M3, M4, M5, M6, M7, M8, M9, M10, M11, M13, M14, M15, M16, SE2
Visual- Tracking **I'm a Little Teapot** **If All the Raindrops**	C5, L15, L25, L27, L28, L29, M20, M22, M23, M24
Animals/Puppets Use **Picture Cards** of birds or **Scarves** to mimic bird movement **Birdie Beat**	C1, C2, C3, C4, C6, C7, C8, C9, C10, C11, C12, C14, C15, L15, L28, L29, M18, M19, M21, M22, M23, SE7, SE13, SE14, SE15
Body Parts **Loop De Loop**	L27, SE10
Mirror Time **Where is Thumbkin?**	L15, L22, L25, L27, M18, M19, M21, M22, M23, SE4, SE5, SE7, SE10, SE11, SE14

Affection/Bonding **Always in My Heart**	SE6, SE8, SE9
Massage/Bedtime Routine **Goodnight, My Sweet One**	L15, L24, L29, M18, M19, M21, M22, M23, SE7, SE13, SE14
Goodbye Song **It's Time to Go**	L13, L17, L18, L27

The following developmental skills are addressed or can be seen in all sessions and all songs for ages 12–18 months:

C15

C19

C20

L10

L11

L12

L14

L15

L16

L26

L28

L32

L33

L35

L36

L37

L38

L39

L40

M15

M27

M28

SE20

SE21

SE23

SE24

SE25

SE29

Bright Start Music   12–18 Month Group   Session Plan #1

SKILL AREAS & SONGS	DEVELOPMENTAL SKILLS ADDRESSED
Hello Song **When I Meet a New Friend**	L17, L18, L19
Sing and Sign Songs **La La La Lullaby** **Skye Boat Song** **My World**	L17, L18, L19, L27, SE31
Instruments- Rhythm Instruments **Playing Along**	C16, C17, C18, L29, L30, M23, M24, M25, M29, M32, M36, M41, SE18, SE26, SE29, SE30
Movement **The Owl**	L17, L18, L25, L27, M30, M31, M39, SE31
Visual- Scarves **I Can Name The Color**	C18, L25, L27, L29, L30, M23, M25, M29, M41, SE18, SE26, SE29, SE30, SE31
Animals/Puppets **Hello Mr. Animal**	C16, C18, L25, L29, L30, M23, M25, M29, M32, M41, SE18, SE19, SE26, SE29, SE30, SE31
Books **Ten Little Monkeys** (Big Book)	L27, L29, L30, L41, M38, M40, SE22
Body Parts **Loop De Loop**	L31, M35, SE31
Mirror Time **Look in the Mirror**	C18, L30, M23, M25, M29, M32, SE18, SE27, SE28, SE29, SE30, SE31

Movement **Hot Air Balloon**	L27, M39, SE31
Affection/Bonding **In My Own Little Way**	SE8
Goodbye Song **It's Time to Go** (using sign language)	L13, L17, L18, L27, SE31

Bright Start Music   12–18 Month Group Session Plan #2

SKILL AREAS & SONGS	DEVELOPMENTAL SKILLS ADDRESSED
Hello Song **When I Meet a New Friend**	L17, L18, L19
Sing and Sign Songs **La La La Lullaby** **Skye Boat Song** **My World**	L17, L18, L19, L27, SE31
Instruments- Rhythm Instruments **Playing Along**	C16, C17, C18, L29, L30, M23, M24, M25, M29, M32, M36, M41, SE18, SE26, SE29, SE30
Movement **The Owl**	L17, L18, L25, L27, M30, M31, M39, SE31
Visual- Scarves **I Can Name the Color**	C18, L25, L27, L29, L30, M23, M25, M29, M41, SE18, SE26, SE29, SE30, SE31
Animals/Puppets **Hello Mr. Animal**	C16, C18, L25, L29, L30, M23, M25, M29, M32, M41, SE18, SE19, SE26, SE29, SE30, SE31
Books **Ten Little Monkeys** (Big Book)	L27, L29, L30, L41, M38, M40, SE22
Body Parts **You Do the Same** Incorporate rolling and throwing small balls	L31, M26, M33, M34, M35,M37, SE31, L31, M35, SE31
Mirror Time **Look in the Mirror**	C18, L30, M23, M25, M29, M32, SE18, SE27, SE28, SE29, SE30, SE31

Movement **Hot Air Balloon**	L27, M39, SE31
Affection/Bonding **In My Own Little Way**	SE8
Goodbye Song **It's Time to Go** (using sign language)	L13, L17, L18, L27, SE31

Bright Start Music   12–18 Month Group Session Plan #3

SKILL AREAS & SONGS	DEVELOPMENTAL SKILLS ADDRESSED
Hello Song **When I Meet a New Friend**	L17, L18, L19
Sing and Sign Songs **La La La Lullaby** **Skye Boat Song**	L17, L18, L19, L27, SE31
Instruments- Rhythm Instruments **Razzle Dazzle 'Em**	C16, C17, C18, L29, L30, M23, M24, M25, M29, M32, M36, M41, SE18, SE26, SE29, SE30
Movement **The Owl**	L17, L18, L25, L27, M30, M31, M39, SE31
Visual- Scarves **I Can Name The Color**	C18, L25, L27, L29, L30, M23, M25, M29, M41, SE18, SE26, SE29, SE30, SE31
Animals/Puppets **Animal Song**	C16, C18, L25, L29, L30, M23, M25, M29, M32, M41, SE18, SE19, SE26, SE29, SE30, SE31
Books **Mulberry Bush** (Big Book)	L27, L29, L30, L41, M38, M40, SE22
Body Parts **Look in the Mirror**	L31, M35, SE31
Mirror Time **This is How I Look**	C18, L30, M23, M25, M29, M32, SE18, SE27, SE28, SE29, SE30, SE31

Movement **Pitter Patter** Can incorporate rain sticks or ocean drums	L27, M39, SE31
Affection/Bonding **In My Own Little Way**	SE8
Goodbye Song **It's Time to Go** (using sign language)	L13, L17, L18, L27, SE31

Bright Start Music   12–18 Month Group   Session Plan #4

SKILL AREAS & SONGS	DEVELOPMENTAL SKILLS ADDRESSED
Hello Song **When I Meet a New Friend**	L17, L18, L19
Sign Language Song **Brown Bear, Brown Bear**	L17, L18, L19, L27, SE31
Instruments- Rhythm Instruments **Playing Along**	C16, C17, C18, L29, L30, M23, M24, M25, M29, M32, M36, M41, SE18, SE26, SE29, SE30
Movement **Let's Go for a Ride**	L17, L18, L25, L27, M30, M31, M39, SE31
Visual- Scarves **I Can Name the Color**	C18, L25, L27, L29, L30, M23, M25, M29, M41, SE18, SE26, SE29, SE30, SE31
Animals/Puppets **Monkey Hug**	C16, C18, L25, L29, L30, M23, M25, M29, M32, M41, SE18, SE19, SE26, SE29, SE30, SE31
Books **Farmer in the Dell** (Big Book)	L27, L29, L30, L41, M38, M40, SE22
Body Parts **You Do the Same** Incorporate rolling and throwing small balls	L31, M26, M33, M34, M35, M37, SE31
Mirror Time **This is How I Look**	C18, L30, M23, M25, M29, M32, SE18, SE27, SE28, SE29, SE30, SE31

Movement **There's a Tickle Under My Skin**	L27, M39, SE31
Affection/Bonding **Doo Wop Love**	SE8
Goodbye Song **It's Time to Go** (using sign language)	L13, L17, L18, L27, SE31

Bright Start Music   **12–18 Month Group**   **Session Plan #5**

SKILL AREAS & SONGS	DEVELOPMENTAL SKILLS ADDRESSED
Hello Song When I Meet a New Friend	L17, L18, L19
Sign Language Song Brown Bear, Brown Bear	L17, L18, L19, L27, SE31
Instruments- Rhythm Instruments Razzle Dazzle 'Em	C16, C17, C18, L29, L30, M23, M24, M25, M29, M32, M36, M41, SE18, SE26, SE29, SE30
Movement Let's Go for a Ride	L17, L18, L25, L27, M30, M31, M39, SE31
Visual- Scarves I Can Name the Color	C18, L25, L27, L29, L30, M23, M25, M29, M41, SE18, SE26, SE29, SE30, SE31
Animals/Puppets Animal Song with Picture Cards	C16, C18, L25, L29, L30, M23, M25, M29, M32, M41, SE18, SE19, SE26, SE29, SE30, SE31
Books This Old Man (Big Book)	L27, L29, L30, L41, M38, M40, SE22
Body Parts Look in the Mirror	L31, M35, SE31
Mirror Time I Feel Silly	C18, L30, M23, M25, M29, M32, SE18, SE27, SE28, SE29, SE30, SE31

Movement **Pitter Patter**	L27, M39, SE31
Affection/Bonding **Baby, Baby**	SE8
Goodbye Song **It's Time to Go** (using sign language)	L13, L17, L18, L27, SE31

Bright Start Music   12–18 Month Group Session Plan #6

SKILL AREAS & SONGS	DEVELOPMENTAL SKILLS ADDRESSED
Hello Song **When I Meet a New Friend**	L17, L18, L19
Sign Language Song **Brown Bear, Brown Bear**	L17, L18, L19, L27, SE31
Instruments- Rhythm Instruments **Playing Along**	C16, C17, C18, L29, L30, M23, M24, M25, M29, M32, M36, M41, SE18, SE26, SE29, SE30
Movement **Let's Go for a Ride**	L17, L18, L25, L27, M30, M31, M39, SE31
Visual- Scarves **I Can Name the Color**	C18, L25, L27, L29, L30, M23, M25, M29, M41, SE18, SE26, SE29, SE30, SE31
Animals/Puppets **Mr. Animal** with **Picture Cards**	C16, C18, L25, L29, L30, M23, M25, M29, M32, M41, SE18, SE19, SE26, SE29, SE30, SE31
Books **Nine Ducks Nine** (Big Book)	L27, L29, L30, L41, M38, M40, SE22
Body Parts **You Do the Same** Incorporate rolling and throwing small balls	L31, M26, M33, M34, M35, M37, SE31
Mirror Time **I Feel Silly**	C18, L30, M23, M25, M29, M32, SE18, SE27, SE28, SE29, SE30, SE31

Movement **There's a Tickle Under My Skin**	L27, M39, SE31
Affection/Bonding **Baby, Baby**	SE8
Goodbye Song **It's Time to Go** (using sign language)	L13, L17, L18, L27, SE31

Bright Start Music   12–18 Month Group   Session Plan #7

SKILL AREAS & SONGS	DEVELOPMENTAL SKILLS ADDRESSED
Hello Song **When I Meet a New Friend**	L17, L18, L19
Sign Language Song **Polar Bear, Polar Bear** (with Big Book)	L17, L18, L19, L27, SE31
Instruments- Rhythm Instruments **Click! Click! Click! Go the Castanets**	C16, C17, C18, L29, L30, M23, M24, M25, M29, M32, M36, M41, SE18, SE26, SE29, SE30
Movement **Tree Hug**	L17, L18, L25, L27, M30, M31, M39, SE31
Visual- Picture Cards **My Favorite Spot**	C18, L25, L27, L29, L30, M23, M25, M29, M41, SE18, SE26, SE29, SE30, SE31
Animals/Puppets **Animal Song**	C16, C18, L25, L29, L30, M23, M25, M29, M32, M41, SE18, SE19, SE26, SE29, SE30, SE31
Books **Walking Through the Jungle** (Big Book)	L27, L29, L30, L41, M38, M40, SE22
Body Parts **You Do the Same** Incorporate rolling and throwing small balls	L31, M26, M33, M34, M35, M37, SE31
Mirror Time **I Feel Silly**	C18, L30, M23, M25, M29, M32, SE18, SE27, SE28, SE29, SE30, SE31

Movement **Pitter Patter** Can incorporate rain sticks or ocean drums.	L27, M39, SE31
Affection/Bonding **Baby, Baby**	SE8
Goodbye Song **It's Time to Go** (using sign language)	L13, L17, L18, L27, SE31

Bright Start Music   12–18 Month Group   Session Plan #8

SKILL AREAS & SONGS	DEVELOPMENTAL SKILLS ADDRESSED
Hello Song **When I Meet a New Friend**	L17, L18, L19
Sign Language Song **Polar Bear, Polar Bear** (with Big Book)	L17, L18, L19, L27, SE31
Instruments- Rhythm Instruments **Click! Click! Click! Go the Castanets**	C16, C17, C18, L29, L30, M23, M24, M25, M29, M32, M36, M41, SE18, SE26, SE29, SE30
Movement **Flower Power**	L17, L18, L25, L27, M30, M31, M39, SE31
Visual- Picture Cards **My Favorite Spot**	C18, L25, L27, L29, L30, M23, M25, M29, M41, SE18, SE26, SE29, SE30, SE31
Animals/Puppets **Monkey Hug**	C16, C18, L25, L29, L30, M23, M25, M29, M32, M41, SE18, SE19, SE26, SE29, SE30, SE31
Books **Panda Bear, Panda Bear, What Do You See?** (Big Book)	L27, L29, L30, L41, M38, M40, SE22
Body Parts **My Hand on My Head**	L31, M35, SE31
Mirror Time **Look in the Mirror**	C18, L30, M23, M25, M29, M32, SE18, SE27, SE28, SE29, SE30, SE31

Movement **There's a Tickle Under My Skin**	L27, M39, SE31
Affection/Bonding **Doo Wop Love**	SE8
Goodbye Song **It's Time to Go** (using sign language)	L13, L17, L18, L27, SE31

Bright Start Music   12–18 Month Group   Session Plan #9

SKILL AREAS & SONGS	DEVELOPMENTAL SKILLS ADDRESSED
Hello Song **When I Meet a New Friend**	L17, L18, L19
Sign Language Song **Polar Bear, Polar Bear** (with Big Book)	L17, L18, L19, L27, SE31
Instruments- Rhythm Instruments **I'm the Sun**	C16, C17, C18, L29, L30, M23, M24, M25, M29, M32, M36, M41, SE18, SE26, SE29, SE30
Movement **Flower Power**	L17, L18, L25, L27, M30, M31, M39, SE31
Visual- Picture Cards **My Favorite Spot**	C18, L25, L27, L29, L30, M23, M25, M29, M41, SE18, SE26, SE29, SE30, SE31
Animals/Puppets **Animal Song**	C16, C18, L25, L29, L30, M23, M25, M29, M32, M41, SE18, SE19, SE26, SE29, SE30, SE31
Books **Wheels on the Bus** (Big Book)	L27, L29, L30, L41, M38, M40, SE22
Body Parts **You Do the Same** Incorporate rolling and throwing small balls	L31, M26, M33, M34, M35, M37, SE31
Mirror Time **This is How I Look**	C18, L30, M23, M25, M29, M32, SE18, SE27, SE28, SE29, SE30, SE31

Movement **Hot Air Balloon**	L27, M39, SE31
Affection/Bonding **Doo Wop Love**	SE8
Goodbye Song **It's Time to Go** (using sign language)	L13, L17, L18, L27, SE31

Bright Start Music   12–18 Month Group   Session Plan #10

SKILL AREAS & SONGS	DEVELOPMENTAL SKILLS ADDRESSED
Hello Song When I Meet a New Friend	L17, L18, L19
Sign Language Song Birdie Beat	L17, L18, L19, L27, SE31
Instruments- Rhythm Instruments I'm the Sun	C16, C17, C18, L29, L30, M23, M24, M25, M29, M32, M36, M41, SE18, SE26, SE29, SE30
Movement Tree Hug	L17, L18, L25, L27, M30, M31, M39, SE31
Visual- Picture Cards My Favorite Spot	C18, L25, L27, L29, L30, M23, M25, M29, M41, SE18, SE26, SE29, SE30, SE31
Animals/Puppets Hello Mr. Animal	C16, C18, L25, L29, L30, M23, M25, M29, M32, M41, SE18, SE19, SE26, SE29, SE30, SE31
Books Ten Little Monkeys (Big Book)	L27, L29, L30, L41, M38, M40, SE22
Body Parts My Hand on My Head	L31, M35, SE31
Mirror Time This is How I Look	C18, L30, M23, M25, M29, M32, SE18, SE27, SE28, SE29, SE30, SE31

Movement **Hot Air Balloon**	L27, M39, SE31
Affection/Bonding **In My Own Little Way**	SE8
Goodbye Song **It's Time to Go** (using sign language)	L13, L17, L18, L27, SE31

Bright Start Music   12–18 Month Group   Session Plan #11

SKILL AREAS & SONGS	DEVELOPMENTAL SKILLS ADDRESSED
Hello Song When I Meet a New Friend	L17, L18, L19
Sign Language Song Birdie Beat	L17, L18, L19, L27, SE31
Instruments- Rhythm Instruments Click! Click! Click! Go the Castanets	C16, C17, C18, L29, L30, M23, M24, M25, M29, M32, M36, M41, SE18, SE26, SE29, SE30
Movement Tree Hug	L17, L18, L25, L27, M30, M31, M39, SE31
Visual- Picture Cards My Favorite Spot	C18, L25, L27, L29, L30, M23, M25, M29, M41, SE18, SE26, SE29, SE30, SE31
Animals/Puppets Animal Song	C16, C18, L25, L29, L30, M23, M25, M29, M32, M41, SE18, SE19, SE26, SE29, SE30, SE31
Books Mulberry Bush (Big Book)	L27, L29, L30, L41, M38, M40, SE22
Body Parts You Do the Same Incorporate rolling and throwing small balls	L31. M26, M33, M34, M35, M37, SE31
Mirror Time I Feel Silly	C18, L30, M23, M25, M29, M32, SE18, SE27, SE28, SE29, SE30, SE31

Movement **Hot Air Balloon**	L27, M39, SE31
Affection/Bonding **In My Own Little Way**	SE8
Goodbye Song **It's Time to Go** (using sign language)	L13, L17, L18, L27, SE31

Bright Start Music   12–18 Month Group   Session Plan #12

SKILL AREAS & SONGS	DEVELOPMENTAL SKILLS ADDRESSED
Hello Song **When I Meet a New Friend**	L17, L18, L19
Sign Language Song **Birdie Beat**	L17, L18, L19, L27, SE31
Instruments- Rhythm Instruments **Click! Click! Click! Go the Castanets**	C16, C17, C18, L29, L30, M23, M24, M25, M29, M32, M36, M41, SE18, SE26, SE29, SE30
Movement **Flower Power**	L17, L18, L25, L27, M30, M31, M39, SE31
Visual- Picture Cards **My Favorite Spot**	C18, L25, L27, L29, L30, M23, M25, M29, M41, SE18, SE26, SE29, SE30, SE31
Animals/Puppets **Monkey Hug**	C16, C18, L25, L29, L30, M23, M25, M29, M32, M41, SE18, SE19, SE26, SE29, SE30, SE31
Books **Farmer in the Dell** (Big Book)	L27, L29, L30, L41, M38, M40, SE22
Body Parts **My Hand on My Head**	L31, M35, SE31
Mirror Time **I Feel Silly**	C18, L30, M23, M25, M29, M32, SE18, SE27, SE28, SE29, SE30, SE31

<u>Movement</u> **The Owl**	L27, M39, SE31
<u>Affection/Bonding</u> **Baby, Baby**	SE8
<u>Goodbye Song</u> **It's Time to Go** (using sign language)	L13, L17, L18, L27, SE31

The following developmental skills are addressed or can be seen in all sessions and all songs for ages 18–24 months:

C19

C20

C22

C24

L26

L28

L36

L38

L39

L43

L44

L45

L46

L47

L48

L50

M27

SE32

SE33

SE37

SE38

SE39

SE40

SE41

SE46

Bright Start Music   18–24 Month Group   Session Plan #1

SKILL AREAS & SONGS	DEVELOPMENTAL SKILLS ADDRESSED
Hello Song How Do You Doodle	L17, L18, L19, C23
Instruments- Tambourines and/or Drums Listen to How I Beat My Drum Clean Up	C21, C27, L42, M41, M43, M44, SE 34, SE35, SE44 C28
Movement We're Gonna Dance, We're Gonna Wiggle	C23, M30
Body Parts/Gestures Hello, Salutations	L17, L18, C23, C26, L31, SE48
Animals/Picture Cards Marty Monkey Clean Up	C21, C25, C27, L42, L49, M41, M43, M44, SE34, SE35, SE44 C28
Body Parts Tony Chestnut	C23, L31
Emotions/Dramatic Play Monkey Moves!	C23, SE36, SE43
Movement The Owl	L17, L18, C23, M30, SE36
Affection/Bonding La La La Lullaby	SE42, SE43
Goodbye Song It's Time to Go (using sign language)	L17, L18, L19, C23

Bright Start Music   18–24 Month Group Session Plan #2

SKILL AREAS & SONGS	DEVELOPMENTAL SKILLS ADDRESSED
Hello Song How Do You Doodle	L17, L18, L19, C23
Instruments- Rhythm Instruments Leader of the Band Clean Up	C21, C27, L42, M41, M43, M44, SE 34, SE35, SE44 C28
Movement We're Gonna Dance, We're Gonna Wiggle	C23, M30
Body Parts/Gestures Loop De Loop	L17, L18, C23, C26, L31, SE48
Animals/Picture Cards Mouse in My House Clean Up	C21, C25, C27, L42, L49, M41, M43, M44, SE34, SE35, SE44 C28
Body Parts Tony Chestnut	C23, L31
Emotions/Dramatic Play I Feel Silly	C23, SE36, SE43
Movement I Roll The Ball to You	L17, L18, C23, M30, M42, M45, SE36
Affection/Bonding La La La Lullaby	SE42, SE43
Goodbye Song It's Time to Go (using sign language)	L17, L18, L19, C23

Bright Start Music   18–24 Month Group Session Plan #3

SKILL AREAS & SONGS	DEVELOPMENTAL SKILLS ADDRESSED
Hello Song How Do You Doodle	L17, L18, L19, C23
Instruments- Rhythm Instruments 1,2,3, Play with Me Clean Up	C21, C27, L42, M41, M43, M44, SE 34, SE35, SE44 C28
Movement It's Time for Parade	C23, M30
Body Parts/Gestures The Body Language Song	L17, L18, C23, C26, L31, SE48
Animals/Puppets Animal Parade Clean Up	C21, C25, C27, L42, L49, M41, M43, M44, SE34, SE35, SE44, SE47 C28
Song Book Mouse in My House	M40, M47, SE45
Body Parts Tony Chestnut	C23, L31
Emotions/Dramatic Play What's Your Name?	C23, SE36, SE43
Movement Monkey Moves!	L17, L18, C23, M30, SE36
Affection/Bonding Never Let Me Go	SE42, SE43
Goodbye Song It's Time to Go (using sign language)	L17, L18, L19, C23

Bright Start Music   18–24 Month Group   Session Plan #4

SKILL AREAS & SONGS	DEVELOPMENTAL SKILLS ADDRESSED
Hello Song How Do You Doodle	L17, L18, L19, C23
Instruments- Rhythm Instruments 1,2,3, Play with Me Clean Up	C21, C27, L42, M41, M43, M44, SE 34, SE35, SE44 C28
Movement It's Time for Parade	C23, M30
Body Parts/Gestures Hello, Salutations	L17, L18, C23, C26, L31, SE48
Animals/Puppets Animal Parade Clean Up	C21, C25, C27, L42, L49, M41, M43, M44, SE34, SE35, SE44, SE47 C28
Song Book Mouse in My House	M40, M47, SE45
Body Parts Tony Chestnut	C23, L31
Emotions/Dramatic Play The Emotion Song	C23, SE36, SE43
Movement Dance to the Music	L17, L18, C23, M30, SE36
Affection/Bonding Never Let Me Go	SE42, SE43
Goodbye Song It's Time to Go (using sign language)	L17, L18, L19, C23

Bright Start Music   18–24 Month Group   Session Plan #5

SKILL AREAS & SONGS	DEVELOPMENTAL SKILLS ADDRESSED
Hello Song How Do You Doodle	L17, L18, L19, C23
Instruments- Tambourines and/or Drums Listen to How I Beat My Drum Clean Up	C21, C27, L42, M41, M43, M44, SE 34, SE35, SE44 C28
Movement Dance to the Music	C23, M30
Body Parts/Gestures Loop De Loop	L17, L18, C23, C26, L31, SE48
Animals/Picture Cards Marty Monkey Clean Up	C21, C25, C27, L42, L49, M41, M43, M44, SE34, SE35, SE44 C28
Body Parts When I Wake Up	C23, L31
Emotions/Dramatic Play Mood Groove	C23, SE36, SE43
Movement I Roll The Ball to You	L17, L18, C23, M30, M42, M45, SE36
Affection/Bonding Do Wop Lullaby	SE42, SE43
Goodbye Song It's Time to Go (using sign language)	L17, L18, L19, C23

Bright Start Music   18–24 Month Group   Session Plan #6

SKILL AREAS & SONGS	DEVELOPMENTAL SKILLS ADDRESSED
Hello Song How Do You Doodle	L17, L18, L19, C23
Instruments- Tambourines and/or Drums Listen to How I Beat My Drum Clean Up	C21, C27, L42, M41, M43, M44, SE 34, SE35, SE44 C28
Movement Dance to the Music	C23, M30
Body Parts/Gestures The Body Language Song	L17, L18, C23, C26, L31, SE48
Animals/Picture Cards Marty Monkey Clean Up	C21, C25, C27, L42, L49, M41, M43, M44, SE34, SE35, SE44 C28
Body Parts When I Wake Up	C23, L31
Emotions/Dramatic Play I Feel Silly	C23, SE36, SE43
Movement It's Time for Parade	L17, L18, C23, M30, SE36
Affection/Bonding Do Wop Lullaby	SE42, SE43
Goodbye Song It's Time to Go (using sign language)	L17, L18, L19, C23

Bright Start Music   18–24 Month Group Session Plan #7

SKILL AREAS & SONGS	DEVELOPMENTAL SKILLS ADDRESSED
Hello Song How Do You Doodle	L17, L18, L19, C23
Instruments- Rhythm Instruments Leader of the Band Clean Up	C21, C27, L42, M41, M43, M44, SE 34, SE35, SE44 C28
Movement Monkey Moves!	C23, M30
Body Parts/Gestures Hello, Salutations	L17, L18, C23, C26, L31, SE48
Animals/Puppets A Rustle in a Bush Clean Up	C21, C25, C27, L42, L49, M41, M43, M44, SE34, SE35, SE44, SE47 C28
Body Parts When I Wake Up	C23, L31
Emotions/Dramatic Play What's Your Name?	C23, SE36, SE43
Movement The Bicycle	L17, L18, C23, M30, SE36
Affection/Bonding La La La Lullaby	SE42, SE43
Goodbye Song It's Time to Go (using sign language)	L17, L18, L19, C23

Bright Start Music   **18–24 Month Group**   **Session Plan #8**

SKILL AREAS & SONGS	DEVELOPMENTAL SKILLS ADDRESSED
Hello Song How Do You Doodle	L17, L18, L19, C23
Instruments- Rhythm Instruments 1,2,3, Play with Me Clean Up	C21, C27, L42, M41, M43, M44, SE 34, SE35, SE44 C28
Movement Monkey Moves!	C23, M30
Body Parts/Gestures Loop De Loop	L17, L18, C23, C26, L31, SE48
Animals/Puppets A Rustle in a Bush Clean Up	C21, C25, C27, L42, L49, M41, M43, M44, SE34, SE35, SE44, SE47 C28
Body Parts When I Wake Up	C23, L31
Emotions/Dramatic Play The Emotion Song	C23, SE36, SE43
Movement I Roll The Ball to You	L17, L18, C23, M30, M42, M45, SE36
Affection/Bonding La La La Lullaby	SE42, SE43
Goodbye Song It's Time to Go (using sign language)	L17, L18, L19, C23

Bright Start Music   18–24 Month Group   Session Plan #9

SKILL AREAS & SONGS	DEVELOPMENTAL SKILLS ADDRESSED
Hello Song How Do You Doodle	L17, L18, L19, C23
Instruments- Rhythm Instruments 1,2,3, Play with Me Clean Up	C21, C27, L42, M41, M43, M44, SE 34, SE35, SE44 C28
Movement The Bicycle	C23, M30
Body Parts/Gestures The Body Language Song	L17, L18, C23, C26, L31, SE48
Animals/Puppets Animal Parade Clean Up	C21, C25, C27, L42, L49, M41, M43, M44, SE34, SE35, SE44, SE47 C28
Songbook Mouse in My House	M40, M47, SE45
Body Parts If I Arr a Pirate	C23, L31, SE36
Emotions/Dramatic Play Mood Groove	C23, SE36, SE43
Movement We're Gonna Dance, We're Gonna Wiggle	L17, L18, C23, M30, SE36
Affection/Bonding Never Let Me Go	SE42, SE43
Goodbye Song It's Time to Go (using sign language)	L17, L18, L19, C23

Bright Start Music   18–24 Month Group   Session Plan #10

SKILL AREAS & SONGS	DEVELOPMENTAL SKILLS ADDRESSED
Hello Song How Do You Doodle	L17, L18, L19, C23
Instruments- Rhythm Instruments Leader of the Band Clean Up	C21, C27, L42, M41, M43, M44, SE 34, SE35, SE44 C28
Movement It's Time for Parade	C23, M30
Body Parts/Gestures Hello, Salutations	L17, L18, C23, C26, L31, SE48
Animals/Puppets Animal Parade Clean Up	C21, C25, C27, L42, L49, M41, M43, M44, SE34, SE35, SE44, SE47 C28
Songbook Mouse in My House	M40, M47, SE45
Body Parts If I Arr a Pirate	C23, L31, SE36
Emotions/Dramatic Play I Feel Silly	C23, SE36, SE43
Movement The Bicycle	L17, L18, C23, M30, SE36
Affection/Bonding Never Let Me Go	SE42, SE43
Goodbye Song It's Time to Go (using sign language)	L17, L18, L19, C23

Bright Start Music   18–24 Month Group   Session Plan #11

SKILL AREAS & SONGS	DEVELOPMENTAL SKILLS ADDRESSED
Hello Song **How Do You Doodle**	L17, L18, L19, C23
Instruments- Tambourines and/or Drums **Listen to How I Beat My Drum** **Clean Up**	C21, C27, L42, M41, M43, M44, SE 34, SE35, SE44 C28
Movement **We're Gonna Dance, We're Gonna Wiggle**	C23, M30
Body Parts/Gestures **Loop De Loop**	L17, L18, C23, C26, L31, SE48
Animals/Picture Cards **Marty Monkey** **Clean Up**	C21, C25, C27, L42, L49, M41, M43, M44, SE34, SE35, SE44 C28
Body Parts **If I Arr a Pirate**	C23, L31, SE36
Emotions/Dramatic Play **What's Your Name?**	C23, SE36, SE43
Movement **I Roll the Ball to You**	L17, L18, C23, M30, M42, M45, SE36
Affection/Bonding **Do Wop Lullaby**	SE42, SE43
Goodbye Song **It's Time to Go** (using sign language)	L17, L18, L19, C23

Bright Start Music   18–24 Month Group   Session Plan #12

SKILL AREAS & SONGS	DEVELOPMENTAL SKILLS ADDRESSED
Hello Song **How Do You Doodle**	L17, L18, L19, C23
Instruments- Tambourines and/or Drums **Listen to How I Beat My Drum** **Clean Up**	C21, C27, L42, M41, M43, M44, SE 34, SE35, SE44 C28
Movement **Dance to the Music**	C23, M30
Body Parts/Gestures **The Body Language Song**	L17, L18, C23, C26, L31, SE48
Animals/Puppets **A Rustle in a Bush** **Clean Up**	C21, C25, C27, L42, L49, M41, M43, M44, SE34, SE35, SE44, SE47 C28
Body Parts **If I Arr a Pirate**	C23, L31, SE36
Emotions/Dramatic Play **The Emotion Song**	C23, SE36, SE43
Movement **The Bicycle**	L17, L18, C23, M30, SE36
Affection/Bonding **Do Wop Lullaby**	SE42, SE43
Goodbye Song **It's Time to Go** (using sign language)	L17, L18, L19, C23

ALPHABETICAL LYRIC AND CHORD SHEETS

"1, 2, 3, Play with Me" by Jessy Rushing

G7
1, 2, 3, can you play with me

G7
I'll tell you when, just listen

G7
Hold your instrument with all your might

G7
Get ready to play way up high!

      C7
And....PLAY

      G7
And....PLAY

      D7   C7
And....PLAY

      G7
And....PLAY

Optional actions:

Side to side

Super fast

Like a plane

To the sky

Soft as like a whisper

Other ideas: incorporate counting for anticipation of playing/stopping or, once they are familiar with the song, to let them know what is coming next.

"A Rustle in a Bush" by Jessy Rushing

```
        A       F#m     Bm      E
I heard a rustle in a bush

        A       F#m     Bm      E
I heard a rustle in a bush

        A       F#m     Bm      E
I heard a rustle in a bush and what did I see

        A
I saw a cat going meow, meow, meow

    F#m
I saw a dog going woof, woof, woof

    Bm
I saw a mouse going squeak, squeak ,squeak

            E-E7
That's what I saw.
```

I heard a noise in a barn

I heard a noise in a barn

I heard a noise in a barn and what did I see

I saw a pig going oink, oink, oink

I saw a hen going cluck, cluck, cluck

I saw a rooster going cock-a-doodle do

That's what I saw.

I heard a splash in a pond

I heard a splash in a pond

I heard a splash in a pond and what did I see

I saw a fish going glub, glub, glub

I saw a frog going ribbit, ribbit, ribbit

I saw a bee going buzz, buzz, buzz

That's what I saw.

I heard a sway in the jungle

I heard a sway in the jungle

I heard a sway in the jungle and what did I see

I saw a monkey going oooo ooo ahah eeee

I saw a giraffe going munch, munch, munch

I saw a snake going ssssss, ssssss, ssssss

That's what I saw.

"The Alphabet Song" Traditional Children's Song

```
A       D  A
A B C D E F G
```

```
E  A  E      A
H I J K L M N O P
```

```
A   DA  E
Q R S T U V
```

```
ADA      E
W X Y and Z
```

```
A            D    A
Now I know my A-B-Cs.
```

```
E        A      E    A
Next time won't you sing with me?
```

"Always in My Heart" by Jennifer Peyton

```
C                   G         F          C
You've got the sweetest eyes, and the cutest little smile

Am          Em        F              G7
I could hold you in my arms for the longest while

     C       G         F              C
Your belly full of laughs, your fingers and your toes

Am              Em        F           G7          F            G7
Where they all will take you, only Heaven knows (OR: no one really knows).


      F         C         F            C
Whenever you're awake, and even when you sleep

F            C          F          G7
You are making memories, forever mine to keep


C              G         F         C
I love all there is of you, every tiny part

Am          Em              F          G7
No matter how big you get, you're always in my heart

      F     G7    C
You are always in my heart.
```

"Animal Parade" by Jenn Batey   Capo 3

A   D
Here's what I'd do on my favorite day

    E7   A
I'd go to the zoo and watch a great parade

                      D
Not one of people, not one of cars

A   E7
The Animals, the Animals

                    A
They would be the stars...

            A
        1- went the octopus (1)

            D
        2- went the turtles (1-2)

            E7
        3- went the zebras (1-2-3)

            A
        4- went the flying birds (1-2-3-4)

            A
        5- went the monkeys (1-2-3-4-5)

            D
        6- went the elephants (123-456)

        E7   A
        7-8-9-10, let's count them once again

Repeat*

*Last time through ending:

        E7   A
        7-8-9-10 , and now my song is done.

"Animal Song" by Julie Avirett

D
I hear a cat. I hear a cat. I hear a cat.

                           A7
What do you think about that?

I hear her sing her little song

                   D
I hear her sing this song

         G
She goes a meow meow, meow

She goes a meow meow, meow

       D   A7
All day long singing this song.

D
I hear a dog. I hear a dog. I hear a dog.

                           A7
What do you think about that?

I hear him sing, his little song

                   D
I hear him sing this song

        G
He goes a woof, woof, woof

He goes a woof, woof, woof

       D   A7
All day long singing this song.

I hear a cow. I hear a cow. I hear a cow.

What do you think about that?

I hear her sing her little song

I hear her sing this song

She goes a moo, moo, moo

She goes a moo, moo, moo

All day long singing her song.

I hear a duck. I hear a duck. I hear a duck.

What do you think about that?

I hear him sing his little song

I hear him sing this song

He goes a quack, quack, quack

He goes a quack, quack, quack

All day long singing his song.

I hear a pig. I hear a pig. I hear a pig.

What do you think about that?

I hear him sing his little song

I hear him sing this song

He goes a oink, oink, oink

He goes a oink, oink, oink

All day long singing his song.

Doo, doo, doo, doo, doo, doot.

"The Ants Go Marching" Traditional Children's Song

Am   C
The ants go marching one by one, hurrah, hurrah

Am   C
The ants go marching one by one, hurrah, hurrah

                      G7   Am   E
The ants go marching one by one, the little one stops to suck his thumb

        C G7 Am   E   Am
And they all go marching down to the ground to get out of the rain,

(single note: E   F#   G#)
            BOOM! BOOM! BOOM!

The ants go marching two by two…The little one stops to tie his shoe…

The ants go marching three by three…The little one stops to climb a tree…

The ants go marching four by four…The little one stops to shut the door…

The ants go marching five by five…The little one stops to take a dive…

The ants go marching six by six…The little one stops to pick up sticks…

The ants go marching seven by seven…The little one stops to pray to heaven…

The ants go marching eight by eight…The little one stops to shut the gate…

The ants go marching nine by nine…The little one stops to check the time…

The ants go marching ten by ten…The little one stops to say "THE END"

And they all go marching down to the ground,

To get out of the rain, BOOM! BOOM! BOOM!

"The Ants Go Marching" *Shortened Version* Traditional Children's Song

Am   C
The ants go marching one by one, hurrah, hurrah

Am   C
The ants go marching two by two, hurrah, hurrah

                    G7   Am   E
The ants go marching three by three, the little one stops to climb a tree

        C G7 Am E   Am
And they all go marching down to the ground to get out of the rain,

(single note: E   F#   G#)
        BOOM! BOOM! BOOM!

Am   C
The ants go marching four by four, hurrah, hurrah

Am   C
The ants go marching five by five, hurrah, hurrah

                    G7   Am   E
The ants go marching six by six, the little one stops to pick up sticks

        C G7 Am E   Am
And they all go marching down to the ground to get out of the rain,

BOOM! BOOM! BOOM!

Am   C
The ants go marching seven by seven, hurrah, hurrah

Am   C
The ants go marching eight by eight, hurrah, hurrah

                    G7   Am   E
The ants go marching nine by nine, the little one stops to check the time

        C G7 Am E   Am
And they all go marching down to the ground to get out of the rain,

BOOM! BOOM! BOOM!

                    G7   Am   E
The ants go marching ten by ten, the little one stops to say "THE END!"

        C G7 Am E   Am
And they all go marching down to the ground to get out of the rain.

BOOM! BOOM! BOOM! BOOM! BOOM! BOOM! BOOM!

"The Bicycle" by Jenn Batey   Capo 2

Verse 1

```
    D  A      D  A     D  A
```
The bicycle, the bicycle the bicycle

```
A
```
He called out to the fast car, the fast car, the fast car

```
                    E7
```
He said I'm going to beat you, I'll beat you, I'll beat you

```
                      G
```
He said I'm going to try... Could he do it? NO

Verse 2

```
    D  A      D  A      D  A
```
The fast car, the fast car, the fast car

```
A
```
He called out to the steam train, the steam train, the steam train

```
                    E7
```
He said I'm going to beat you, I'll beat you, I'll beat you

```
                      G
```
He said I'm going to try... Could he do it? NO

(Verse 3 & 4 = same pattern)

The Steam Train- called out to the Airplane- Could he do it? NO

The Airplane called out to the Rocket- Could he do it? NO

Verse 5

The rocket, the rocket, the rocket,

He called out to the airplane, the airplane, the airplane,

He said I'm going to beat you, I'll beat you, I'll beat you

He said I'm going to try...Could he do it? YES!!!

Verse 6

The airplane, the airplane, the airplane,

He called out to the steam train, the steam train, the steam train

He said I'm going to beat you, I'll beat you, I'll beat you

He said I'm going to try...Could he do it? YES!!!

 (Verse 7 & 8= same pattern)

The steam train, called out to the fast car- Could he do it? YES!!!

The fast car, called out to the bicycle- Could he do it? YES!!!

"Big Bright Moon" by Julie Avirett

A D A   D   A
Big bright moon shining all around

   D   A   D   E
It illuminates the world for my precious little one.

 A D   A   D   A
It's time to dream and drift off to sleep

      D   A D   A
Thinking how would we love to play some more

       D   E   A
And dance upon the moon.

A D A   D   A
Big bright moon shining all around

D   A
Twinkling stars for you.

 D   E
Not a cloud in sight

A   D   A   D   A
Catch a falling star. Close your eyes where you are.

        D   A   D   A
Knowing when you wake, I'll be here for you

           D   E   A
With loving arms to hold you near.

"BINGO" Traditional Children's Song

C   F   C   G   C
There was a farmer had a dog, and Bingo was his name-o.

C   F
B - I - N - G - O.

G   C
B - I - N - G - O.

Am   F   G   C
B - I - N - G – O, and Bingo was his name-o!

"Birdie Beat" by Julie Avirett

A little birdie said to me while he was sitting in a tree

Beedee dee dee dee dee

Beedee dee dee dee dee.

A little birdie said to me while he was sitting in a tree

When he flies he feels free, whooeee

When he flies he feels free, whooeee.

A little birdie said to me while he was sitting in a tree

The whirling wind makes this sound, Swishoo

The whirling wind makes this sound, Swishoo.

Activities:

The primary goal is to exercise gross motor skills through moving both arms simultaneously to create the beat. Once children are able to replicate the rhythmic pattern with consistency, transition to exercising gross motor skills to create a flying movement with arms.

For younger children, the primary goal is to exercise verbal skills through singing the vowel sounds.

"Blow Me Some Bubbles" by Jessy Rushing

Capo 1

E   022100

Amaj7 x02120

Am   x02210

A2/F# 202200

C7   032310

(Verse 1)

E   Amaj7   E   Amaj7
Bubbles, blow me some bubbles

                             Am   E
They float through the air, at them I'll stare

E   Amaj7   E   Amaj7
Bubbles, blow me some bubbles

                 Amaj7   Am
They come in all different sizes, so full of surprises

(Chorus 1)

A2/F#
A bunch of little ones too many to count

   C7
Or one great big one-- watch it wobble about.

Bubbles, blow me some bubbles

All around the room, I'll watch them zoom

Bubbles, blow me some bubbles

I don't need a reason, bubbles are so pleasin'

The pop, pop, pop fills me with glee

Oh how much fun bubbles can be

Bubbles, blow me some bubbles

As the sun light beams, so many colors can be seen

Bubbles, blow me some bubbles

Just give a little blow, and round and round they'll go

On my finger I'll try to hold, the thing about the bubbles is they never get old

Oh bubbles!

"The Body Language Song" by Steve Sandler

G   D
Shrug your shoulders, you don't care

C   G
Lift your brows you're surprised what's there.

C   G   D   C   D G
Pat your tummy if you are full, wrinkle your nose and away we go.

CHORUS

C
Move, move your body,

G
Move, move your body,

D   C
Move, move your body,

D   G
And Stop! Here we go…

REPEAT

"Click! Click! Click! Go the Castanets" by Jennifer Peyton

A   E
Click! Click! Click! Go the castanets

          E7   A
Click! Click! Click! Go the castanets

          A7   D
Click! Click! Click! Go the castanets

A   E7   A   D   A
We make the castanets go click, click, click.

Boom, boom, boom goes the drum…

Rat tat tat goes the kokiriko…

Ring, ring, ring go the bells…

Jingle, jingle, jingle goes the tambourine…

Rattle, rattle, rattle go the shakers…

Scratch, scratch, scratch goes the guiro…

Scrape, scrape, scrape goes the cabasa…

"Dance to the Music" by Jenn Batey   Capo 2

D
Dance to the music, dance to the music

A   D
Dance to the music, dance to the music

D
Dance to the music, dance to the music

A   D (mute)
Dance until I say STOP AND FREEZE!

D
Jump to the music, jump to the music

A   D
Jump to the music, jump to the music

D
Jump to the music, jump to the music

A   D (mute)
Jump until I say STOP AND FREEZE!

D
Twist to the music, twist to the music

A   D
Twist to the music, twist to the music

D
Twist to the music, twist to the music

A   D (mute)
Twist until I say STOP AND FREEZE!

Other movements:

Turn

Walk

Reach up and down

Sway like a tree

Float like a leaf- float to the floor

"Doo Wop Love" by Judy Nguyen Engel

G7 C   Am   F   G7
Your laugh took me by surprise, the twinkle in your eye it's baby love ooh,

         C   Am   F   G7
The bounce in your step what a sight to see, your first words they call it love ooh,

      C   Am   F   G7
Can't get you out of my mind, ooh, ooh, sha la la la, wah, wah, wah

    C   Am   F   G7
Your smile melts my heart your funny ways, it's baby love ooh,

      C   Am   F   G7
The hugs you give so pure and sweet, just like your heart they call it love ooh,

      C   Am   F   G7
Can't get you out of my mind, ooh, ooh, sha la la la wah, wah, wah

     C Am   F   G7
Your little hands so curious, I am amazed it's baby love ooh,

     C   Am   F   G7
The simple things brings me joy, you're so much fun they call it love ooh,

     C   Am   F   G7 C
Can't get you out of my mind, ooh, ooh, sha la la la wah, wah, wah.

"Five Green and Speckled Frogs" Traditional Children's Song

G
Five green and speckled frogs

C
Sitting on a speckled log

G   D
Eating the most delicious bugs – Yum yum!

G
One jumped into the pool

C
Where it was nice and cool

G   D7   G
Now there are four speckled frogs – Glub glub!

Four green and speckled frogs…

Three green and speckled frogs…

Two green and speckled frogs…

One green and speckled frog…

…Now there are no more speckled frogs!

"Five Little Ducks" Traditional Children's Song

D   A
Five little ducks went out one day

A7   D
Over the hills and far away

D   A
Mama duck said, "Quack, quack, quack, quack,"

A7   G   A7   D
but only four little ducks came back...

Four little ducks...

Three little ducks...

Two little ducks...

One little duck...

"Five Little Monkeys" Traditional Children's Song

Chant

Five little monkeys jumpin' on the bed

One fell off and bumped his head.

Mama called the doctor and the doctor said,

"No more monkeys jumping on the bed!"

Four little monkeys...

Three little monkeys...

Two little monkeys...

One little monkey...

"Flower Power" by Jaden South

```
C         C
I am a lily, I am a rose

C                   G
I am a pansy, and I will grow

            F                   C
So give me water, water, water and sun, sun, sun


            G               C
And I will bloom and be so much fun.


C         C
I am a daisy, I am a mum

C                   G
I am a tulip, and bees will come.


            F                   C
So give me water, water, water and sun, sun, sun


            G                   C
And I will bloom and be so much fun.


C         C
I am an iris, I am a phlox

C                   G
I am a daffodil, and I will POP!


            F                       C
So give me water, water, water and sun, sun, sun


            G                   C
And I will bloom and be so much fun.
```

"Funga A La Feeya" Traditional Welome Chant   Ghana, West Africa

Chant

Fune-gah a la fee-yuh

Ah-shay ah-shay

Fune-gah a la fee-yuh

Ah-shay ah-shay

Cow-ah ey-lah-bah

Ah-shay ah-shay

Cow-ah ey-lah-bah

Ah-shay ah-shay

Translation:

I welcome you into

My heart today

I welcome you into

My heart today

"Going Over the Sea" Traditional Children's Song

C   G7   C
When I was one, I swallowed a bun, going over the sea.

                                                          G7   C
I jumped aboard a sailor ship and the sailor said to me.

Going over, going under, stand at attention, like a soldier,

          F   G7   C
With a one, two, three.

When I was two, I tied my shoe, going over the sea...

When I was three, I climbed a tree, going over the sea...

When I was four, I shut the door, going over the sea...

When I was five, I danced the jive, going over the sea...

When I was six, I picked up sticks, going over the sea...

When I was seven, I counted to eleven, going over the sea...

When I was eight, I learned to skate, going over the sea...

When I was nine, I towed the line, going over the sea...

When I was ten, I started again, going over the sea...

"Goodnight, My Sweet One" by Judy Nguyen Engel

```
D7     G                    Am            D7                        G
       Goodnight, my sweet one, close your eyes and dream a dream come true.


D7         G              Am            D7                      G
           Feel safe right in my arms, I'll hold you tight and keep you safe from harm.


D7     G                  Am           D                    G
       Goodnight, my sweet one, the day is done and time for sleep has come,


D7         G               Am          D                  G
           Sleep well, all through the night I will wake you in the early morn.


        C          Am           D              G
        I whisper softly in your ear, my hopes and dreams for you,


        C           Am                D          D7
        Quiet reflections of things hoped for and things not yet seen.


          G                Am              D             G
          Goodnight, my sweet one, the sun has set and now the moon will rise


D7         G           Am           D         G
           The sounds of the earth are still and quiet for the night.


          C          Am           D              G
          I whisper softly in your ear, my hopes and dreams for you


        C            Am                D          D7
        Quiet reflections of things hoped for and things not yet seen.


          G              Am             D7                       G
          Goodnight, my sweet one, close your eyes and dream a dream come true


D7         G               Am               D7                   G  C  G
           Feel safe right in my arms, I'll hold you tight and keep you safe from harm.
```

"Had a Little Rooster" Traditional Children's Song

```
G                                                      D
Had a little rooster by the barnyard gate, that little rooster was my playmate
G                     C
That little rooster went cock-a-doodle-doo,
      G          C        D        G
Dee-doodle-dee, doodle-dee, doodle-dee-doo.
G                                                D
Had a little cat by the barnyard gate, that little cat was my playmate
G
That little cat went meow, meow, meow
G                     C
That little rooster went cock-a-doodle-doo,
      G          C        D        G
Dee-doodle-dee, doodle-dee, doodle-dee-doo.
G                                                D
Had a little dog by the barnyard gate, that little dog was my playmate
G                                       D
That little dog went arf, arf, arf, that little cat went meow, meow, meow
G                     C
That little rooster went cock-a-doodle-doo,
      G          C        D        G
Dee-doodle-dee, doodle-dee, doodle-dee-doo.
```

Had a little duck by the barnyard gate, that little duck was my playmate

That little duck went quack, quack, quack, that little dog went arf, arf, arf,

That little cat went meow, meow, meow

That little rooster went cock-a-doodle-doo,

Dee-doodle-dee, doodle-dee, doodle-dee-doo.

Had a little pig by the barnyard gate, that little pig was my playmate

That little pig went oink, oink, oink, that little duck went quack, quack, quack,

That little dog went arf, arf, arf, that little cat went meow, meow, meow

That little rooster went cock-a-doodle-doo,

Dee-doodle-dee, doodle-dee, doodle-dee-doo.

Had a little sheep by the barnyard gate, that little sheep was my playmate,

That little sheep went baa, baa, baa, that little pig went oink, oink, oink,

That little duck went quack, quack, quack, that little dog went arf, arf, arf,

That little cat went meow, meow, meow

That little rooster went cock-a-doodle-doo,

Dee-doodle-dee, doodle-dee, doodle-dee-doo.

Had a little cow by the barnyard gate, that little cow was my playmate,

That little cow went moo, moo, moo, that little sheep went baa, baa, baa,

That little pig went oink, oink, oink, that little duck went quack, quack, quack,

That little dog went arf, arf, arf, that little cat went meow, meow, meow

That little rooster went cock-a-doodle-doo,

Dee-doodle-dee, doodle-dee, doodle-dee-doo.

Had a little horse by the barnyard gate, that little horse was my playmate,

That little horse went neigh, neigh, neigh, that little cow went moo, moo, moo,

That little sheep went baa, baa, baa, that little pig went oink, oink, oink,

That little duck went quack, quack, quack, that little dog went arf, arf, arf,

That little cat went meow, meow, meow

That little rooster went cock-a-doodle-doo,

Dee-doodle-dee, doodle-dee, doodle-dee-doo.

"Head, Shoulders, Knees, and Toes" Traditional Camp Song

G
Head, shoulders, knees and toes, knees and toes.

                          D
Head, shoulders, knees and toes, knees and toes.

    G   C
And eyes, and ears, and mouth, and nose.

D   G
Head, shoulders, knees and toes, knees and toes.

"Hello Mr. Animal" by Jennifer Peyton

```
G          C        G   C   D7  G
```
One day I was <u>walking</u> on a <u>farm</u>, and I saw a <u>pig</u>

```
              C            G   C   D7  G
```
He was <u>pink</u> and this is what he said: "<u>oink, oink, oink</u>"

```
              C      G  C   D7    G
```
So then I said, "Hello Mr. <u>Pig</u>! Hi my name is <u>Joey</u>."

```
                    C          G   C   D7  G
```
But he looked at me and this is what he said: "<u>oink, oink, oink</u>."

One day I was <u>swimming</u> in a <u>lake</u>, and I saw a <u>frog</u>

He was <u>green</u> and this is what he said: "<u>ribbit, ribbit, ribbit</u>"

So then I said, "Hello Mr. <u>Frog</u>! Hi my name is <u>Anne</u>"

But he looked at me and this is what he said: "<u>ribbit, ribbit, ribbit</u>."

One day I was <u>walking</u> in the <u>park </u>and I saw a <u>dog</u>

He was <u>brown</u> and this is what he said: "<u>ruff, ruff, ruff</u>"

So then I said, "Hello Mr. <u>Dog</u>! Hi my name is ____"

But he looked at me and this is what he said: "<u>ruff, ruff, ruff</u>."

One day I was <u>climbing </u>up a <u>tree</u> and I saw a <u>cat</u>

She was <u>grey</u> and this is what she said: "<u>meow, meow, meow</u>"

So then I said, "Hello Mrs. <u>Cat</u>! Hi my name is _____"

But she looked at me and this is what she said: "<u>meow, meow, meow</u>."

One day I was <u>splashing</u> in a <u>pond </u>and I saw a <u>duck</u>

She was <u>yellow</u> and this is what she said: "<u>quack, quack, quack</u>"

So then I said, "Hello, Mrs. <u>Duck</u>! Hi, my name is ____"

But she looked at me and this is what she said: "<u>quack, quack, quack</u>."

**Underlined words can be accompanied with sign language or can be illustrated for a picture book
**Illustrations available on pages 446-458

"Hello, Salutations" by Jessy Rushing


```
G        A    D   G
Hello, Hello, salutations
```

```
G        A            D
Hello, Hello, Hello, Hello
```

```
D            Dsus2/G  em        A
Let's make some music, do it my way
```

```
D        Dsus2/G      em   A
Pat your knees while your name I play
```

```
D      Dsus2/G em       A
Katie, Katie it's   nice to see you
```

```
D      Dsus2/G      em        A
Katie, Katie pat your knees with me.
```


```
:G      D: x2 A
```

```
     [motion]
```


```
G      A    D G
Hello, Hello, salutations
```

```
G        A            D
Hello, Hello, Hello, Hello
```

```
D            Dsus2/G  em        A
Let's make some music, do it my way
```

```
D        Dsus2/G      em    A
Blink your eyes while your name I play
```

```
D      Dsus2/G em         A
Sam, Sam it's     nice to see you
```

```
D      Dsus2/G      em        A
Sam, Sam blink your eyes with me.
```


```
:G      D: x2 A
```

```
     [motion]
```


Other movements: Nod your head, Tap your feet, Clap your hands

"(Here We Go) Loop De Loop" Traditional Children's Song

```
C                                    G7
Here we go loop de loop, here we go loop de lie
C                       G7          C
Here we go loop de loop, all on a Saturday night.
C
You put your right hand in, you take your right hand out
```

```
                                    G7          C
You give your hand a shake, shake, shake, and turn yourself about.
```

Here we go loop de loop, here we go loop de lie

Here we go loop de loop, all on a Saturday night.

You put your left hand in, you take your left hand out

You give your hand a shake, shake, shake, and turn yourself about.

Here we go loop de loop, here we go loop de lie

Here we go loop de loop, all on a Saturday night.

Other verses:

You put your right foot in

You put your left foot in

You put your whole self in

"Hokey Pokey" Traditional Children's Song

C
You put your right foot in.

You put your right foot out.

                           G
You put your right foot in and you shake it all about!

You do the Hokey Pokey and you turn yourself around.

                    C
That's what it's all about!

You put your left foot in…

You put your right arm in…

You put your left arm in…

You put your head in…

You put your whole self in…

"Hot Air Balloon" by Julie Avirett

```
G9                C9              G9
Let's go for ride in a hot air balloon

C9          Em7 D C9  G9
Just for the af-  ternoon

 G9                       C9           G9
I wonder what we'll see when we get up there

C9       Em7  D C  G
Let's go for   a  ride.
```

```
G9                  C9            G9
I see a big blue bird floating in the air

C          Em7 D    C9 G9
Free without      a  care

 G9                   C9                G9
I wonder what he sees when he's flying with me

C9       Em7     D C G
Let's go for  a  ride.
```

```
G9                        C9      G9
I see the bright yellow sun shining so high

C9      Em7 D   C9 G9
It's warming the  sky

 G9                 C9                    G9
I wonder what it sees when it's shining down on me

C9       Em7 D C G
Let's go for a ride,
```

```
C9       Em7 D C G
Let's go for a ride.
```

"How Will You Grow?" by Julie Avirett   Capo 4

```
G       D       G
I wonder how you'll grow

      C       G
And what will you know

          C       D
Will you be strong and brave

      G
Love to laugh and play

   C           D
Be kind to those in need?


G       D       G
I wonder how you'll grow

      C       G
And what will you know

          C    D
Will you chase butterflies

      G
Capture leaping frogs

   C               D
Find new adventures each day?


   C       D
The world is yours

      G
Reach for your dream

      C       D   G
But today your work is done

      C       D
So close your eyes

G
Know deep inside

      C       D   G
That I love you very much.
```

"Humpty Dumpty" Traditional Nursery Rhyme

Chant:

Humpty Dumpty sat on a wall,

Humpty Dumpty had a great fall.

All the King's horses, and all the King's men

Couldn't put Humpty together again!

"Hush Little Baby" Traditional Lullaby

D   A7   D
Hush, little baby, don't say a word, Mama's going to buy you a mockingbird.

                 A7   D
If that mockingbird won't sing, Mama's going to buy you a diamond ring.

                 A7   D
If that diamond ring turns brass, Mama's going to buy you a looking glass.

                 A7   D
If that looking glass gets broke, Mama's going to buy you a billy goat.

              A7   D
If that billy goat won't pull, Mama's going to buy you a cart and bull.

                 A7   D
If that cart and bull turn over, Mama's going to buy you a dog named Rover.

              A7
If that dog named Rover won't bark,

                        D
Mama's going to buy you a horse and cart.

              A7
If that horse and cart fall down,

                        D
You'll still be the sweetest little baby in town.

"I Can Name the Colors" by Jennifer Peyton

A   E
Colors, colors, I can name the colors

                E7   A
Colors, colors, you can name them, too.

A   E
<u>Red</u>, <u>red</u>, I know this is <u>red</u>

         E7   A
<u>Red</u>, <u>red</u>, see what I can do.

Orange, yellow, green, blue, purple, pink, white, brown, black, etc.

"I Feel Silly" by Jessy Rushing   4/4 each chord gets 2 beats

Intro: G C G C

```
G               C      G C        G C G  C
Sometimes from deep down inside, I feel silly
  G        C       G        C       G   C  G   C
It tingles in my fingers and tickles my toes I feel silly.
          D                   D
With my thumb on my nose I wiggle my hand
   C9              C9
I stick out my tongue as far as I can
       G  C  G  C
I feel silly.
```

Sometimes from deep down inside, I feel angry

It rumbles in my tummy and it makes me so mad, I feel angry

So scrunch my face nice and tight

Cross my arms left over right

I feel angry.

Sometimes from deep down inside, I feel happy

I may jump up and down or give a high five, I feel happy

I open my eyes big and wide

I give a great big smile from side to side

I feel happy.

Sometimes from deep down inside, I feel sad

I get kind of quiet and sometimes I cry, I feel sad

So cock my head down to the side

Stick out my lip and close my eyes

I feel sad.

Sometimes from deep down inside, I get excited

My body just wants to move, I am excited

So I throw my arms up in the air

And I wave them around like I just don't care

I get excited.

G C G C

       G C G C
I feel silly

       G C G   C
I feel angry

         D
I feel happy

        C9
I feel sad

       G C G   C   G
I get excited

"If All the Raindrops were Lemon Drops and Gum Drops" Traditional Children's Song

C   G7   C
If all of the raindrops were lemon drops and gum drops

          G7   C
Oh what a rain it would be!

C   G7   C   G7
I'd stand outside with my mouth open wide singing,

C   G7   C   G7
"Ah, ah, ah, ah, ah, ah, ah, ah, ah, ah."

C   G7   C
If all of the raindrops were lemon drops and gum drops,

          G7   C
Oh what a rain it would be!

"If I Arr a Pirate" by Jessy Rushing

A7 D   A7
If I arr a pirate as I might well be

A7
I'd have a **patch on my eye**

      D
Yes I'd have me

D   G
A patch on my eye and this is where it'd be

  D   A7   D
If I arr a pirate as I might well be

If I arr a pirate as I might well be

I'd have a **bandana on my head**

Yes I'd have me

A bandana on my head,

A patch on my eye, and this is where it'd be

If I arr a pirate as I might well be

If I arr a pirate as I might well be

I'd have a **parrot on my shoulder**

Yes I'd have me

A parrot on my shoulder,

A bandana on my head,

A patch on my eye, and this is where it'd be

If I arr a pirate as I might well be

Earring in my ear...

One wooden leg...

Sword on my hip...

372   Supplemental Materials

"If You're Happy and You Know It" Traditional Children's Song *Modified*

C   G7
If you're happy and you know it, clap your hands

                                          C
If you're happy and you know it, clap your hands

              F   C
If you're happy and you know it, then your face will surely show it

        G7   C
If you're happy and you know it, clap your hands.

If you're sad and you know it, say boo hoo (boo hoo!)

If you're sad and you know it, say boo hoo (boo hoo!)

If you're sad and you know it, then your face will surely show it

If you're sad and you know it, say boo hoo (boo hoo!).

If you're mad and you know it, say grrrr (grrrr!)

If you're mad and you know it, say grrrr (grrrr!)

If you're mad and you know it, then your face will surely show it

If you're mad and you know it, say grrrr (grrrr!).

If you're excited and you know it say hoo-ray (hoo-ray!)

If you're excited and you know it say hoo-ray (hoo-ray!)

If you're excited and you know it, then your face will surely show it

If you're excited and you know it say hoo-ray (hoo-ray!).

"I'm a Little Teapot" Traditional Children's Song

G
I'm a little teapot

C   G
Short and stout.

D7   G
Here is my handle

D7   G
Here is my spout.

G
When I get all steamed up

C   G
Here me shout,

 D7
"Tip me over and

      G
Pour me out."

"I'm the Sun" by Steve Sandler

```
G                       D
I'm the sun, I rise and chase away the dew

 C                                  G
I wake the noisy rooster, he screams cock a doodle doo

  C                      G
He wakes up your mom she stumbles out of bed

        D
Then she whispers in your ear, "Wake up my sleepy head!"

     C                      G
It's a special new day for the world, little friend

 D                      G
It never came before and will never come again

         C                  G
When the full moon rises and my shine slips away

    D
You'll fall asleep and dream of all the wonders of the day

       C                      G
When I rise again tomorrow and your Mommy wakens you

   Am                   G
I'll do my best to keep you warm in everything you do

  C              G
If clouds should come and rain drops fall

   Am                      D
I'm hiding just behind them, you don't even have to call

  C              G
I'll pop back out and try to make a shiny day

        D                  C  D  G
I'm the star shining brightest in your Milky Way

        D                  C  D  G
I'm the star shining brightest in your Milky Way.
```

"In My Own Little Way" by Jennifer Peyton

```
G     Em    C                 D
I love you, I know you love me, too

       G         Em    C           D
In my own little way, I tell you every day

          C           G
When I hug you real tight

          C           G
When I kiss you goodnight

          Em       C       D7     G
I love you, and I know you love me, too.
```

"It's Time for Parade" by Julie Avirett   (Q-Chord March background)

C
It's time for parade. Hip Hooray!

            G
It's time for parade today.

Wave your hands in the air.

          C
Wave your hands everywhere.

C
It's time for parade. Hip Hooray!

            G
It's time for parade today.

March along to our song.

            C
March your feet down the street.

C
It's time for parade. Hip Hooray!

            G
It's time for parade today.

Clap along to our song.

          C
Clap your hands on the beat.

C
It's time for parade. Hip Hooray!

            G
It's time for parade today.

Dance along to our song.

          C
Dance your feet down the street.

C
It's time for parade. Hip Hooray!

                                   G
It's time for parade today.

Grab an instrument. Make a song.

                                    C
Grab an instrument and play along.

C
It's time for parade. Hip Hooray!

                                   G
It's time for parade today.

Wave to a friend. It's near the end.

                           C
It's time for parade today.

                   G   C
It's time for parade today.

"It's Time to Go" author unknown   A capella with sign language

It's time to go

It's time to go

Will you wave goodbye?

Will you wave goodbye?

It's time to go

It's time to go

Will you wave goodbye?

And say goodbye?

"Itsy Bitsy Spider" Traditional Nursery Rhyme

D
The itsy bitsy spider

     A7   D
Crawled up the water spout

Down came the rain

     A7   D
And washed the spider out

Out came the sun

     A7   D
And dried up all the rain

And the itsy bitsy spider

     A7   D
Crawled up the spout again.

"I've Been Working on the Railroad" Traditional Folk Song

G   C   G
I've been working on the railroad, all the livelong day

G   A7   D7
I've been working on the railroad, just to pass the time away

                         G   C   B7
Can't you hear the whistle blowing? Rise up so early in the morn

C   G   D7   G
Can't you hear the captain shouting, "Dinah, blow your horn."

G   C
Dinah, won't you blow, Dinah, won't you blow

D7   G
Dinah, won't you blow your horn?

G   C
Dinah, won't you blow, Dinah, won't you blow

D7   G
Dinah, won't you blow your horn?

G
Someone's in the kitchen with Dinah

                         D7
Someone's in the kitchen I know

G   C
Someone's in the kitchen with Dinah

 D7   G
Strumming on the old banjo. And singing

Fie, fi, fiddly i o

              D7
Fie, fi, fiddly i o

G   G7 C
Fie, fi,   fiddly i o

D7   G
Strumming on the old banjo.

"Kemo Kimo" Appalachian Folk Song

C
A froggie went a courting and he did ride

       D7   G
King kong kitchie kitchie ki-me-o

      C
With a sword and a pistol by his side

       G7   C
King kong kitchie kitchie ki-me-o

CHORUS

C
Ki-mo-ke-mo Ki-mo-ke

F   D7   G
Way down yonder in a hollow tree

      C
With an owl and a bat and a bumble bee

       G7   D
King kong kitchie kitchie ki-me-o

He rode until he came to Miss Mousie's door
King kong kitchie kitchie ki-me-o
And there he knelt upon the floor
King kong kitchie kitchie ki-me-o

CHORUS

He took Miss Mouse upon his knee
King kong kitchie kitchie ki-me-o
And he said little mouse will you marry me
King kong kitchie kitchie ki-me-o

CHORUS

They went to the park on the very next day
King kong kitchie kitchie ki-me-o
And left on their honeymoon right away
King kong kitchie kitchie ki-me-o

CHORUS

Now they live far off in a hollow tree...

Where they now have wealth and children three...

"Kookabura" Traditional Australian Children's Song

```
C          F       C
Kookabura sits in the old gum tree.

C             G7        C
Merry, merry king of the bush is he.

F                C
Laugh, Kookabura! Laugh, Kookabura!

C
Gay your life must be.

C          F       C
Kookabura sits in the old gum tree,

C             G7      C
Eating all the gumdrops he can see.

F                C
Stop, Kookabura! Stop, Kookabura!

C
Leave some there for me!
```

"La La La Lullaby" by Jenn Batey   Capo 3

Finger pick:

Intro

```
C                 F         C    G
La la la la, La la la la, La la la la Oh Lullaby

      C         F          C       G    C
La la la la, La la la la, I'm going to sing you a lullaby...

C                         Cmaj7
I like to kiss you, I love to hold you

      Em7                F
I love to tell you that you are mine

        C                 Cmaj7
I love to hug you, I want to be with you

        G                 F    Fsus F
I'm going to tell you all of the time....
```

Strum:

```
C       Cmaj7    G    F        C    Cmaj7
That I love you, that I love you, that I love you

              G                F   Fsus F
I'm going to love you all of the time.
```

Finger pick:

```
          C                Cmaj7
On days you're great, on days you're good

        Em7              F
On days you don't do what you should

        C                 Cmaj7
I'm going to love you, I'm going to see you through

        G                 F   Fsus F
I'm going to help you out all of the time.... because
```

Strum:

```
C    Cmaj7      G    F          C    Cmaj7
I love you, because I love you, because I love you,

  G              F   Fsus F
I Love you all of the time... Repeat La La La Intro
```

"Leader of the Band" by Darcy Walworth

```
C                 G7
```
<u>Susie</u> is the leader of the band,

```
                  C
```
<u>Susie</u> is the leader of the band

```
C7                F
```
<u>Susie</u> is the leader of the band,

```
      C     G7    C    F    C
```
She tells us when to start and stop

Start!..............Stop!

<u>Ethan</u> is the leader of the band,

<u>Ethan</u> is the leader of the band

<u>Ethan</u> is the leader of the band,

She tells us when to start and stop

Start!..............Stop!

*Fill in the blank with different names or the MT's name for different verses

"Let's Get Ready" by Jennifer Peyton

Tune: "Here We Go 'Round the Mulberry Bush"

C   G7   C
Let's get ready to <u>play the drum</u>, <u>play the drum</u>, <u>play the drum</u>

                                     G7   C
Let's get ready to <u>play the drum</u>, here we go.

This is how to <u>play the drum</u>, <u>play the drum</u>, <u>play the drum</u>

This is how to <u>play the drum</u>, this is how.

Together we can <u>play the drum</u>, <u>play the drum</u>, <u>play the drum</u>

Together we can <u>play the drum</u>, <u>play the drum.</u>

Let's get ready to: clean up, pick up toys, brush our hair/teeth, say goodbye, etc.

"Let's Go for a Ride" by Julie Avirett   (Q-Chord Dance background)

F
Let's go for a ride

   C
Let's head outside

Feel in the wind in our face

    F
Blowing in our hair

Ready, Set, Go

F
Broom, broom, broom,

Broom, broom, broom,

     C
Let me hear you go zoom, zoom, zoom,

     F
Let me hear you go zoom, zoom, zoom.

"Listen to How I Beat My Drum" by Jenn Batey A capella with a tambourine or drum

CHORUS

Listen to how I beat my drum

I'm telling you a story

Listen to how I beat my drum

I'm telling you how I would go.

VERSE 1

If I were a snake, I'd go slither, slithering through the town

(Repeat)

CHORUS

VERSE 2

If I were a turtle, I'd stroll along, slowly, slowly moving

If I were a turtle, I'd stroll along, slowly through the town.

CHORUS

VERSE 3

If I were a horse, I'd giddy app, galloping, galloping giddy app

Galloping, galloping giddy app, galloping through the town.

CHORUS

VERSE 4

If I were a cheetah, I'd run so fast, I'd be the fastest runner

If I were a cheetah, I'd run so fast, running through the town.

CHORUS

VERSE 5

If I were an elephant, I'd take big steps

Pounding, pounding, pounding

If I were an elephant I'd take big steps

Pounding through the town.

"Little Red Caboose" Traditional Children's Song

C
Little red caboose chug, chug, chug.

Little red caboose chug, chug, chug.

            G7
Little red caboose behind the train, train, train, train.

Smokestack on her back, back, back, back.

Comin' down the track, track, track, track.

            C
Little red caboose behind the train. Whoo! Whoo!

*For a variation of this song listen to Lisa Loeb's version on the album:

"Catch the Moon"

"London Bridge Is Falling Down" Traditional Nursery Rhyme

C
London bridge is falling down,

G7   C
Falling down, falling down,

C
London bridge is falling down,

G7   C
My fair lady.

"Look in the Mirror" by Steve Sandler

```
C                          F
I look in the mirror and what do I see?
             C                     F    C  G
Why it's me, yes it's me looking back at me.
        C               F   C    G    C              F   C  G
I see two eyes and a mouth and a nose, I see two feet with 10 little toes.
          C                      F
You look in the mirror and what does it do?
        C                    G
It has a perfect picture of you, yes it's you.
            C              F   C      G
You see two ears on the sides of your head
          C                F   C    G
That help you hear everything that is said.
          C                     F
We look in the mirror and what do we see?
              C                      G
Why it's us, yes it's us, we're happy as can be.
            C          F     C    G
We have two eyes a mouth and a nose.
            C                      F   C   G
We each have two feet with ten little toes.
            C                   F   C    G
We both have ears on the sides of our head
            C                F    C    G
That help us hear everything that is said.
              C                          F
We're kind of the same but we're different you and me
            C                  G
Just look in the mirror and you will see.
            C                  F    C   G
We both have two eyes a mouth and a nose
            C              F    C    G
And two little feet with ten little toes.
```

```
    C                   F   C    G
We both have ears on the sides of our head

      C                                  F   C    G
But our mommies know the difference when they put us in bed.

      C                            F   C    G
Our mommies know the difference when they put us in bed.

       C                          F   C    G
Yes, daddies know the difference when they put us in bed.
```

"Marty Monkey" by Jenn Batey   Capo 3

A   D   A E7
Marty Monkey ate bananas

      A   D   A   E7
That grew up in a banana tree.

A   D   A   E7
When he was hungry he would climb up

                                    A
Up and up and up the banana tree.

          A   D   A   E7
          1-2-3-4-5-6-7-8

          A   D   A E7 A
          1-2-3-4-5-6-7-8

A   D   A E7
Marty Monkey ate bananas

      A   D A   E7
That grew up in a banana tree,

        A   D   A   E7
And when he finished eating the bananas

                          A
He'd climb down the banana tree.

          A   D   A   E7
          8-7-6-5-4-3-2-1

          A   D   A E7 A
          8-7-6-5-4-3-2-1

A   D   A E7
Marty Monkey ate bananas

        A   D A   E7
That grew up in a banana tree.

    A   D   A   E7
When he finished eating the bananas

                              A
He'd take a nap on the jungle leaves (x2)

A D   A E7   A   D A E7 A
1-2-3-4-5-6-7-8   8-7-6-5-4-3-2-1

**Illustrations available on pages 459-462

"Mister Golden Sun" Traditional Children's Song

C   F
Mister Sun, Sun, Mister Golden Sun

G7   C
Please shine down on me.

C   F
Mister Sun, Sun, Mister Golden Sun

G7
Hiding behind a tree.

C   G7
These little children are asking you

     C   G7
To please come out so we can play with you.

      C   F
Mister Sun, Sun, Mister Golden Sun

G7   C
Please shine down on me.

Supplemental Materials

"Monkey Moves!" by Jaden South   INTRO: G C G D x2

```
        G              C
Can you jump? Can you groove?

     G        D      G
If you can, do the monkey move!

        G              C
Can you hop? Can you spin?

     G        D    G
If you can, do the monkey grin!

        G            C
Can you sway? Can you sleep?

     G        D       G
If you can, do the monkey squeak!

        G            C
Can you swing? Can you glide?

     G        D       G
If you can, do the monkey slide!

        G        C
So if you can, do it again

        G      D      G
And you are our monkey friends!
```

REPEAT

"Mood Groove" by Julie Avirett   (Basic blues progression throughout)

Chorus

E   E7
We're doing our mood, mood groove, doo doo doo doo doo

A7   E
'Cause I have so many feelings

B7   E
Come on and join our groove.

E   E7
Some days I'm happy

A7   E
Some days I'm happy

B7   A7   E   E   E
When I'm happy I like to laugh, "Haa haa haa Haa haa haa." (Repeat Chorus)

Some days I feel sad

Some days I feel so sad

When I'm sad I cry, "Boo hoo, Boo hoo." (Repeat Chorus)

Other days I'm silly

Other days I'm silly

When I'm silly I make a funny sound Bliop, Bliop. (Repeat Chorus)

Other days I worry

Other days I worry

When I worry I frown, Oh no, Oh no! (Repeat Chorus)

And some days I get real mad

Some days I get stomp'n mad

When I'm mad I like to yell, "Ahh Ahh." (Repeat Chorus)

Tag to end

B7   E   E7 E
Come and join our groove.

"The More We Get Together" Traditional Nursery Rhyme

C
The more we get together,

  G7   C
Together, together,

C
The more we get together,

   G7   C
The happier we'll be.

  G7   C
For your friends are my friends,

   G7   C
And my friends are your friends.

C
The more we get together,

   G7   C
The happier we'll be!

"Mouse in My House" by Jenn Batey   Capo 3

CHORUS

```
C      G         C          F         C      G    F
```
There is a mouse in my house, house, house and I don't know what to do

```
      C      G          C     F      C    G      C
```
So I'll paint him a picture of the way back home and this is what he'll see...

VERSE 1 Am   Em   F   C
Green is the grass in the countryside, green is the color of the leaves

```
      Am              Em      F              G
```
Yellow is the sun in the afternoon and, yellow are the bumblebees...

CHORUS

VERSE 2 Am   Em   F   C
Red are tomatoes on the vine and red are the ladybugs

```
      Am              Em      F              G
```
Blue is the color of the sky and blue is the color of the sea, ohh...

CHORUS

VERSE 3

White are the clouds in the sky above, soft and light and clean...

Brown is the color of the mud and brown are the chipmunks, ohh...

CHORUS

VERSE 2

Pink are the flowers in the fields and purple are the flowers, too

Orange are the pumpkins and tangerines and orange are the oranges too, ohh...

ENDING:

```
C      G         C          F         C      G    F
```
There is a mouse in my house, house, house and I know just what to do

```
C          G        C    F      C      G     C  F C
```
The mouse, mouse, mouse can have the house- I'm going outside to play.

**Illustrations available on pages 463-467

"Move Your Scarves" by Jenn Batey   Capo 3 or 4

Move your scarves up and down, up and down, in the air

    Make a circle - make a circle

    Make a circle - in the air

Move your scarves up and down, up and down, in the air

    Throw your scarves- higher, higher

    Throw your scarves- in the air

    When it falls down, catch it, catch it, catch it, catch it, in the air

Move your scarves up and down, up and down, in the air.

    Other movements:

    Hide it, find it   Take it swimming

    Shake your scarf   Sway ...

"My Favorite Spot" by Julie Avirett

C   F
When the weather is hot and the sun is out

G   C
I like to go down to my favorite spot.

CHORUS

C
Singing la da da da

F
La da da dee

G   C
Bah da bah da bah da

G   C
Bah da.

C   F
I look around fine a spot on the ground

G   C
Pull out my chair and smell the ocean air.

CHORUS

C   F
I hear the waves go in and the waves go out

G   C
I love to be in my favorite spot.

CHORUS

C   F
Look there in the air

```
G              C
Dolphins are jumping everywhere.
```

CHORUS

```
C            F
I see some sand and I want to play

G             C
I make a castle for the rest of the day.
```

CHORUS

```
C              F
The warmth of the sun is fading away

G                 C
I must pack my things and get on my way.
```

CHORUS

```
G  C
Bah da

G  C
Bah da

G  C
Bah da.
```

The primary goal for **"My Favorite Spot" is vocalization of vowel sounds. The pauses between verses create opportunities for absorption of new material, imitation of vowel sounds, and imitation of rhythmic response.

**A baby ocean drum can be utilized to focusing on tracking and/or imitating simple rhythmic patterns. Scarves are another visual stimuli to encourage tracking and rhythmic movement.

**The Q-Chord with rhythm cartridge on beat 14 can be used to create background sound.

Illustrations available on pages 467-470

"My Hand on My Head" Traditional Irish Children's Song

C   G7   C
My hand on my **head**, what have I here? This is my top-notcher, my Mama dear
C   G7
Top-notcher, top-notcher, Dickey, dickey doo,

G7   C (pat   pat)
That's what I learned in my school. Boom! Boom! (slap thighs)

My hand on my **eye**, what have I here? This is my eye blinker, my Mama dear

Eye blinker, top-notcher, Dickey, dickey doo

That's what I learned in my school. Boom! Boom! (slap thighs)

My hand on my **nose**, what have I here? This is my smell sniffer, my Mama dear

Smell sniffer, eye blinker, top-notcher, Dickey, dickey doo

That's what I learned in my school. Boom! Boom! (slap thighs)

My hand on my **mouth**, what have I here? This is my food grinder, my Mama dear

Food grinder, smell sniffer, eye blinker, top-notcher, Dickey, dickey doo

That's what I learned in my school. Boom! Boom!

My hand on my **knee**, what have I here? This is my knee bender, my Mama dear

Knee bender, food grinder, smell sniffer, eye blinker, top-notcher, Dickey, dickey doo

That's what I learned in my school. Boom! Boom! (slap thighs)

My hand on my **foot**, what have I here? This is my foot stomper, my Mama dear

Foot stomper, knee bender, food grinder, smell sniffer, eye blinker, top-notcher,

Dickey, dickey doo, that's what I learned in my school. Boom! Boom! (slap thighs)

"My Right Hand Says Hello" by Darcy Walworth

D   A7
Hello, <u>Gracie</u>, how are you today?

                                  D
My right hand says hello and is giving you a wave!

             A7
Hello, <u>Gracie</u>, how are you today?

                  D
My right hand is waving hello!

Hello, <u>Ben</u>, how are you today?

My right hand says hello and is giving you a wave!

Hello, <u>Ben</u>, how are you today?

My right hand is waving hello!

*Fill in the blank with each child's name

"Never Let Me Go" by Jenn Batey   Capo 2 or 3 (finger pick)

A
Hold me and want me and tell me you love me

   E   A
And never let me go.

A
Kiss me and hug me and squeeze me and tell me

    E   A
You'll never let me go.

      D
Lead me I'll follow

        A
And love me tomorrow

      D   E
But kiss me just for today.

A
I'll hold you, I'll want you, I'll tell you I love you

   E   A
I'll never let you go.

      D
Follow me I'll lead you

        A
And love you tomorrow

      D   E
But kiss me just for today.

A
Hold me and want me and tell me you love me

   E   A
And never let me go.

"Oh Where Has My Little Dog Gone?" Traditional Nursery Rhyme

C   G7
Oh where, oh where has my little dog gone?

                                 C
Oh where, oh where can he be?

                             G7
With his ears cut short and his tail cut long

                             C
Oh where, oh where can he be?

"Old MacDonald" Traditional Children's Song


```
C              F    C      G7 C
Old MacDonald had a farm, Ee i ee i oh!

                   F       C          G7 C
And on that farm he had some chickens, Ee i ee i oh!

C
With a cluck-cluck here, and a cluck-cluck there

C
Here a cluck, there a cluck, Everywhere a cluck-cluck

              F    C      G7 C
Old MacDonald had a farm Ee i ee i oh!

                   F       C       G7 C
And on that farm he had some dogs, Ee i ee i oh!

C
With a woof-woof here, and a woof-woof-woof there

C
Here a woof, there a woof, everywhere a woof-woof

              F          G7  C
Old MacDonald had a farm, Ee i ee i oh!

                   F       C       G7  C
And on that farm he had some cows, Ee i ee i oh!

C
With a moo-moo here, and a moo-moo there

C
Here a moo, there a moo, everywhere a moo-ooo

              F          G7  C
Old MacDonald had a farm, Ee i ee i oh!
```


Other Animals: cats, geese, goats, horses, pigs, roosters, sheep

"One, Two, Buckle My Shoe" Traditional Nursery Rhyme

Chant

One, two, buckle my shoe

Three, four, shut the door

Five, six, pick up sticks

Seven eight, lay them straight

Nine, ten, let's do it again!

"The Owl" by Julie Avirett   Capo 1st Fret

D   A7   D
Hoo Hoo, Hoo Hoo, Hoo Hoo, says the owl

D   A7   D
Hoo Hoo, Hoo Hoo, Hoo Hoo, says the owl

D
And she flies so high

Soaring through the sky,

D   A7   D
Hoo Hoo, Hoo Hoo, Hoo Hoo, says the owl

"Pajarito" Traditional Mexican Children's Song

Verse 1
```
G      C      G  C      D  C      G
```
Pajarito Cantas Tu, Cantas Tu, Cantas Tu

```
G        C      G   C      D  G
```
Pajarito Cantas Tu, Cantas Para Mi

Verse 2
```
G      C      G  C      D  C      G
```
Pajarito Vuelas Tu, Vuelas Tu, Vuelas Tu

```
G        C      G  C      D   G
```
Pajarito Vuelas Tu, Vuelas Para Mi

Verse 3
Pajarito Comes Tu

Verse 4
Pajarito Besas Tu

Verse 5
Pajarito Saltas Tu

Verse 6
Pajarito Duermes Tu

Verse 7
Pajarito Dispierta Tu

Translation:

Little bird sing to us, sing to us, sing to us

Little bird sing to us, sing with me

Verse 2- Fly

Verse 3- Eat

Verse 4- Kiss

Verse 5- Hop

Verse 6- Sleep

Verse 7- Wake up

"Pat a Cake" Traditional Nursery Rhyme

Chant

Pat a cake, pat a cake, baker's man

Bake me a cake as fast as you can

Roll it, pat it, and mark it with a B

And put it in the oven for baby and me!

"Peek-A-Boo" by Julie Avirett

G   D
I love you. Yes I do. I gotta game that's just for you.

G
Close your eyes and a big surprise

D   G
Here we go!

            D   G
Peek-A-Boo Peek-A-Boo Peek-A-Boo

D   G
I love you!

"Pitter Patter" by Julie Avirett

A
Pitter patter rain is coming down.

            E   A
Pitter patter falling to the ground.

A
Pitter patter makin' things new.

             E   A   A E A
Pitter patter little song for you.

A
Splish splash playin' in the water.

           E   A
Splish splash stompin in the mud.

A
Splish splash havin' so much fun.

         E   A   A E A
Splish splash until the rain is done.

Activities:
Finger movement to represent falling rain, pitter patter, and splish splash are utilized to exercise fine motor skills. A rainstick may be incorporated to increase sensory awareness, increase tracking visual stimuli, and exercise gross motor skills. Feet stomping can be included to increase attention to task, group listening, and increase motor skills. In addition using finger, hands, and feet enhance a child's ability to identify body part and increase language.

"Playing Along" by Judy Nguyen Engel

A7   D   E7
       Come play along with me; come join the fun with me,

   A7   D
We can play anyway we wanna play

A7   D   G
       Come play along with me, pretend along with me

   A7   D
We can do anything we wanna do.

                            G A7 D
Walking on the moon, bouncing up and down

A7   D
Swimming underwater with fishes in the sea

                            G A7 D
Climbing up a mountain, stretch my arms up high

A7   D
Tiptoe in the forest looking out for deer.

A7   D   E7
       Come play along with me; come join the fun with me,

   A7   D
We can play anyway we wanna play

A7   D   G
       Come play along with me, pretend along with me

   A7   D
We can do anything we wanna do.

                            G A7 D
Rowing the boat, going fast upstream

A7   D
Casting your rod, like a fisherman

                          G   A7 D
Hopping on lily pads, like the green, green frog

A7   D
Flying through the sky, like an aeroplane.

A7   D   E7
     Come play along with me; come join the fun with me,

   A7   D
We can play anyway we wanna play

A7   D   G
     Come play along with me, pretend along with me

   A7   D G A7 D-A7-D
We can do anything we wanna do.

"Pollito, Chicken" Traditional Spanish Song

G   D7
Pollito, chicken; Gallina, hen.

                           G
Lapiz, pencil, y Pluma, pen.

                           D7
Ventana, window; Puerta, door.

                        G
Maestra, teacher, y Piso, floor.

G   D7
Pollito, chicken; Gallina, hen.

                           G
Lapiz, pencil, y Pluma, pen.

                           D7
Ventana, window; Puerta, door.

                        G
Maestra, teacher, y Piso, floor.

"Razzle Dazzle 'Em" by Judy Nguyen Engel

A
Let's get together and razzle dazzle 'em

E7
Let's get together and razzle dazzle 'em

A   E7   A
Let's get together and razzle dazzle 'em, razzle dazzle 'em now!

                        E7   A
Razzle them playing <u>fast</u>! Razzle them playing <u>slow</u>!

                        E7   A
Razzle them playing <u>up</u>! Razzle them playing <u>down</u>!

Let's get together and razzle dazzle 'em

E7
Let's get together and razzle dazzle 'em

A   E7   A
Let's get together and razzle dazzle 'em, razzle dazzle 'em now!

*underlined, replace with variety of actions

"Row, Row, Row Your Boat" Traditional Nursery Rhyme

A
Row, row, row your boat

Gently down the stream.

Merrily, merrily, merrily, merrily

E   A
Life is but a dream.

"Shake, Shake, Shake!" by Darcy Walworth

C
You've gotta shake, shake, shake!

                     G7
You've gotta shake, shake, shake!

            C
You've gotta shake, shake, shake!

G7   C
Shake it all the day long!

C
You've gotta shake it way up high!

                     G7
You've gotta shake it way up high!

           C
You've gotta shake it way up high!

G7   C
Shake it all the day long!

Other verses:

You've gotta shake it way down low…

You've gotta shake it to the right…

You've gotta shake it to the left…

You've gotta shake it all around

"Siyahamba" Traditional South African Song

C
Siyahamba kukhenyeni kwenkhos'

   G   C
Siyahamba kukhenyeni kwenkhos'

C
Siyahamba kukhenyeni kwenkhos'

   G   C C7
Siyahamba kukhenyeni kwenkhos'

F   C
Siyahamba oh oh Siyahamba oh oh

   G   C C7
Siyahamba kukhenyeni kwenkhos'

F   C
Siyahamba oh oh Siyahamba oh oh

   G   C
Siyahamba kukhenyeni kwenkhos'.

"Skip to My Lou" Traditional Folk Song

C
Skip, skip, skip to my Lou.

G
Skip, skip, skip to my Lou.

C
Skip, skip, skip to my Lou.

G   C
Skip to my Lou my darlin'.

C
Flies in the buttermilk, Shoo fly, shoo!

G
Flies in the buttermilk, Shoo fly, shoo!

C
Flies in the buttermilk, Shoo fly, shoo!

G   C
Skip to my Lou my darlin'.

"Soon the Moon Will Rise" by Steve Sandler

```
Bm7                 C     G        C
Soon the moon will rise, time for a lullabye

   Bm7              C             D
She stirs our dreams and gently lights the evening skies.


   Bm7            Em   Bm7           C
Soon the moon will glow, different each time she shows

   Bm7          C              D
So many shapes she knows, where do the slivers go?


   Bm7          C     G        C
Soon the moon will disappear, silent as she goes

   Bm7          C        D
Soon the moon will rise and fast asleep you'll go.


  Bm7           Cmaj7
Soon the moon will rise,

Bm7            Em
Soon the moon will rise,

Bm7           Cmaj7
Soon the moon will rise

        C D      G
And fast asleep you'll go.
```

"Ten in the Bed" Traditional Nursery Rhyme

C
There were ten in a bed and the little one said, "Roll over, roll over."

                       G7   C
So they all rolled over and one fell out.

C
There were nine in a bed and the little one said, "Roll over, roll over."

                       G7   C
So they all rolled over and one fell out.

There were eight in a bed and the little one said, "Roll over, roll over."

So they all rolled over and one fell out.

There were seven in a bed and the little one said, "Roll over, roll over."

So they all rolled over and one fell out.

There were six in a bed and the little one said, "Roll over, roll over."

So they all rolled over and one fell out.

There were five in a bed and the little one said, "Roll over, roll over."

So they all rolled over and one fell out.

There were four in a bed and the little one said, "Roll over, roll over."

So they all rolled over and one fell out.

There were three in a bed and the little one said, "Roll over, roll over."

So they all rolled over and one fell out.

There were two in a bed and the little one said, "Roll over, roll over."

So they all rolled over and one fell out.

                                        F G C
There was one in a bed and the little one said, "Good night!"

"There's a Tickle Under My Skin" by Jessy Rushing

(*Starting at a slower tempo*)

A
There's a tickle forming under my skin

         D   A
There's an itch, and it's comin' from within

         A7   dm
I got a tingle under my toes...(pause)

(*Increase tempo*)

NC   A   E7   A
I've got to move, it's time to go

A
Clap your hands, to the beat

A   E7   A
Clap your hands, as you move your feet

A   A7   dm
Clap your hands, when the moment is right

A   E7   A
Clap your hands, when the urge you can't fight.

More Actions:

Stomp your feet

Wave your arms

Shake your hips

Jump in place

"This is How I Look" by Jennifer Peyton

A   E7
This is how I look when I am <u>sad</u>:   (*make corresponding face*)

                              A
This is how I look when I am <u>sad</u>:   (*make corresponding face*)

 D   A
I make a face to show you what I feel inside

 E   E7   A
I make a face I cannot hide.   (*make corresponding face*)

This is how I look when I am: glad, mad, scared, etc.

This is how I look when I'm: surprised, confused, etc.

"This is How We Rock" by Judy Nguyen Engel

```
C                     Am
This is how we rock; this is how we roll

F             G7                           C
This is how we stop ------- and this is how we stroll.

C     Am    F     G7   C   Am     F      G7
Rock,  roll,  stop,  stroll... rock, roll,   stop,   stroll!

C                     Am
This is how we rock; this is how we roll

F             G7                           C
This is how we stop ------ and this is how we stroll

C     Am    F     G7   C   Am     F      G7
Rock,  roll,  stop,  stroll... rock, roll,   stop,   stroll!

C                     Am
This is how we rock; this is how we roll.

F             G7                           C
This is how we stop ------- and this is how we stroll.
```

"This Old Man" Traditional Nursery Rhyme

G   C   D
This old man, he played one, he played knick-knack on my thumb
G   C   D   G
With a knick-knack paddywhack, give a dog a bone, this old man came rolling home.

This old man, he played two, he played knick-knack on my shoe

With a knick-knack paddywhack, give a dog a bone, this old man came rolling home.

This old man, he played three, he played knick-knack on my knee

With a knick-knack paddywhack, give a dog a bone, this old man came rolling home.

This old man, he played four, he played knick-knack on my door

With a knick-knack paddywhack, give a dog a bone, this old man came rolling home.

This old man, he played five, he played knick-knack on my hive

With a knick-knack paddywhack, give a dog a bone, this old man came rolling home.

This old man, he played six, he played knick-knack on my sticks

With a knick-knack paddywhack, give a dog a bone, this old man came rolling home.

This old man, he played seven, he played knick-knack up in heaven

With a knick-knack paddywhack, give a dog a bone, this old man came rolling home.

This old man, he played eight, he played knick-knack on my gate

With a knick-knack paddywhack, give a dog a bone, this old man came rolling home.

This old man, he played nine, he played knick-knack on my spine

With a knick-knack paddywhack, give a dog a bone, this old man came rolling home.

This old man, he played ten, he played knick-knack once again

With a knick-knack paddywhack, give a dog a bone, this old man came rolling home.

"Tingalayo" Traditional West Indies Folk Song

```
G   C G D           G
```
Tingalayo, run my little donkey run.

```
G   C G D           G
```
Tingalayo, run my little donkey run.

```
            C           G
```
My donkey walk, my donkey talk,

```
            D           G
```
My donkey eat with a knife and fork.

```
            C           G
```
My donkey walk, my donkey talk,

```
            D           G
```
My donkey eat with a knife and fork.

```
G   C G D           G
```
Tingalayo, run my little donkey run.

```
G   C G  D          G
```
Tingalayo, run my little donkey run.

```
            C           G
```
My donkey eat, my donkey sleep,

```
            D           G
```
Don't get too close to his hind feet.

```
            C           G
```
My donkey eat, my donkey sleep,

```
            D           G
```
Don't get too close to his hind feet.

```
G   C G D           G
```
Tingalayo, run my little donkey run.

Tingalayo, run my little donkey run.

Tingalayo, run my little donkey run.

Tingalayo, run my little donkey run.

"Tree Hugs" by Jaden South

VERSE 1

```
C            F
Big and green, tall and strong

C                    G
Many little branches that birds sit on

C              F
Bring your friends stay all day

C            G
Climb around and play!
```

CHORUS

```
C    F          C        G
Oh the little children, they come and play in my shade,

C    F          C        G
Oh the little children, they come and play in my shade.
```

BREAK

C F C G x 2 (they come and play, in my shade)

VERSE 2

```
C                    F
If you were as tall as me, as tall as me

C                        G
There would be so many things that you'd see.

C          F
Old and wise, the things I know

C        G
Help me to grow!
```

CHORUS

CHORUS OUT

"Twinkle, Twinkle, Little Star" Traditional Lullaby

```
C           F   C  F   C    G7    C
Twinkle, twinkle, little star, how I wonder what you are.

    F      C     G7 C   F     C   G7
Up above the world so high, like a diamond in the sky.

C           F   C  F   C    G7     C
Twinkle, twinkle, little star, how I wonder what you are!
```

When the blazing sun is gone, when he nothing shines upon,

Then you show your little light, twinkle, twinkle, all the night.

Twinkle, twinkle, little star, how I wonder what you are!

Then the traveler in the dark, thanks you for your tiny spark;

He could not see which way to go, if you did not twinkle so.

Twinkle, twinkle, little star, how I wonder what you are!

In the dark blue sky you keep, while you through my window peep,

And you never shut your eye, till the sun is in the sky,

Twinkle, twinkle, little star, how I wonder what you are!

"Two Little Blackbirds" Traditional Children's Song

Tune: The Alphabet Song

```
C                   F    C
Two little blackbirds sat on a hill,

F        C    G7        C
One named Jack and one named Jill.

C      F    C      G7
Fly away, Jack; fly away, Jill.

C        F    C        G7
Come back, Jack; come back, Jill.

C                   F    C
Two little blackbirds sat on a hill,

F        C    G7        C
One named Jack and one named Jill.
```

Two little blackbirds, sitting in a row.

One flies fast, one flies slow.

Fly away, fast! Fly away, slow!

Come back, fast! Come back, slow!

Two little blackbirds, sitting on a cloud.

One sings soft, one sings loud.

Fly away, soft! Fly away, loud!

Come back, soft! Come back, loud!

"We Circle Around" Traditional Arapaho Native American Song

Em
We circle around, we circle around

   G   D   Em
The boundaries of the Earth,

G   D   Em
The boundaries of the Earth.

Em
We circle around, we circle around

   G   D   Em
The boundaries of the Earth,

G   D   Em
The boundaries of the Earth.

Em   G D Em
Wearing our long wing feathers as we fly,

Em   G D Em
Wearing our long wing feathers as we fly.

Em
We circle around, we circle around,

   G   D   Em
The boundaries of the sky.

Em
We circle around, we circle around,

   G   D   Em
The boundaries of the sky.

"We're Gonna Dance, We're Gonna Wiggle" by Jessy Rushing

E
We're gonna dance

E
And yell, "Hurray, hurray."

                                        B7
We're gonna wiggle, we're gonna sway

           E
No one can stop us once we start

            A7   B7   E
We're gonna move, we're gonna groove our body parts.

           A7
Clap your hands, hands, hands

           E
Twist your hips, hips, hips

           B7
Stomp your feet, feet, feet

           E
Move with this, this, this.

We're gonna dance

And yell, "Hurray, hurray."

We're gonna wiggle, we're gonna sway

No one can stop us once we start

We're gonna move, we're gonna groove our body parts

Shake your head, head, head

Rock your knees, knees, knees

And turn around

Once with me.

We're gonna dance

And yell, "Hurray, hurray."

We're gonna wiggle, we're gonna sway

No one can stop us once we start.

We're gonna move, we're gonna groove our body parts.

Tip toe, tip toe, tip toe

Walk, walk ,walk.

Run, run, run

And then we stop.

"Whack That Drum" by Steve Sandler

```
C               G
Sammy, can you play that drum?

F    G    C
Hit it hard. Have alotta fun.

F      G   C      A
Now let Sara play that drum.

F            G            C
Bangaalanga, whackalaka, tum, tum, tum.

F      G      C      A
Keep the rhythm. Play that drum.

F            G          C
Bangalanga, Whakalacka, tum, tum, tum.
```

Repeat with Sara and the next child, etc.

"What's Your Name?" by Jessy Rushing

A+ A
When, I

D   DM7   D6   DM7
Walk down the street people ask me all the time,

                em7 em6 em em6
"What's your name?"

A+ A
So, I

D   DM7   D6   DM7
Look them in the eye and tell them loud and proud,

          em7 em6 em em6
"My name is

A+ A
_____,

D   DM7   D6   DM7   em7 em6 em em6
_____, _____, _____ that's my name!"

*Repeat all substituting different places at the very beginning.

Go to school

Come to music

Play at the park

Meet new people

Go to a party

"When I Meet a New Friend" by Jenn Batey

```
C                        F
Oh... the first thing that I do

      C        G
When I meet a new friend,

           C              F
Oh... the first thing that I do

    C       G7   C
Is say hello to them.

C
Hello, Adah

F
Hello, Adah

C            G
Hello, Adah girl.

C
Hello, Joshua

F
Hello, Joshua

C      G7    C
Hello, Joshua boy.
```

"When I Wake Up" by Jaden South

SECTION 1:

```
D              G           D    D           G           D
When I wake up I love to get dressed, I take off my PJ's and I grab my shirt.

D              G           D         G                    D
I put one arm up and then the other one, I pull my shirt on and feel really cool.

A                            D
Can't wait to go watch Elmo and Dora, too!

D              G                    D
Who knew getting dressed was so much fun?!
```

SECTION 2:

```
D         G           D
Well then I thought, "Hey, I need some pants!"

D         G     D
So I grabbed my jeans and put them on,

D                      G            D
Kinda the same way as the shirt but with my legs (of course!)

G                              D
I never know what Mom laid out but I know it's neat

A              D
Everyday is like a brand new treat.

D              G             D
Who knew getting dressed was so much fun?!
```

SECTION 3

```
    D         G           D
Now when I wake up I try to do it myself

D         G             D
And I know I'll always need some help,

G                      D
That's OK with me, 'cause I'm learning new things.

A                      D
One day I'll be able to do everything!

D              G              D
When I wake up... Getting dressed is always FUN!
```

"Where is Thumbkin?" Traditional Children's Song

C   G7 C
Where is Thumbkin?

C   G7 C
Where is Thumbkin?

C G7 C
Here I am!

C G7 C
Here I am!

C   F C G7 C
How are you today, sir?

C   F   C G7 C
Very well, I thank you.

C   G7
Run away.

Run away.

Other verses:

How are you today sir? I am feeling sad…

How are you today sir? I am feeling happy…

How are you today sir? I am feeling mad…

How are you today sir? I am feeling joyful…

"You Are My Sunshine" Traditional Folk Song

```
C                              C7
You are my sunshine, my only sunshine

              F              C
You make me happy when skies are gray

          F                      C
You'll never know, dear, how much I love you

                  G7      C
Please don't take my sunshine away.
```

```
C                              C7
The other night, dear, as I lay sleeping

          F            C
I dreamed I held you in my arms

      F              C
When I awoke, dear, I was mistaken

          G7        C
And I hung my head and cried.
```

```
 C                             C7
You are my sunshine, my only sunshine

              F                  C
You make me happy when skies are gray

          F                      C
You'll never know, dear, how much I love you

                  G7        C
Please don't take my sunshine away.
```

"You Do the Same" by Jennifer Peyton

```
C    G    C         G    C
```
Look at me, I'm <u>dancing</u>. You do the same.

```
C    G    C    F  G    C  F  G    C
```
Look at me, I'm <u>dancing</u>. You do the same. You do the same.

```
C       G    C              G    C
```
What am I doing with my <u>arms</u>? You do the same.

```
C       G    C         F  G    C  F  G    C
```
What am I doing with my <u>feet</u>? You do the same. You do the same.

Look at me, I'm: moving, hopping, twirling, spinning, walking, jogging, marching, hugging, shaking, etc.

What am I doing with my: hands, legs, head, body, hips, ears, nose, eyes, etc.

"Zum Gali Gali" Traditional Song from Israel

Em entire song

Zum, Zum, Zum, Zum, Zum, Zum, Zum

Zum, Zum, Zum, Zum, Zum, Zum, Zum

Zum gali gali gali,

Zum gali gali.

Zum gali gali gali,

Zum gali gali.

Hechalutz le maan avoda

(translated: Pioneers all work as one)

Avoda le maan hechalutz

(translated: Work as one all pioneers)

Hechalutz le maan avoda

(translated: Pioneers all work as one)

Avoda le maan hechalutz

(translated: Work as one all pioneers)

CHORUS

Ha shalom le maan ha amin

(translated: Peace shall be for all the world)

Ha amin le maan ha shalom

(translated: All the world shall be for peace)

Ha shalom le maan ha amin

(translated: Peace shall be for all the world)

Ha amin le maan ha shalom

(translated: All the world shall be for peace)

INDEXED SONGS

ANIMAL SONGS

A Rustle in a Bush
Animal Parade
Animal Song
Had a Little Rooster
Hello Mr. Animal
Old MacDonald

BODY PARTS SONGS

The Body Language Song
Head, Shoulders, Knees, and Toes
Hello, Salutations
If I Arr a Pirate
My Hand on My Head

BONDING SONGS

Always In My Heart
Big Bright Moon
Doo Wop Love
Goodnight, My Sweet One
How Will You Grow?
Hush Little Baby
In My Own Little Way
La La La Lullaby
Never Let Me Go
Peek-A-Boo
Soon the Moon Will Rise

BOOK SONGS

Marty Monkey
Mouse in My House
My Favorite Spot

EMOTION SONGS

I Feel Silly
If You're Happy and You Know It
Look in the Mirror
This is How I Look

HELLO SONGS

Hello, Salutations
My Right Hand Says Hello
What's Your Name?
When I Meet a New Friend
When I Wake Up

INSTRUMENT SONGS

1,2,3, Play with Me
The Alphabet Song
BINGO
Click! Click! Click! Go the Castanets
Five Green and Speckled Frogs
Five Little Ducks
Five Little Monkeys
Funga A La Feeya
Going Over the Sea
Humpty Dumpty
If All the Raindrops
I'm the Sun
Kookabura
Leader of the Band
Let's Get Ready
Listen to How I Beat My Drum
London Bridge
Mister Golden Sun
My Favorite Spot
Oh Where Has My Little Dog Gone?
One, Two, Buckle My Shoe
Pajarito
Pat a Cake
Pitter Patter
Pollito, Chicken
Razzle Dazzle 'Em
Row, Row, Row Your Boat
Shake, Shake, Shake!
Siyahamba
Ten in the Bed
This Old Man
Tingalayo
Tree Hugs
Twinkle, Twinkle, Little Star
Two Little Blackbirds
Whack That Drum
Where is Thumbkin?
You Are My Sunshine
Zum Gali Gali

MOVEMENT SONGS

The Ants Go Marching
The Bicycle
Birdie Beat
Dance to the Music
Five Little Ducks
Five Little Monkeys
Flower Power
Going Over the Sea
Head, Shoulders, Knees, and Toes
Hello, Salutations
(Here We Go) Loop De Loop
Hokey Pokey
Hot Air Balloon
I'm a Little Teapot
It's Time for Parade
Itsy Bitsy Spider
I've Been Working on the Railroad
Kemo Kimo
Let's Go for a Ride
Little Red Caboose
Monkey Moves!
Mood Groove
The More We Get Together
The Owl
Pajarito
Pitter Patter
Playing Along
Skip to My Lou
Ten in the Bed
There's a Tickle Under My Skin
This is How We Rock
We Circle Around
We're Gonna Dance, We're Gonna Wiggle
You Do the Same

SIGN LANGUAGE SONGS*

The Alphabet Song
It's Time to Go
*Purchasing **Baby Sing & Sign** by Anne Meeker
Miller is recommended for other sign language songs
incorporated into session plans.*

VISUAL TRACKING/SCARVES SONGS

Blow Me Some Bubbles
I Can Name the Colors
Little Red Caboose
Move Your Scarves

VISUAL AIDS

Illustration accompanies **"Hello Mr. Animal"** page 359

Illustration accompanies **"Hello Mr. Animal"** page 359

Illustration accompanies **"Hello Mr. Animal"** page 359

Illustration accompanies **"Hello Mr. Animal"** page 359

Illustration accompanies **"Hello Mr. Animal"** page 359

Illustration accompanies **"Hello Mr. Animal"** page 359

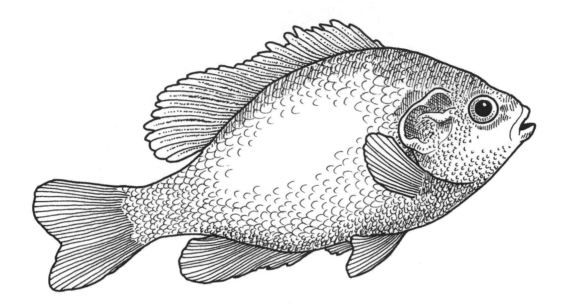

Illustration accompanies **"Hello Mr. Animal"** page 359

Illustration accompanies **"Hello Mr. Animal"** page 359

Illustration accompanies **"Hello Mr. Animal"** page 359

Illustration accompanies **"Hello Mr. Animal"** page 359

Illustration accompanies **"Hello Mr. Animal"** page 359

Illustration accompanies **"Hello Mr. Animal"** page 359

Illustration accompanies **"Hello Mr. Animal"** page 359

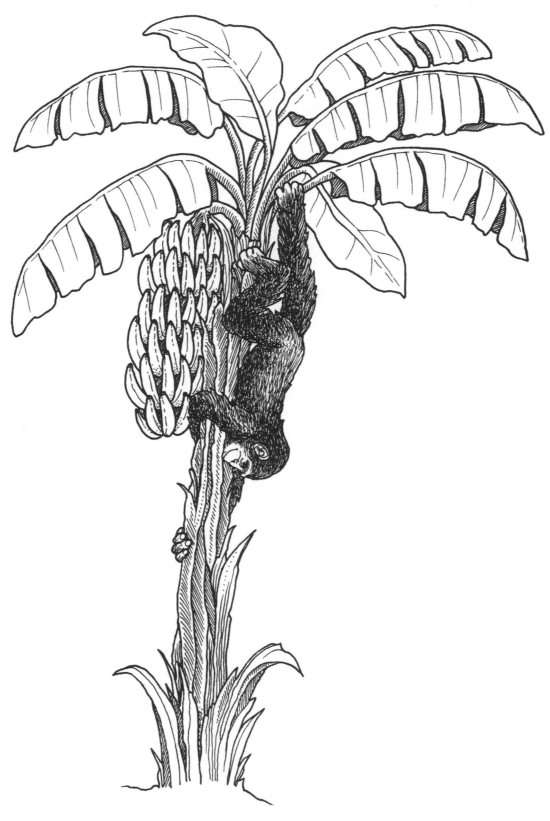

Illustration accompanies **"Marty Monkey"** page 392

Illustration accompanies **"Marty Monkey"** page 392

Illustration accompanies **"Mouse in My House"** page 397

Illustration accompanies **"Mouse in My House"** page 397

Illustration accompanies **"Mouse in My House"** page 397

Illustration accompanies **"Mouse in My House"** page 397

Illustration accompanies **"Mouse in My House"** page 397, **"My Favorite Spot"** page 399

Illustration accompanies **"My Favorite Spot"** page 399

Illustration accompanies **"My Favorite Spot"** page 399

Illustration accompanies **"My Favorite Spot"** page 399

INSTRUMENT AND MATERIALS LIST
(*suggested websites*)

Big Books

(*www.booksource.com*)

> *Brown Bear, Brown Bear, What Do You Hear?* by Bill Martin Jr. & Eric Carle
> *Farmer in the Dell*
> *Mulberry Bush*
> *Nine Ducks Nine*
> *Polar Bear, Polar Bear, What Do You See?* by Bill Martin Jr. & Eric Carle
> *Ten Little Monkeys Jumping on the Bed*
> *This Old Man*
> *Walking Through the Jungle*
> *Wheels on the Bus*

Bubbles—Gazillion Bubble brand

(*http://www.toysrus.com/product/index.jsp?productId=2316269&CAWELAID=112213294&pla=plat&cagpspn=pla*)

Folkmanis Animal Puppets

(*www.folkmanis.com*)

Hand-held mirror—small plastic single-sided

Hohner Plastic Finger Castanets

(*http://www.musiciselementary.com/mie2/index.php?cPath=36_187&sort=4a&page=1&osCsid=jth0inutjmcpjtum3q56g7d562*)

Multicolor Scarf Kit

(*http://www.discountschoolsupply.com/Product/ProductDetail.aspx?product=30188&es=237970000ESC&utm_source=CSE&utm_medium=weblink&utm_campaign=shoppingcom*)

Nino Percussion Ball Shakers

(*http://www.westmusic.com/1002405-kids/k5030-kids-percussion/k5030f-shakers/nino-nino509-ball-shaker.htm*)

Playful Harmonies Baby Maracas

(*http://www.musiciselementary.com/mie2/index.php?cPath=36_187&sort=4a&page=1&osCsid=jth0inutjmcpjtum3q56g7d562*)

Playful Harmonies Maracitos

(*http://www.musiciselementary.com/mie2/index.php?cPath=36_187&sort=4a&page=1&osCsid=jth0inutjmcpjtum3q56g7d562*)

Playful Harmonies 8" and 16" Rainbomaker Rainsticks

(*http://www.musiciselementary.com/mie2/index.php?cPath=36_187&sort=4a&page=1&osCsid=jth0inutjmcpjtum3q56g7d562*)

Playful Harmonies 8" Tambourines

(http://www.musiciselementary.com/mie2/index.php?cPath=36_187&sort=4a&page=1&osCsid=jth0inutjmcpjtum3q56g7d562)

Playful Harmonies Train Whistle

(http://www.musiciselementary.com/mie2/index.php?cPath=36_187&sort=4a&page=1&osCsid=jth0inutjmcpjtum3q56g7d562)

Remo Lynn Kleiner Baby Drums with Mallets

(http://www.westmusic.com/1002405-kids/k5050-under-age-3/k5050b-drums/remo-lynn-kleiner-hd-2005-lk-baby-drum.htm)

Remo Lynn Kleiner Ocean Drums

(http://www.westmusic.com/1002405-kids/k5020-kids-drums/k5020h-ocean/remo-lynn-kleiner-lk-0309-8s-pre-tuned-ocean-drum.htm)

Remo Kids Lollipop Drums with Mallets

(http://www.westmusic.com/1002405-kids/k5020-kids-drums/k5020g-lollipop/remo-kids-lollipop-drums.htm)

Toy Train Engine with a pull-along string

REFERENCES

Adamson, L. B., & Bakeman, R. (2004). The development of symbol-infused joint engagement. *Child Development, 75*, 1171–1187.

Balter, M. (2004). Seeking keys to music. *Science, 306*, 1120–1122.

Bricker, D., Squires, J., Mounts, L., Potter, L., Nickel, R., Twombly, E., et al. (1999). *Ages & Stages Questionnaire® (ASQ): A parent completed, child-monitoring system* (2nd ed.). Baltimore, MD: Brookes.

Cornish, A. M., McMahon, C. A., Ungerer, J. A., Barnett, B., Kowalenko, N., & Tennant, C. (2005). Postnatal depression and infant cognitive and motor development in the second postnatal year: The impact of depression chronicity and infant gender. *Infant Behavior and Development, 28*, 407–417.

Donohue, P. K. (2002). Health related quality of life of preterm children and their caregivers. *Mental Retardation and Developmental Disabilities Research Reviews, 8*, 293–297.

Field, T., Pickens, J., Prodromidis, M., Malphurs, J., Fox, N., Bendell, D., et al. (2000). Targeting adolescent mothers with depressive symptoms for early intervention. *Adolescence, 35*, 381–414.

Gourgey, C. (1998). Music therapy in the treatment of social isolation in visually impaired children. *RE:view, 29*, 157–162.

Klassen, A. F., Lee, S. K., Raina, P., Chan, H. W. P., Matthew, D., & Brabyn, D. (2004). Health status and health related quality of life in a population-based sample of neonatal intensive care unit graduates. *Pediatrics, 113*, 594–600.

Laakso, M.-L., Poikkeus, A.-M., Eklund, K., & Lyytinen, P. (1999). Social interactional behaviors and symbolic play competence as predictors of language development and their associations with maternal attention-directing strategies. *Infant Behavior and Development, 22*, 541–556.

Littleton, D. (1991). Influence of play settings on preschool children's music and play behaviors. *Dissertation Abstracts International, 52*(04), 1198A. (UMI No. 9128294)

Miller, A. M. (2007). *Baby sing & sign: Communicate early with your baby: Learning signs the fun way through music and play.* New York, NY: Marlowe & Company.

Morales, M., Mundy, P., & Rojas, J. (1998). Following the direction of gaze and language development in 6-month-olds. *Infant Behavior and Development, 21*, 373–377.

Msall, M. E., & Tremont, M. R. (2002). Measuring functional outcomes after prematurity: Developmental impact of very low birth weight and extremely low birth weight status on childhood disability. *Mental Retardation and Developmental Disabilities Research Reviews, 8*, 258–272.

Odom, S. L., & Wolery, M. (2003). A unified theory of practice in early intervention/early childhood special education: Evidence-based practices. *Journal of Special Education, 37*, 164–173.

Rautava, P., Lehtonen, L., Helenius, H., & Sillanpää, M. (2003). Effect of newborn hospitalization on family and child behavior: A 12-year follow-up study. *Pediatrics, 111*, 277–283.

Standley, J. M. (2008). Does music instruction help children learn to read? Evidence of a meta analysis. *Update: Applications of Research in Music Education, 27*, 17–32.

Standley, J., Walworth, D., & Nguyen, J. (2007, March). *Effect of parent/child group music activities on toddler development: A pilot study.* Paper presented at the 17th International Symposium for Research in Music Behavior, Baton Rouge, LA.

http://www.aap.org/

http://www.asha.org

http://www.dbpeds.org

http://firstwords.fsu.edu/

CD SONGS LIST

1. 1,2,3 Play with Me
2. A Rustle in a Bush
3. Always In My Heart
4. Animal Parade
5. Animal Song
6. Ants Go Marching
7. Big Bright Moon
8. Bingo
9. Birdie Beat
10. Blow Me Some Bubbles
11. Click! Click! Click! Go the Castanets
12. Dance to the Music
13. Doo Wop Love
14. Five Green and Speckled Frogs
15. Five Little Ducks
16. Five Little Monkeys
17. Flower Power
18. Funga A La Feeya
19. Going Over the Sea
20. Goodnight, My Sweet One
21. Had a Little Rooster
22. Head, Shoulders, Knees, and Toes
23. Hello Mr. Animal
24. Hello, Salutations
25. Hokey Pokey
26. Hot Air Balloon
27. How Will You Grow?
28. Humpty Dumpty
29. Hush Little Baby
30. I Can Name the Colors
31. I Feel Silly
32. If All the Raindrops
33. If I Arr a Pirate
34. If You're Happy and You Know It
35. I'm a Little Teapot
36. I'm the Sun
37. In My Own Little Way
38. It's Time for Parade
39. It's Time to Go
40. Itsy Bitsy Spider
41. I've Been Working on the Railroad
42. Kemo Kimo
43. Kookabura
44. Kookabura Round
45. La La La Lullaby
46. Leader of the Band
47. Let's Get Ready
48. Let's Go For a Ride
49. Listen to How I Beat My Drum
50. Little Red Caboose
51. London Bridge
52. Look in the Mirror
53. Loopty Loop
54. Marty Monkey

55. Mister Golden Sun
56. Monkey Moves!
57. Mood Groove
58. Mouse in My House
59. Move Your Scarves
60. My Dog Rags
61. My Favorite Spot
62. My Hand on My Head
63. My Right Hand Says Hello
64. Never Let Me Go
65. Oh Where Has My Little Dog Gone
66. Old MacDonald
67. One, Two, Buckle My Shoe
68. Over in the Meadow
69. Pajarito
70. Pat a Cake
71. Peek-A-Boo
72. Pitter Patter
73. Playing Along
74. Pollito, Chicken
75. Razzle Dazzle 'Em
76. Row, Row, Row your Boat
77. Shake, Shake, Shake!
78. Siyahamba
79. Skip to My Lou
80. Soon the Moon Will Rise
81. Ten in the Bed
82. The Alphabet Song
83. The Bicycle
84. The Body Language Song
85. The More We Get Together
86. The Owl
87. This is How I Look
88. This is How We Rock
89. This Old Man
90. There's a Tickle Under My Skin
91. Tingalayo
92. Tree Hugs
93. Twinkle, Twinkle, Little Star
94. Two Little Blackbirds
95. We Circle Around
96. We're Gonna Dance
97. Whack That Drum
98. What's Your Name
99. When I meet a New Friend
100. When I Wake Up
101. Where is Thumbkin?
102. You Are My Sunshine
103. You Do the Same
104. Zum Gali Gali